talking at the boundaries

for Saludo
affectionately
david

david antin

talking at the boundaries

A New Directions Book

Grateful acknowledgement is made to the editors and publishers
of books and magazines in which some of the selections in this
volume first appeared: *Alcheringa, Big Deal, Boundary-2, New
Directions in Prose and Poetry 29, Sixpack, Vort,* and *Wch Way.*

Manufactured in the United States of America
First published clothbound and as New Directions Paperbook 416
in 1976
Published simultaneously in Canada by McClelland & Stewart, Ltd.

Library of Congress Cataloging in Publication Data
Antin, David.
    Talking at the boundaries.

    I. Title.
PS3551.N75T36   1976   811'.5'4   76-15374
ISBN 0-8112-0559-2
ISBN 0-8112-0560-6 pbk.

New Directions Books are published for James Laughlin
by New Directions Publishing Corporation,
333 Sixth Avenue, New York 10014

*for the last few years ive been working at talks that ive
been calling "talk poems"   because i see all poetry as
some kind of talking   which is some kind of thinking
and because ive never liked the idea of going into a
closet to address myself over a typewriter   what kind
of talking is that?   ive gotten into the habit of going
to some particular place   with something on my mind
but no particular words in my mouth   looking
for a particular occasion to talk to particular people in a
way i hope is valuable for all of us   because these
talks were worked out with no sense of a page in mind
the texts are not "prose"   which is as i see it a kind
of "concrete poetry with justified margins"   while
these texts are the notations or scores of oral poems
with margins consequently unjustified   since
these works could not have been realized without the
kind invitations of many people at many institutions
this book is dedicated to them*

contents

*this poem-talk was improvised at the san francisco poetry
center on the occasion of a joint reading by jerome
rothenberg and myself in april 1973   we had each
been asked by kathy fraser to provide some sort of statement about our own work to provide something of a
context for the audience and for kathys introduction
          i had suggested that i had always had mixed feelings
about being considered a poet   "if robert lowell is a
poet i dont want to be a poet   if robert frost was a
poet i dont want to be a poet   if socrates was a poet
   ill consider it"   kathy using this and the fact that
rothenberg is notably associated with the poetry of
"primitive" cultures and that im notoriously associated
with avant garde art proposed somewhat lightly that it
seemed both appropriate and odd for the two of us to be
  reading together since jerome always seemed to represent to her the ancient past and i the remote future
          i took her at her word   since i had not the
remotest intention of "reading" poetry   because i
had brought no books that i could have read from   i
chose to address myself to the question of what i was
   doing there   references to other poets in the talk
were more or less direct because they happened to be in
the audience*

what am i doing here?

since ive heard jerry before   i was prepared to ask myself
        a somewhat similar question   to the question *cokboy*
seems to have asked   which is   "what am i doing here?"
        the question has some funny aspects to it   one of them is
        i have no intention whatever   of reading   and   that
would seem to put me   outside the general   scope of the
genre   but maybe not   if im characterized by an odd
futureness   science fiction like   which is a sort of funny
        pathetic position   the future   comes relatively
unequipped and bare   a dream of technology so to speak   so
        i came with a small tape recorder   and this is appropriate
        a tape recorder is probably more of a dream than anything else
        because they never work very well   but the point was
        that i was going to ask myself what i was doing here in several
senses   one of these senses is "what am i doing *here?*" in this
kind of ambience?   but what is "this kind of ambience"   i
        havent really wanted to be considered a poet   but i think that
takes refining to make clear what i mean   i dont want to be
considered a poet   if a poet is someone   who adds art to
talking   now i know there are several ways that people look at
        poetry   but there is a passage in bacon   where bacon says
        "if you talk about the manner of speaking that poetry is   its
just a mode of speech   and if you talk about its content   its

3

merely history at pleasure"   which was merely a polite way of
   saying that poetry was a lie   history at pleasure   is history
the way you happen to want to remember it   now the way i
want to remember something   may very well be   the issue
of why im here   to ask myself "why am i here?" in a context
of poetry   which is like asking why   when i do put a book
out in the world   it winds up getting classified   by the
library of congress   under the section called poetry   and
   i find that   puzzling   but logical   because what else
   would they call it?   i looked through the library of congress
classificational system and   was unable to find any classification
called talking   it seemed to me they didnt have that
   classification   they had belles lettres   and they had
   literature and   they had essays and   they had geography
      and they didnt have talking   and i thought   that
something had been left out   but maybe it was because talking
   was not   as it were   imagined to fit into a book
      between   say   telling jokes   and doing something
   else   now   i kept looking around for a place   into
which   i could put what i do   and i asked myself   why
do i do it in such a place anyway   why do i persist in doing it in
a place next to old friends   who call upon the word poet
      to some degree   and to some degree   call upon
something that one might call   the past   though i get very
   dubious about   its past   and   i say to myself   why
did we edit a magazine together   jerome rothenberg and i
      i was the future and he was   the past   and there was
nothing in the present   we might have published an empty book
      consistently   if i had seen how we came out   irregularly
      as these things do   and we   seem to have come together
again   and again   at various times   though weve not
   always been together   weve probably known each other longer
than we havent known each other   at this point   and we
obviously split the world rather peculiarly   maybe we split
   ourselves rather peculiarly   but i notice that   in   the
kind of work   that he's interested in   theres a lot of talking
   because there isnt a lot of writing   the past had a lot more
   talking than it had writing   i'll make a bold hypothesis before

4

there was talking   before there was writing   before there was
   talking there wasnt talking   before there was writing there was
talking   this may not be an immense hypothesis   but its
   certainly true   and   it has consequences   there are
certainly consequences i can draw from this   that before there
   was writing down   and looking up   there was remembering
      when you talked about something that wasnt there you had to
remember it   and you couldnt write it down   and when you
   talked about something that wasnt there   the only way that it
was there was   somehow   it manifested itself   in your
   mouth   and before it manifested itself in your mouth   it
didnt always do that   before it manifested itself in your mouth
it *may* have manifested itself in your head   thats not always true
      because sometimes or maybe even most of the time a new thing
manifests itself in talking before it manifests itself anywhere else
at all   but when we try to remember what was the past   the
past is all remembering   and   if the past is remembering its
   talking too   now i dont want to say that it is always talking
      or at least talking is not always spoken   but its a good
   word to stick with   and its a word that had a grand history
      theres a word close to talking   a word that may finally
   mean talking   but used to have a very grand meaning   a
word myth   which has a very grand meaning for most people
      and   i know that robert duncan has given a lot of attention
to the word "myth"   the one definition he did leave out when
   he rehearsed the definitions for the middle voice greek verb
mytheomai   is to talk   which it was   it was a verb "to
   talk" and "to tell"   and it was a verb meaning "to put a rap
in the air"   when odysseus   the great con-man   the
   trickster gets up to talk in council   he "myths"   and he
"myths" regardless of whether he "myths" the way nobody else
   remembers   and i think the word may not be very prejudicial
at that point   differently now   lets say   if i were to say
   of the president   "he's been mything for a long time"
"he's been mythifying us"   you know   the word seems to
have come down   and to have been coming down for a very long
   time   and if i said that he was talking for a long time   you
   might think i was tired of his talking   but you wouldnt think

that he was lying   or that i was accusing him of lying   id like
to offer a suggestion   about the word "myth"   for a
moment   let me make a negative suggestion about the word
"myth"   the word "myth" is the name given to the lies told by
little brown men   to men in white suits with binocular cases
    because nobody knows of the myth that the man in the white
suit believes   there is one important thing about a story
    told you   by a little brown man   if the story sounds as
if you could have observed it yourself   you being the man in the
white suit   you wouldnt call it a "myth"   youd say "he told
me what happened"   youd say "he told me a fact"   or
    "he told me a story"   now   the story might be a true
story   but whats a true story   well   a true story   is a
    story   something like the one that was told me the other day
    theres a woman   a very hopeful   woman   works in
our office   name is candy   and she   always has bad luck
    and shes always trying again   it doesnt matter what
happens   she always gets up off the floor and has another try at
it   candy came into the office the other day   she had had
many disasters recently   one of her most recent disasters was
that her children   her kids are always getting picked up on dope
    charges   or for burglarizing   or for petty theft or   for
knocking up somebodys child or for letting the goat loose and it
    bites someone or eats his flowers   and shes getting citations
    or driving the car off the road   or talking back to a cop
    and she has troubles with her children   but she has troubles
with other people besides her kids   she has troubles with men
    she mislaid her last husband   and she then   had a
succession   of   couplings   that were temporary and
    transitional   and each one   always looked like it was going
to be very important and meaningful   or had the prospect of
being meaningful   and each time   she would come in
    with the story that there was a new man in her life   and
she would say to everybody in the office   because she was an
    irrepressible talker   teller of truths   that   what had
happened to her   she had met this groovy guy   and he was
    a very distinguished person   but he had a mother and two wives
    whatever it was   it never was working out   but it

6

appeared at last that she had found someone   who she really got
     on very well with   though he was a little old   that is   she
is perhaps in her middle thirties   and he was slightly white haired
     but a very distinguished and elegant guy and   they seem to have
gotten along together   because in spite of the fact that he lived in
san diego he hated nixon and   they talked about the same things
     together   whatever it was it was very romantic   only he
hadnt taken her out yet   and then he asked her out   and he
 took her to one of those steak houses where its very dark and you
cant tell what youre eating   and they had   dinner together
     and they had lobster and drank one of those cold duck wines
or whatever that she really liked   and they went off to his house
     they went off to his place   and she was telling me the story
     and she told me the story with a kind of irrepressible and fierce
energy and i wasnt able to tell what was coming but i knew something
was up   and she said "then we got to the house and he put a
record on   and he put on the record and we danced for a while
     and necked   and then we took off our clothes and we started
to go to bed   and he had three red cherries tattooed on his prick"
     and i said "candy"   "candy   what did you do?"   she
said "i couldnt stop laughing and i went home"   i had heard a
 story   and the office people were saying "did you hear what
happened to candy?"   "did you hear what happened to candy
again?"   and candy was very cheerful   shed managed to shake
 it off i guess   and i said to myself   "if i have to deal with
that story   what do i have to deal with in that story?"   "what
 kind of talking is that story to me?   what is that story?"   do
i have to suppose   think of the horrible issue at stake   candy
     i contemplate the scene   the *debacle*   which i didnt
invent i hate inventing   and i hate imagination   this story was
told me   yesterday   i assure you   and candy   told me
this story and i said "candy how did it come to pass that he had these
     damn things *tattooed* on his prick?"   she said it was in the
marines and it was on a dare   i said "on a dare"   i said "oh
     yeah"   and i keep thinking about it   if i keep thinking
about it that way   i keep thinking about the way that tattooes are
applied   and i dont like that image   i really dont like that
image   and there is a kind of probability distribution for events

that i normally inspect when someone says something to me
but yet there are times when i dont inspect it   this is one of
the times where i inspected it and i thought "tattooed?" "decald?"
          no   she said tattooed   these were tattooed   i dont
know what to say   that is   is this a story told by a little brown
man to a man in a white suit?   i was rapidly acquiring a white
suit   its fairly evident that my binoculars were beginning to feel
heavy   and i thought "well maybe this is not the right way to
think about it   maybe im not considering this thing seriously
in an appropriate manner   what could this mean that
someone   who is really   an adult   35 years old   what
could she have on her mind with such a story?"   what could it
have meant that it happened to her?   and i realized that   this
was the major structure of her life   she had in fact described
the existence that she lived   now   either she had found a man
by great and amazing magical skill   who had done this
exorbitant thing   or she had found a memory of a man who had
done this amazing and exorbitant thing   this was the way candy
represented her entire life   yesterday   and then i said
"well then thats a true story"   because thats really very much like
candy   thats very much like the kind of people candy goes out
with   its very much like everything about her entire life   her
whole career is based upon   coming together with men with 3
cherries tattooed on their prick   there is something about candy
that will always find such a case it is the essence of candy
          now i dont know if thats history at pleasure   or whether its
somewhat more aristotelian   that is   when you think of
aristotle's idea of poetry   his idea was that poetry   was
essential history   it was the kind of history that had to happen
          or the kind of history that might have happened or the kind of
history that should have happened   because it was appropriate that
it happen   and i thought   candy has told me an aristotelian
truth   she told me essential history   now   thats a clearcut
and you may say poeticized image   now you may feel
          and i also   i also draw back somewhat   i draw back from
poetry and poetic justice   i really do draw back from it   even
though im amused by   the truthfulness of candy   who told
me this story   now if i was to take the science myth   if i were

8

to imagine   that the only way   that i could deal with this
story was to corroborate it   on a spatio-temporal grid   in a
   number of ways that are approved   for inspections of this sort
      i would go about   saying   well   what is the possi-
bility that a man did this?   would someone who ran a tattoo
parlor   do such a thing?   how much would you have to pay
   him?   i'd go through the whole number   but forget that
story   forget that story   because its the kind of story that
   science   with all its expensive instrumentation and its totalitarian
   use of language   that is   science is   in a certain sense
         a kind of poetry of terror   it is a very well organized poetry
of terror   what you do is you bring in a student   and i
was educated in science   you bring in a student at a very early
age   and you teach him to speak the way you want him to speak
      and when he doesnt you flunk him   and then   after a
while   after years   after 4 years of undergraduate school
      and two years of a masters and   4 years of a doctorate
      and then you have him practice talking on paper   and you
call that his thesis   by that time he's learned to use the words
   exactly as all the other people in the same community   use the
   words   and this is the hieratic art we call science   now science
      with its sacred art of terror   if we were to take this kind of
enforced consciousness   which is still   consciousness   and
   apply it   to do the best it could to inspect   these events
      or these supposed events   the evidence   would in the end
be   inconclusive   we would probably judge this event   to
   fall   somewhere   outside the line of the probable   but to
fall somewhere within the domain of the possible   and then
      to pass no judgment except to say   we think its got this
probability its possible   but its very unlikely   the confidence
   limits are perhaps exceeded   now thats a rare case   forget it
      how can you forget it?   i cant forget it   but   take
another situation   suppose i try to exercise   upon a past
      my past   not my whimsical past   but a past that i try to
decode   because the only way that i can imagine myself   to be
my self   co-editor of a magazine with a friend   or someone
   who went to some particular place the only way i can imagine my
self   as being the same   person   going by that name

9

besides the fact that i answer by reflex   when   people
call me by that name   and even in that instance   the only way
that   i can conceive of myself   as a personality   is by
an act   of memory   by an act of interrogation of my memory
which is   also talking   the self   itself   is emergent
in discourse   in some kind of discourse   it is probably available
but it comes up under dialogue   and the dialogue   is
conducted with it   and then the self emerges   even though the
self   may not have been there until you called upon it   you
were always under   something   of an assumption that it was
available for discourse   and that it would answer you and if it
doesnt   answer you they call that   forgetting   and if you
forget very gravely   they give that other kinds of names   a
person who cant interrogate himself   and has no impulse to
interrogate himself   is someone   one normally calls a psychopath   that is   a psychopath might be imagined to be a
consciousness distributed always   upon some imaginary point of
the present   one could imagine   that the two   major
historical forms of self   interrogation of self   discovery and
investigation   the two polar forms   the dark historian and
the white historian   might be called schizophrenia and paranoia
in their old fashioned senses   the terms themselves are not terribly
meaningful   but using the older terminology   paranoia
inspects history in the form of anxiety   and the schizophrenic
would   inspect history in   the form essentially   of wish
or dream   or imagination   or desire   and naming
desire as history for the schizophrenic   whatever he wanted
happened   and naming anxiety as history for the paranoid
whatever he feared was history   and closing in   the
paranoid would convert the present in the light of anxiety   the
schizophrenic would convert it in the light   of desire   and the
psychopath has no history to convert at all   he always has
projects   perhaps somewhere into the future   but let us imagine
that these polar positions   are not the ones i intend to undertake
im going to ask myself   seriously   about how i can find
my past   because if i invoke history every time   in a conversation that cannot be held in a particular place   then   after all
the self is a nonliterate society   if you think about it   the

10

self is a preliterate society   because it doesnt proceed by writing
        and it has no absolute repository of any past event   it has no
place to which it can come   to find its past   it has only the
memory   which is a way of proceding and not a treasure trove
        and memory   for all we know may be   inconstant and
changing   so let me try to remember a situation and inspect it
        for a past   my past   if i think of it   i was thinking of
a situation   that occurred   when i was   i dont know how
many years ago   so my memory is already defective   an old
        friend of mine   someone i went to college with   his name
was dick berlinger   he was a jazz musician   he wasnt a jazz
musician   professionally   he could have been a jazz musician
professionally   he was a saxophonist   he played baritone sax
        he'd played with very good people   he sat in with parker
and other good people   at various points   but dick berlinger
was a kind   of person   whose life always had a future   and
        never had a present   im not sure about his past   because he
always had projects   he seemed to be planning always to be doing
        something   that he wasnt doing yet and wasnt ready to do yet
        without ever doing it   except very intermittently   and
planning always to be doing something without ever doing it is
somehow like planning on swimming   my little boy plans to learn
        swimming   he's been planning on swimming for several years
        and each year he goes down to the water and feels   the water
and then   he goes away   he hasnt become much of a swim-
mer yet   well   dick   though capable   as a saxophonist
        was not a jazz musician   and dick did that with all of his life
        and years passed   and we lost sight of him   and then a
friend of mine who had become a painter   and was in new haven
        and had been a close friend of dicks   told me that dick had
been in an asylum   a sanatorium   or whatever   and had
        been there for some time and had come out   and that was kind
of surprising   friends of mine had been falling by the wayside for
        a long time   that is there were other friends who had fallen
        in various places   somewhat similarly   mainly because
their lives only had futures   and nothing ever happened to them
        that ever changed   except they got older   which meant that
the present   really was something like an escalator   or one of

11

those paths in the los angeles airport that are motorized   and
youre moving forward   though youre not moving   and youre
   being carried forward toward something without your moving at
all   at any event   at this time i was married   and i was
living in new york   as a matter of fact i was living in court street
not very far from george oppen   who was living over closer to
the river   in brooklyn   the bay   and i got a call on the
phone   and   i heard a voice   that i vaguely recognized but
   i didnt quite recognize because it was darker and lower   and
older   and i said "hello" and he said "hello this is dick"   and
it was   that i remember   he said it was dick he didnt say who
he was   and by this time i must have known hundreds of other
dicks   and forgotten hundreds of dicks   i mean it was not
very easy and i said "dick who?" and i realized this might be insulting
   and he said "dick berlinger ive got to see you"   and i said "you
have to see me?   about what?"   he said "its very important"
   i said "what do you want?"   again   the urgency   was
really what was puzzling me and putting me off   i remember
   now i think i remember it   i said "well what do you want?"
   he said "i cant tell you i gotta come down"   i said "well
   im busy right now   im going to be going into the city"   ely
kept saying to me   "dont let him come here   he'll kill you" i
said "shut up what are you talking about?"   she has something
   of an anxiety history   "what are you talking about he's an
old friend"   and im holding my hand over the phone saying "let
   me find out what he wants"   i said "dick what is it that you
need?"   and he said "i cant tell you   i cant tell you now
   i'll   i'll tell you when i see you"   i said "all right   i'll
tell you what   im going into the city i have to go to a few galleries
   why dont i meet you   in manhattan"   and we named a
place   which was down near n.y.u.   and we got into the car
and we drove to the city   where we were going anyway   and
   the car we had was a peculiar car it was the only time i ever had
a car that turned out to be an incredible bargain   it was like i got
it for $200 from somebody who kept it on blocks for fourteen
years   it was a 1953 chrysler imperial with electrical windows
and i bought it for $200   and it was a very lovable elderly car
   that was like driving an armored car   it was very high and

12

you looked down on the road   it was a very strange car to drive
   and i loved it it was a big black car   and we drove there and
suddenly i saw dick   he was there   and he hailed us and we
parked the car and we got out to talk to him and i said "well dick
   what did you want?"   he said "i gotta borrow your car"
       and   i guess i should have said no   i guess i should have
said no but   it was an odd situation   and i had a kind of
feeling   of intense pleasure at seeing him out of a sanatorium
       it was a kind of amazing feeling that he was   alive   and i
remembered many occasions   in the 50's   which was like 10
years before that   when on summer nights wed driven in his car
   out to jones beach or something   and gone somewhere or
another   to grants for clams or something   and i remembered
   he had a kind of intense pleasure in handling a car   it calmed
him   and he loved driving   the way some people like to play
tennis   or   some people like to do something physical
       some physical activity in which you take some kind of pro-
found pleasure from both the skill that you display   and the
casualness with which you display it   and i said "yeah   okay
       i have to get somewhere   i have to get somewhere   why
dont you let me off   when can you bring it back?"   and at
   this point   ely was looking at me like i was crazy   and
       now i dont remember that she did but i think she did   and
she said "youll never see it again"   and i said "well he drives very
   well   nothing will happen"   and i told him "all right   drop
us off uptown   where are you taking the car?"   id been sitting
   there getting nervous   "where are you taking it?"   he said "i
have to see someone"   i said "well all right"   and he said
       "i gotta see someone   i gotta help them move"   this was
beginning to get me nervous because i didnt believe it and   i said
"okay you drive then"   he drove and he drove very madly   that
is he drove very peculiarly   now i remember im not sure whether
   he really did drive   now at this point   in the story   i cant
tell you whether i let him sit behind the wheel   before i was
going where i was going   or i didnt   and   finally i said "dick
   where do you have to go?"   and somehow i was driving   i
think he had driven   i think he had driven   to his mother's
house which is where he had lived for a long time   and   having

13

driven there   he had to go upstairs and come down again   and
    while he went upstairs and   was out of the car   i had a
frantic conversation with elly who was much more reasonable about
this i suppose and   said "youre crazy   he's going to do something insane with the car   youll never see the car again but something else is going to happen and youre not insured" and well it went
    on   we went through this serious and reasonable but paranoid
conversation   in which we worried about the car   and about
    things unspoken   like what could conceivably happen that had
nothing to do with losing a $200 car   which was in a certain
sense   not the meaning of the fear entirely   it couldnt have
been   because the anxiety about the mystery of what he was
doing was all so strange   finally he came back down and i said
"look dick   wherever you have to go why dont i drive you   if
you just have to move someone why dont i drive the car   and
        you sit there and   ill take you where you want to go"
        and he started getting very angry   and he didnt say anything
    you know having no claims on the car   except my previous
decision impulsively to lend him the car   he   said "oh   i
have to go   south"   i said "south where?"   you know
youre in manhattan you cant go very south in manhattan   youve
    got the battery on one end   and i said "south where?"   he
said "right near the museum of modern art"   i think we were in
the 80's or 90's on the east side   we drove down to the museum
of modern art and all this time he's getting crazier and crazier
        and i said "where do you want me to take you   what do
you want me to do with the car?"   he said "all right i have to get
    out here i have to get out right here"   and   traffic is very
slow we turned up 53rd street up past the museum of modern art
going west   which is on a street thats one way   westerly
        and   he got out of the car very quickly   and he suddenly
moved off down the street   and   the museum of modern art at
that time   had an empty lot   next to it with a parking lot
        and he ran into the lot   traffic was very slow at that point
    it was a kind of traffic jam that new york often has and the car
wasnt moving   and we were waiting   then all of a sudden   i
saw dick   coming back   walking   in what looked like an
unconcerned   sprint   that is he was coming down the street

14

as if he was walking but really running   very fast toward us
      and i said "dick!"   he didnt pay attention he didnt say a
word he went sailing down past my car and   i couldnt figure out
what was happening   and   then i saw two other people on
the street   and one saying "thats him! thats him!" and a policeman running down the street with a revolver in his hand coming up
and saying "they're with him!"   suddenly this cop came up to
the car with his hand on his revolver he said "lemme see your
license!"   im looking and i say "what?"   and the other two
say "whos he?"   i said "what are you talking about?"   he
said "come on!"   i said "all right" and i started to get out of the
car   he said "no stay right where you are"   i said "stay right
where i am?"   i said "okay   okay   he's a friend of mine"
                  he was gone   and he had been a friend of
mine   and he had tried to steal a car from the lot the policeman
said   and he   had needed a car very badly   for some reason
      he'd walked into the parking lot and he'd turned the ignition on
and tried to drive out   but apparently the owner of the car had
walked in   about the time he was coming out   and this
coincidence had occurred   and he ran   and he ran down the
      street   and there we are   weve got a memory   and a
story   and im talking about it   and there are some elements in
      this   that are true   because that i can remember it at all   i
imagine it to have in it a core of truth   and i remember it this way
      now i ask myself   i said to myself that i did this for this
reason   that elly did this for that reason   that dick wanted the
car for this reason   and i cant remember whether he was driving
      the car whether i was driving the car all the time   whether i was
really more worried about the car or i was worried about him
            now i know that any time i start to concentrate on this story
with any strong sense of conviction   i lose every bit of doubt
      that is as soon as i begin to say that i was driving the car   it
came out of my mouth very nicely   i was driving the car   well
then *i* was driving the car   but i can very easily stop driving the
      car and say "no *he* was driving the car"   now he was driving the
car   now he was sitting next to me and he was driving the car
      doing very odd things in fact now that i say so in fact im sure that i
can remember him nearly hitting another car   but im not really

15

sure that happened and im not really sure he ever hit anything and i
   never knew him to drive in such a way as to ever hit anything even
stone drunk   so im not sure he was driving the car   in which
case i was sitting on the left and he was sitting on the right   and
   now i can remember he was sitting on the right   and now i cant
remember really   what the order of these events was at all
        but i know that this happened   this story is a   straight-
forward story and i dont know whether i was guilty of   putting
   a friend   in a desperate position into a worse position   or
   whether i was behaving reasonably   because he had nearly killed
all of us   sure i can have a great justification for this story he was
driving so badly he nearly drove into a truck   when i saw the
way he was driving i said "my god i cant trust the car to this man!
he'll kill himself he'll kill somebody else   its only a sensible social
   act to prevent him from driving a car"   clearly a straightforward
example of   reasonable ethical concern for the rest of the society
        or   my $200 car with the wire wheels   it was a great car
with wire wheels and electrical windows that you could play with all
day they went up and down   each window had its own little
button you could make the glass go up and the glass go down   i
   have nobody to consult on this story except elly   who was also
there   but elly   as ive said on many occasions in other situations that have been published   has a very bad memory   and
she has a memory thats so bad i would really hesitate to ask her what
   happened   because it would merely make two stories   and
in fact   if i insisted on my story   if i cared more   my story
would probably be her story   and her story would then give
ground to my story before it got entirely off the ground   or we'd
   merge stories at some point   if she really cared we'd probably
   find a merger story   unless she cared and i didnt   because
then it would be her story   but since i cared we'd probably find
a merger story   that was somewhere between the two stories
   and come out with what one would call a group myth   right?
        a group story   now   this story   would lie between us
      that is we could get dick   if we could get hold of dick
        but i dont know where we could get hold of dick   if we
could get hold of dick im sure we couldnt get that story very easily
together again   because we would have dicks image of the story

16

and he may have forgotten the story by now entirely   now
you may think this is trivial   it is and it isnt   it is as trivial
        as the nature of establishing my self is   to me   or as the
nature of establishing your self would be to you   if you have to
define who you are and what youve done   if you feel it necessary to be able to stand behind yourself at any point   you feel it
necessary to decide who you are   and if you know who you are
        you know who you are because of who you remember   it is
because of a kind of continuity that i can say what i did and what
reasons i did it for   now im afflicted by what one might call   a
        doubt   a kind of scientific doubt about myself   thats not
the only kind of doubt   that comes up to me in this   mythical system   in candys story i knew what candy was saying
        and i was quite happy that by the time candy had finished her
story i knew exactly what she meant   regardless i knew what she
meant that is to say i didnt know what she did but i knew what she
meant   that is   i knew what she did regularly   in this
case   i dont know what i mean   i dont know what i meant
        and if i dont know what i meant now i only want to know what
i meant   but supposing i want to find out something that lies
between me and someone else   in a matter of doubt even in the
        area   that should be in the public domain   supposing we
want to talk about history   is there a privileged science of history
that has any other recourse?   lets imagine a situation   it
doesnt take long   one day   i dont know   it may have been
        a very close period in time   george and mary oppen were living
in brooklyn   near me   and it was a very bad time during the
vietnamese war   and johnson had escalated the war to an inordi-
nate degree and the bombs were dropping at a great rate and i believe
at this point the talk was of bombing hanoi   at that point they
were considering the   awful possibility   that hanoi might be
bombed   and elly   was pregnant at that time   and i
remember she looked sort of round   and one evening   we
went over there to talk   and george looked very black   dark
        really quite appalled by it we were all appalled by it   and
        we had this conversation about what it meant   and george
said to me in   what i take to be   very concerned sombre and
        intelligent tones   that theyre trying to get china   that is the

united states   was seriously   attempting to apply   piecemeal
pressure on china   and that we would escalate point by point
until china is provoked into war   so that we could drop the
atomic bomb on them   and bomb them out of existence before
they could become an industrial power   now i remember george
as having thought this at the time and as having argued a convincing
case   now its after the event   china has not been bombed
china has not been attacked   and if george and i were to ask
ourselves the question of was that the strategy   do we really have
a clearcut answer?   that is if i were to say to george "george you
were wrong"   lets say i say that to george "george you were
wrong"   i think george could reasonably answer me   "its not
certain that i was wrong"   and i think we would have to ask
ourselves how could we find out whether he was wrong?   what
system would we use to find out whether or not   a strategy had
changed its course   supposing in fact   the united states
had had among it people who might have been called   its
"intellectual leaders"   its drivers if it were a car   at its controls
someone with a hand on it who was directing it toward a war
with china   and that someone said "get china into the war"
now   the question that would first come up is "why not
attack china?"   george knew why they shouldnt attack china and
it was perfectly understandable   if they attacked china without
a consensus in america   it was conceivable at least then   now
weve had consensus for everything   but in those days it seemed
as though it might be impossible to drop an atomic bomb on
another country   before the other country was brought into
such a state   as to seemingly attack us   so george felt that it
was impossible   for the united states for anyone   malevolent
or intelligent or violent enough to want to bomb china to bomb china
just like that   that is he could give an order and say "bomb china!"
but if he were to bomb china he could worry   that is to say
now we're hypothesizing what happened   the leader might worry
that some large group of people standing up in congress   would
also talk and say "arrest that man!"   we may now feel differently
about the possibility of such a thing   that may never happen
it may now happen that anybody at the controls of the
american government   can do anything in the world   and

18

nobody will stand up and say   "arrest that man!"   or very few
   people will try to arrest that man but in 1965 or so it seemed
   possible that congress might not have allowed it   or that the
   country   might have protested that is   imagine going out on
   protest marches we had half a million people walking on a protest
march once   one might imagine millions of people on a protest
   march   people laying barricades across communication systems
      tearing out their television sets you could imagine terrible things
happening to the culture if china had been bombed   i was a party
   to this belief   george convinced me   i didnt take much convincing we assumed that if china   had been bombed   just like
that it was out of the question   well   if china   could have
   been bombed physically but couldnt have been bombed because of
the anxiety of the president we are now speculating about the presidents beliefs and the presidents hopes and aspirations   and fears
      however realizable they are   and weve got his mind to
contend with   now   let us say   that he took on a strategy
   of tactical escalation   bomb hanoi bomb this bomb that and let
us say that when he bombed in an escalating fashion   what
happened is the country's protest reached such a level that he felt
   perhaps it was not yet auspicious to attack china   and that the
lack of auspiciousness caused him at that moment not to attack china
      and that for a long period of time the intent to attack china
remained in abeyance   until gradually it had eroded   for
   reasons of political reorganization   or whatever   the issue is
serious but im not dealing with the issue seriously   im dealing
   with the question seriously   the question of how could we tell
      if it didnt happen how could we tell it was intended to happen
finally   other than by our theory   and our theory would have
   been that a sensible government   sensible   pathologically
sensible   with an intention to destroy another country   sought
about   to find ways to apply pressure on the other country so that
   the other country would assault us in some trivial manner   by
dropping bombs on us say   or doing something appalling   that
was in this sense trivial because it only took half a million lives or
something like that and then we blew them off the face of the earth
      now this was a sensible but pathological strategy and we could
imagine it   and we did imagine it   but if it didnt happen

that is if this strategy doesnt succeed   the difficulty is how
do you decide whether there was in fact such a strategy?   and the
answer is not forthcoming   i still dont know   i still dont
know whether george was right   or whether i was right
        because i didnt believe this was the strategy   i really didnt
believe it   that is i didnt believe the american government was less
pathological   i believed it was less sensible   it seemed to me
that the american government was not one hand on the driving wheel
        but lots of hands   and hands that were intermittently
reaching for that drivers wheel   and they had lots of other things
they were doing like playing poker in the back   and that various
people with variously strong motivations were driving the car
        and somebody would occasionally step on the gas and the gas
pedal would accelerate   and then somebody would slow it down
and somebody would randomly turn a signal but that on the whole
there was a relative pattern to the insanity   some of the people
took the wheel more commonly than other people   now that
was my theory   now how could i validate that   im really not
certain how we could have validated that one either   and there
we are again   we come back again to   "what am i doing here?"
what is it that im doing here?   im trying to find out   how i
could find out   and what im trying to find out is by
        essentially doing what i think talking does   that is
        talking and thinking may not be the same thing   but i see
thinking as talking   i see it as talking   to a question   which
may give rise to another question   and it may open up some
terrain and lose some terrain and answers come up   but theyre not
the same answers   ive learned something by talking about
        georges opinion   and my opinion   but i didnt learn
which opinion was right   now it doesnt seem to me that thats
terribly different from the career of science   which has consistently interrogated hypothetical entities   and has not validated
their existence   what it has done is to amass more difficult facts
that are more or less appropriate to the type of theory theyve
advanced   for example   not long ago there was a great
achievement in science   and this great achievement consisted
essentially of entering a new candidate for entityhood into physics
        and this was an entity that is to be imagined as having no mass

20

and having the capacity for absorbing electrons   that is really
what science   a scientist   mr wilson imagined   was something that got to be called an electron hole   now you can imagine
   something as absurd as an electron hole   imagining something as
   absurd as an electron hole is as absurd as imagining the shekhina
          the electron hole and the shekhina have a lot in common
        the electron hole is the answer to a question about why it is that
when you know all about resistances in certain kinds of substances
        these substances refuse to provide the resistances that you con-
sider appropriate to them   in the domain of electrical science you
   imagine flows and from this point of view you consider substances
   with respect to their responsiveness to the pressures which create
   these flows   and you name them   so to speak   by their
      ability to transmit or resist these flows   fairly casually as con-
ductors or insulators   and in the course of the history of electrical
science youve spent a fair amount of time classifying these materials
        and ranking them   and by now you see these flows   the
   current   as a flow of entities with a negative charge and you call
these electrons   now youve come to know an awful lot about the
   arrangement of these substances that you subject to these flows
        or you consider that you know a lot about them   and you
   are all very happy with what you know about them and when you
   apply two wires to the sides of this substance and create what you
   like to call a difference of potential   a difference of pressure
        electrical pressure   that is you apply more electrical pressure
to one side of the substance than the other   thats what you like
   to say that youre doing   because you know all about the resistances to this pressure   of the various substances   and when
   you apply these two wires to this piece of substance   you really
know all about what is going to happen   at least in the case of
your favorite substances   certain metals or crystalline compounds
        and you ordinarily only measure the results of this differential
pressure that you apply to take the legitimate satisfaction in what
   you already know   because you know all about the ways and
      habits of these crystals and how they work   and youre very
pleased with your knowledge   as you should be   and you turn
   on the pressure   and it doesnt work   now all this time and
all this money   all of these electrical scientists   have been

21

working out all that they know   and they put the two wires
together and it doesnt work?   all this time and all this money
they said   "and it doesnt work?"   they said "we have too
much invested in it working"   and so entered mr wilson and said
"the electron hole"   the electron hole   as you will see
    made it work   because if you suppose that the structure of
this disappointing substance was augmented   or one might say
    depleted   by a hole where there had no reason to be a hole
    and that this hole would be capable of absorbing electrons
    then the answer that you had   could be made equivalent to
the answer that you wanted   namely by the addition of an electron hole   now this was a difficult task   to convince the rest of
    science because yet science doesnt just say "electron hole"   you
have to do this with an apparatus of appropriate discourse   so what
you say is   you cant merely say there is an electron hole and it
    sits there   everyone knows that electrons are relatively randomly
distributed in this space in accordance with certain laws of probability   so that if you want to trap electrons   to facilitate their
    passage through the jungle of the semiconductor   you have to
provide correspondingly randomly distributed electron holes   and
you give them a more or less probable distribution   and density
    and then you say   they flow through the semiconductor in
such a manner that the outcome you get is the outcome you want
    now this is the form of interrogation   of discourse   that
science   a highly valued   a sacred art   has in fact   conducted to establish the existence of an entity   science is a sacred
    art   it is a hieratic art conducted with a high class technology
    like benin bronze making   that is it is essential to the society
    the society worships it   is mystified by it   and rewards
its practitioners immensely   what else can i say to reemphasize its
    sacredness   the sacred society sat down and came up with this
    answer to an interrogation   and while the answer is laughable
    it is not uncharacteristic   that is it is no different   which is
why i have always said there is a very close relation between poetry
    or talking   and science   the difference is great too
    that is   the kind of talking we conduct is different   they
conduct a sacred talking   in science   a specially sacred talking
    a hierophantic a hieratic talking   a talking that one might

call a fascist talk   they conduct a kind of oligarchic conversation
   with constrained materials and constrained people   and after
   that they should come out with what we come out with anyway?
      the finagle variable?   the finagle variable is any magnitude
      any constant any number any equation anything that you can
associate by any means whatsoever   to the number that you have
   in hand that will give you the number that you want   provided
only that it is proposed with the right manners or in the right dialect
      that is the finagle variable   and it is the profound mode of
interrogation   but they have different purposes and different ways
   of being conducted in our separate arts   and even though
      poetry or talking   talking poetry   poetry and talking
are not precisely the same   ill admit that   i'll admit that not
all talking is poetry   and that not all poetry is talking   i'll
   admit the poetry of the cry   i'll admit the mammalian poetry
      of michael mcclure   roaring   that goes along with lorcas
"aieeeee ignacio!"   i'll admit that   and its not my kind of
   poetry   today   and i   will admit that   there is a kind
of talking that   is responsory   directly responsory   and in
   general i'll say that it is not the habit of poetry   to be open to
interruption   to be entirely vulnerable to interruption   thats
a modest statement   i once told somebody he said "what's
poetry?" i said "uninterruptable discourse"   now i dont know
      there are other kinds of uninterruptable discourse   we have
   among us here many great conversationalists who dont have interruptable discourse   or theyre interruptable   with great difficulty   i confess   myself   to sharing some of these charac-
   teristics   and i would say that that is   a special kind of talking
      now science   is not such a kind of talking   always
      science will let you talk   until you contradict   the
council of elders   when the council of elders feels that your
   contradiction   appropriately phrased   and pronounced from
   the appropriate pulpit   is of such an order   that they must
meet   they say "shut up   and we'll consider it"   and then
   they consider it   that is to say   you publish   then they
experiment   then they publish   that is   there is a form of
dialogue   i could imagine a poetry that would go like this   and
   perhaps today we'll go on that way   with the other kind of

poetry   which   will for the time end uninterruptible discourse
    and open   interruptible discourse   so that   you can
    interrupt what im saying   or what jerrys saying and we can
find out   what it is that you would have liked to say that we have
shut you out from for so long

*the philadelphia art museum and moore college were
cooperating on a series of talks set up loosely to coincide
with the duchamp retrospective that had been organized
by anne d'harnoncourt and kynaston mcshine for the
philadelphia museum and the museum of modern art in
new york   the curatorial staff of the modern was on
strike and the show had opened in philadelphia   i was
one of the contributors to the duchamp catalog   with
a piece i had improvised at a duchamp festival in california
at uc irvine in a small gully between three hills
        because there had been a scheduling problem and
barbara rose had gone on too long   and now that
piece had been published and i had completed another
piece on duchamp the following october   and now
it was halloween of 1973 i was expected to talk once
again to the subject of marcel duchamp and i wasnt sure
there was anything else i wanted to say about him
        that duchamp needed to have said about him or
would have wanted to have said about him   by anyone*

at this time   but first i was going to be talking at
the moore college of art a girls college that had no such
expectations   in fact   no expectations whatever
because   i suspect   they had no idea who i was or
what i am   and when diane vanderlip the curator of
their gallery had to introduce me she was worried that
there might be too few people in the auditorium to hear
me   which didnt worry me at all since i figured that
if there were too few for the auditorium they could all
come down to the front and we could have a conversation
    when we got there things werent as bad as all that
but diane decided to set up the public address system
and pipe the sound into the cafeteria where a lot of the
students were eating   in the hope of attracting a few
more to the auditorium   i started talking and gradually
more and more people drifted into the auditorium
    till by the end the auditorium was nearly filled with
people whod heard at least half of the talk

is this the right place?

when i was asked what i wanted to talk about   before i came here
        i picked up the telephone   in san diego and   bill miller
from the philadelphia art museum   spoke to me on the phone
        said "what are you going to talk about?"   and   i had
about   five seconds   to decide   and in the five seconds
        i realized   that theres something peculiar about talking on a
telephone   when youre three thousand five hundred miles away
        which is approximately the distance   long winded crows
        take when they go directly from san diego   to philadelphia
        and i remembered philadelphia very vaguely   as i kept trying
to think of   philadelphia   im an old new yorker as youll probably recognize from my accent   which is fairly marked   and
i thought of philadelphia "what does philadelphia have?"   well
        it has all sorts of things   i remembered the rodin museum
        the franklin institute   a ninety mile drive which seemed to
take hours   that i couldnt put together with ninety mile drives in
california   because in california when you drive ninety miles you
make it in about an hour and a half or less   and when you drive
        from new york to philadelphia you dont make it in an hour and a
half   so that space was different   and there was the friendly
voice on the other side of the telephone and i said   "well   ill
talk about 'is this the right place?'"   because i had a feeling
        that it might be the right place and   it might not be the

27

right place   but the rightness of place is something you learn
    progressively   apparently   not something you know
instantly   when i came here   in the plane   this time
    and ive come back and forth so many times now im beginning
to suffer from air shock between flights   when i got on the plane
    i had the feeling   i started out early in the day   it was
about 12 oclock   to be on a plane   12 oclock on a plane is in
some ways the worst possible time to get on a plane because
        what happens is   you start out in the daylight and you
wind up in the night and there never was any day   and its odd you
    feel that youre travelling into the past   though technically youve
gone into the future and lost the present   but you cant really
come to terms with that   somehow youve lost the day and youve
    gone into some time thats anterior to your time   and you dont
know what to make of it   youve been enveloped by night
        you look out of the window   you know   youre sitting
on a plane   and you start investing in anything possible that
happens on planes   earphones drinks whatever   and you plug
in everything   because you may as well do the plane experience
        otherwise why do it at all?   and you pay your two dollars
for earphones your dollar fifty for a bloody mary   although its
earlier in the day than you would ever drink in your life and
    you turn on the sound system and there is this odd sound
coming out   quickly you turn   you want to know whether
    you should turn on "corporate art"   theres a lecture thats going
    on about "art as business"   and i thought that was terrific
        but i couldnt get it   because someone was talking about
mergers   theres a ninety minute cycle   the problem of time
    keeps coming up   and someone is talking about mergers
        mergers of conglomerates   and at that moment i wasnt
interested in mergers because i didnt have a conglomerate i wanted to
    merge   i wanted to hear about art as business but art as business
was forty-five minutes away and i wasnt going to make it   so i
turned on music and   i tried for the music i thought would be in-
    teresting   and i hoped i was going to get brahms third symphony
and i came up in the middle of *schelomo*   and it went on and it was
interesting because it was very muddy   you know the earphones
    are   i suppose theyre as good earphones as they would get on

    28

an airplane   and what you get is a sound that you vaguely recognize   the element of recognition in this is more than anything
else   because no pitch is very distinct   so chords have for
example one note you hear and two notes you guess   which is a
rather impressive conceptual art form   and for a while you
listen   and then they put on a movie   and you dont really
want to hear the movie   because there is a movie about a rodeo
clown   you know this because you see his face and its all white
and somebody is beating him up and   you dont know why and
you dont really care   but you watch it and   people come by
and someone is computing his expense account next to you
and you say to yourself "what place is this?"   "is this a right
place?"   and "where am i going in this right place?"   somehow
im over kansas   and you look down and you say "this must be
kansas because thats how long ive been travelling"   but you cant
see kansas   what you see are rifts in clouds and you wonder
"what place is that under there?"   it doesnt have a big label   i
know that john baldessari went around california marking the letters
"C" "A" "L" "I" "F" "O" "R" "N" "I" "A" so that you could see
them from planes   which was a great service to california   or
to psa   and he took photographs of it later   and then at least
you knew where you were   if you looked all the time   though
if you lost three letters you might not know   you might have
thought it was CAFONIA   or you might have forgotten each
letter as you came to the next one   but the point is youd have a
chance to figure it out   but i kept wondering where i was going
      in coming to philadelphia   there was something of a ques-
tion   i would never go to the rodin museum again   no hostility
involved   its just that no reason in the world   that im now
aware of   would bring me to look at another rodin   and i
kept saying to myself "what am i going to do in philadelphia?   im
going to talk about   duchamp?   no   im not going to talk
about duchamp when i get there   thats the last thing in my mind
to talk about when i get to philadelphia   is to talk once again
about duchamp"   ive written too much about duchamp
      duchamp had talked too much about duchamp   and he was
very careful not to talk too much about duchamp   all his life he
spent trying not to bore people   very carefully not to bore

people   and now theyre going to make him bore people   the
institutions are going to propose that duchamp will be a bore
      and he hadnt wanted to be a bore   all his life he kept three
quarters of his work hidden   very carefully so that it could only
offend people who deserved to be offended by it in an appropriate
manner   and i felt that he had a right   to the obscurity he had
claimed for parts of his work   and to the crankiness he had
claimed for other parts of his work   and im going to protect that
      but thats another lecture another talk   another poem and
thats what i propose to do tomorrow but   im coming here i realized   im coming to a college   now colleges are not all the
same   and an art college   is not the same as any other   and
i teach in a place i teach in a college   in california   and   the
people who come to colleges are   there with expectations
      some kind of expectations   theres a transient quality to a
college   youre there hoping for some   change of status   that
is   youre there in some preparational state   and its not
entirely clear what   teaching in a college is either   as far as im
concerned   its neither clear what teaching in a college is   nor
is it clear what learning in a college is   or attending a college is
      im older than most people who go to colleges   most not all
      younger than others   but the fact is   i once went to
college   and i keep trying to think of that when i teach in a
college   because teaching in college is something for me of an
inquiry   that is a way of trying to find something or trying to
find a way to something   which may help other people to find a
way to something   because ive been to other places before them
      and itll turn out they go to other places than the places i
intended to go   there is a terrible problem   the notion of a
teacher   is that experience   will help you   you know?
      and there is a terrible lurking fear   in my mind   and ive
always had this fear   that experience prepares you for what will
never happen again   and its a terrible challenge   to anybody
who has experience   to find out what its worth   you know it
must be worth something   and i think its worth something   i
dont think its worth nothing   on the other hand im very nervous
about what it is that i can effectively offer   thats not trivial
      to someone who doesnt have this experience   thats not also

30

merely boring   everybody has on occasion been bored by somebody elses experience   you sit down and they tell you "LET ME
TELL YOU..." they say and you dont want to be told and youre
told and told and told   and ive experienced that too   in college
     although ive experienced other things in college   i kept
saying to myself "what is it about a college   that is the most
experience-like experience of it?"   i mean there are a lot of
  things in life that are not experiences   you dont regard them as
experiences   you go through them and you say "that wasnt an
  experience   that wasnt an experience   that wasnt an experience   that was an experience!"   in fact everybody has some
notion as to what is an experience and what is not an experience
     and a lot of it has to do with what you think is either beneficial
or real   it doesnt have to be beneficial   it might just simply
  be real   and your definition of the real has a lot to do with your
notion of what an experience should be   because your definition
of the real is more like a hope about things that should prove to be
  real   the real is like a construction   something that you
build   piece by piece   and then it falls on you   or you
  move into it   and then youre sorry or youre delighted   you
built a house out of it and you moved into it and then you furnished
  the house   well the ambiguity of this act   of constructing
  the real   is something that i wanted to talk about   because
its an art question as much as a life question   though its not
obligatory that we make it an art question   when i moved to
california i came from new york   which is a great thriving enclave
  of activity   there were millions of people all around and most of
them seem to have been artists   of some sort or another
     maybe i was mistaken but it seemed to me there were all sorts
of artists   there were many more artists than there were audiences
     which was all right   artists went to see each others work
     and we were all very excited with everything we were doing
and we were all doing everything   it seemed   but it became
  tiring after a while   very tiring   it was very friendly   one
of the things about new york that most people dont seem to know
  about it is that it was an extraordinarily friendly place   and
pretty soon we got tired of hearing each others gossip   or each
others work because it was very familiar   and you had the feeling

that there was a world somewhere that wasnt that   and that that
world outside it   was not better but maybe interesting   that
one might want to find out what it was that was not art   it was
as if the walls of new york were lined with art and you couldnt see
anything but art   the subways were art the streets were art the
actions were art there was nothing that didnt seem to be art-ful
      and overly artful   and everybody was an art critic   all
artists were art critics   and you looked at something and you said
"mmm   not bad"   it was getting very tiring   nothing
seemed to be at stake in any sense   i have to restrain myself   i
go to new york and i see these great subways moving with these
concrete poems   paco 135   rosilda 207   all over the subway
system with spray paint   and finally there arent enough subway
cars for these great art works   and they appear on trees and
rocks   and central park has been taken over and you expect the
whole city to become one vast art gallery   and though its pleasing
its nerve racking   there was something very tiring about watching
the world transformed into art the way you might watch cows get
transformed into hamburger   and somehow there must be cows
that are not hamburger   so   it was an accident   i accepted
a job in california   it was really an accident   i mean all my life
i stood preparing for other things than what happened to me   i
was in the process of taking a doctorate in linguistics and moon-
lighting as a curator for an institute of contemporary art in boston
      to which i commuted   i flew back and forth there during the
middle of the week and   i had all set a career in theoretical linguistics   a career?   i was interested in theoretical linguistics
and trained in it   and someone said to me "how would you like
to take a job teaching art in the university of california?   and you
could be curator of our gallery"   i said "what would i do in
california?   what would i teach?"   and he said "youd teach
art"   and i said "wow!   id teach art?   what art?   any
art?   to who?"   he said "theyre students   they come
regularly   every day students come into school   they come
into school   some of them bring notebooks   they sit down
      and you can talk to them"   and i thought this was so freaky
i said "wow im going to california"   and i went to california
      we went to california and we moved into   we drove out

my wife and i   my wifes an artist   you see theres art all
around   we drove out to california and we arrived in a nightmarish
situation   we arrived in california the day after we came to
phoenix   we came into phoenix the day andy warhol had just
been shot   which may have been about a week after i had last
seen him   and that same night   i was about to check out of
our motel   i was standing at the checkout desk   ely and blaise
were waiting in the car outside   and i heard a man saying over
and over again in a soft voice into the telephone "i dont know how
it happened" and it was like a *deja vu*   like i was back in benson
street in a house in the bronx we were subletting from a dentist who
was travelling in the far east when we heard that john kennedy was
shot   and suddenly   i dont know how   i knew that this
kennedy had been shot too   i had been watching him on television that evening in the motel dining room   before the big win
in california   and now he was shot and we had this mad scene of
driving across the desert   in a world that had just changed   i
didnt know whether andy was dead   and i didnt know whether
kennedy was dead   and i knew who had shot andy   and i had
no idea who had shot kennedy   whom i didnt know   and i
had this   peculiar feeling of driving across a chaos   and i
suppose its appropriate that a desert should be a chaos   that is
     the desert that lies between phoenix arizona and san diego is
not a profoundly dangerous or exciting desert anymore   i mean
you can get water and there are hotdog stands and whatever   but
you say "desert" and it feels dangerous and exciting   the anza-
borrego desert   and it was at night and it felt like chaos had been
restored to that place between arizona and california and it had
been repopulated with monsters   and it was hot when we arrived
in midmorning   having come through the mountain chain skirting
the coast   and my little boy got sick   he suddenly threw up
and we had to find a place where there was a doctor because we were
a little scared   and we found a medical center where all the
doctors were out to lunch   suddenly we were in solana beach
and everybody was out to lunch   and i said to somebody in a
shoestore "what do you do if somebody gets sick during lunch?"
     and they said "theres a medical center right up the hill"   and
i drove to the medical center   and there was a medical center

in california a medical center is unlike anything youve ever seen
unless youre a californian   medical centers depend on redwood trees   because theyre made out of redwood trees and iceplant   because what they do is level off an area   whatever was
there they take a bulldozer and level it off   if there were eucalyptus trees they knock them down they push things out of the way
    and then what they dont cover with redwood and blacktop they
cover with iceplant   wherever you go theres iceplant   its a
kind of squishy water-retaining plant that flowers very prettily
    its a bizarre plant and its rubbery and it forms a lawn all over
southern california   and no matter what you do southern
california is characterized by iceplant   it grows like crazy
    normally there would be a coastal desert   but there is this
iceplant and theres the medical center   and the medical center
has these large open spaces cooled by rooflike structures that are not
exactly rooves   theyre strips of redwood that cast shade wherever
they go   and there are these genteel offices   sometimes with
muzak   and theres nobody in the offices   that is   there
are a few people around   a nurse or a clerk   but nobodys
there   its lunchhour   and you say "whats going on?   i
mean here i am in california and i cant find a doctor"   and they
say "oh well   its lunch hour"   and i say "well maybe i can call
the university and find out whats happening"   and i call the
university and nobody answers the phone   and they say   "oh
well   theyre closed   i guess theyre pretty liberal there"
and i didnt know whether she meant that they were closed
because kennedy was dying and that was liberal   or they were
liberal about lunch hours   i had no way of knowing   in any
event this medical center   which was a place where a collocation
of specialists   come together in warmth and collegial friendliness
    is a place called a medical center   and there was in this
medical center a man called a dentist   a strange morose man
    into whose office nobody ever came   i went there once
    and i felt i had made a mistake   he felt i had made a mistake
    he had been sitting there looking out of his window at the ice-
plant and now he looked at me as if i was annoying him   now he
had to stop looking at his iceplant and look at my teeth   so he
looked at me disapprovingly as though he was silently trying to

persuade me to go away   so he could go back to looking at his
   iceplant   and i went away   and he looked as if he felt a bit
better   and i later learned that he had gone away too   that he
   was no longer there   and a young man   a very beautiful
young man   named laurence riedlinger   a very beautiful
young man came and took his practice   that is he bought his
practice   i dont know why he bought his practice   i was
   sitting on the floor in somebodys house   while the university
was erupting   the university was protesting the cambodian war
   and many of us had gone out to visit people to explain why the
   university was indignant about the cambodian venture   or
maybe it was the kent state thing   by now ive forgotten   and i
was sitting on the floor with other people and we were talking sanely
of why it is that students   the people who come to universities
   regularly   found it appalling   and there sitting across from
me were a lot of nice people from the town   usually the people
   who were rather pleasant and tolerant and really were not appalled
about anything   and there was this very beautiful blond young
man sitting there and he turned out to be someone who had come
   there   to take over this reluctant dentists practice   and i
couldnt believe it   he was so golden   handsome   young
      gentle   and he was going to move into this   life   and
i asked him "what are you doing here?"   he said he had just
graduated from the university of southern california and he had
   studied dentistry there and he had taken over this practice   and i
saw him a few times   and he would be sitting there not doing
   apparently very much till he got up to clean my teeth   and he
   would go off to tennis games after he finished cleaning my teeth
      or he would come in from a tennis game just in time to clean
my teeth when i got there   and i have a feeling that very few
people came to this dentist   because these centers get set up as
   speculations about the future population that will yet come
      now there are plenty of people with toothaches in california
and there are plenty of dentists   at least in the areas where there
are plenty of people   but most of the people go to the dentists
   who are overcrowded and before you go to a new dentist some sort
of revolution must take place before people come in   in any
event he would sit morosely and he would tell me every time i saw

him how his life was planned   he had gone to school for four
   years   then he had gone to dental school   and hed been
lucky and found this practice   and his wife was a teacher and she
   was going to teach for a while   till they got a little established
   and she could have a baby   and she was a beautiful golden
   child just like him   and it was very sad   and i would see him
every year   or every other year   maybe to get my teeth
   cleaned   or maybe id run into him in the postoffice or coming
out of the mayfair market   and each year he looked older and
   greyer   and i realized he had prepared this life   he had a
   terrifically prepared life   and he was waiting for it to begin
      and i kept feeling it would be interesting for him to have asked
      if it was the right place for it to begin   because he was aware
that the place he was at was not the place where it was beginning
      and he was waiting for something to happen   and i realized
that there was something typical about this thats a students problem
      this culture develops   a feeling   in one or in ones life
      that this is not the right place   no matter where you are it
isnt the right place   because its not the right time   the whole
feeling is youre getting ready for something   youre always
getting ready   you know?   you go off and you   expect to
   be benefited   by something   you go into school and you
take notes   i had one notebook through all my undergraduate
   career   i had one notebook that was filled with doodles   and
i studied   but i never took anything down with notes   it didnt
   seem to make any sense   but i had the notebook   it gave me
   a good feeling   that i was doing something   i used to like the
exercise of writing   and i was there and i remember that sense
   that where i was was not really a place   that is it was not really a
place it was like a passageway   i had the feeling i was in a school
   and it was a passageway   i had the feeling i was going to be an
   artist   of some kind   thats why im talking about it here
      i had the feeling i was going to be an artist but   going to be
an artist was like a whole "going to be"   and it was all futurity
was involved in this thing   you were getting ready   how were
   you getting ready?   what was i going to get ready to do?   i
   was going to get ready for something that somebody had already
   done   now the one thing about what everybody had already done

is that if you were going to do it it would be a disaster   the one
   thing you cant afford to do is whats already been done   because
its already been done and done and done and theres nothing meaningful in doing it all over again   but those were the 1950s   and
   the feeling that it was beneficial to do what everybody had already
done   was all around you   i mean everybody in the 50s knew
that what you should do was only what everybody had already done
   in those days   i remember a friend of mine   who was
taking a course   now people didnt take courses because they
   expected to learn something specific   they werent that naive
         i had a friend named corky   who was taking a course in
narrative writing   i think it was called creative writing but nobody
believed that   it was called narrative writing   which meant
   that you wrote stories   and everybody knew what a story was
      in those days there was no one who didnt know what a story
was because a story had an "epiphany"   and you may not know
what that word is   but it was a favorite critical term for something
   that turned things around   that is   at some point somebody
who had been doing   not very much   realized something
      when he realized something that was the epiphany   it was a
very famous type of story   you know it was somehow as if a
subtle bolt of lightning hit him and he said "wow!"   and it was
   based on a reading of james joyces dubliners which were very popular
   at that time   naturally   since it was forty-seven or
forty-some years after theyd been written   they were a little less
   popular when they were written   and with the audience for
which they were written   i said to corky one night "what are you
   doing lately?"   he said "what do you mean?"   "you know"
i said "what do you do?"   he said "oh   i guess im a novelist"
      i said "why?"   and he said "well because im not writing
novels this year"   he was getting ready to write a novel   he
was not writing novels   he was preparing to write a novel
      you researched novels   i was going to write a novel then too
      i dont know why i was going to write a novel but i had an image
of a life as an artist that had a definitive career   and a career
accumulated   lets say a novelists career   how did a novelists
   career accumulate?   there was an empty bookshelf and gradually
   it filled up with books   your books   and what you did is

you wrote book 1 and book 2 and after a while you had a lot of
books on that bookshelf that were by you   and i had an image
    of what they looked like   probably a little bit like french novels
        you know those beautiful lemon colored covers and then they
became white colored covers and they were published by gallimard
        and it was nice   i saw each one   and the novels would be
like by flaubert   well written   because obviously they had to
be well written   and you would choose the right words to write
them in   because well written novels are always written in the
    right words   and youd think a lot about those words   youd
    write 200 words a day   150 words a day   but they would be
the right 150 words   because they would be better than the
other 150 words you might have written   and this was a universal
    thing   it didnt matter whether you were writing novels or
making paintings   because if you made paintings you made
paintings of that type   that is you knew how a painting was made
        and you recognized it by its frame   and inside of it you had
a very clear expectation of what would be a good one   and i had
a friend who was learning how to make good ones   he was working at it   he drew very well   that is he drew very well in terms
    of what they thought drawing was   and he made marks that
looked like things in the external world and then   he would blot
them in certain ways   he would use a wet paper   and it would
look energetic and   impressionistic   or vaguely picassoid
        in a certain phase of picassos early work   and you knew
that he was in training   and he was going to make paintings of
the right sort   after a while   and later he sure enough did
        he went off and he got a fulbright to italy   and he drew
monks riding around on motorcycles   and he added some
italianate aspects to his style   and he came back and became an
    illustrator   which had not been his expectation   because his
expectation was that he was going to be an artist   and he didnt
    turn out to be an artist   and then other people turned out to be
artists who had no such expectation   and thinking back on this
situation of expectation   the question has become what had we
all been doing?   we had sat there in these classes   walked
there through those halls   spent a lot of time in the cafeteria
        probably as much time in the cafeteria as we spent in anything

38

else   probably it was more beneficial than most of the classes
       not because of the food but because there were people who
talked in the cafeteria   it was a conversation place   and among
these people   there were a few   contrast people   who
didnt do it that way   by way of endless preparation   i had a
friend who suddenly appeared   his name was gene   gene
appeared one day   and i dont know how i knew he was a friend
       but i knew it and thats one of the things youre sometimes more
certain about when youre younger than when youre older   anyway he suddenly appeared and he said to me "look ive made these
paintings   cmon i want you to look at my paintings im an artist"
       and this was very bold and was very unlike anything that
happened in a college cafeteria in the 1950s   he said "look at my
paintings   what do you think of them?"   he said "come up
to my loft and look at my paintings"   so i went to his loft and
looked at his paintings   and i dont know exactly what i thought
of them   it didnt too much matter   it was interesting that
someone should come to me and say "these are my paintings" not
like "im training to be a painter"   i was sort of shocked   and
he said "well what do you think of them" and i said "they look
energetic   why do you draw that way?"   you know?   and
he said "de kooning likes them"   i said "well   thats nice
       whos de kooning?"   i didnt know who de kooning was
       that was a mistake   soon i found out   and gene took
himself very seriously   which was unlike a student   and he
went to a philosophy class   and it was a gentle   genteel
philosophy class   in ethics   and he came around   im not
sure whether he was registered for the class or not   i think he
used to go around the school looking for things he might be interested in   and it was a class taught by a sweet man   a vaguely
friendly left wing   grey haired man who smoked a pipe   and
thought   ethics   and somehow somewhere in the middle of
the class gene was beginning to get nervous   because we were
talking about the things that might lead people to hold certain
values   or the professor was talking about that   and you were
beginning to look like you were   weighing things   and you had
six pounds of value and six pounds of negative value and   you
put them in the scale and   before you knew it   you made a

39

decision   that is   its a toss-up   or its not a toss-up   its
better to kill your mother   than to die or   its worse to kill
your mother than to die   and gene suddenly bristled and he said
to the professor "what about the unconditioned?"   and the
professor said "what? what do you mean?"   "what about the
unconditioned?   what about that which has no conditioned
grounds?"   and the professor just repeated "what do you
mean?"   and gene simply shook his head and said "being is one"
       now while this may seem a little absurd it was very serious and
quite simple   gene didnt want to be had by all this "weighing"
       because weighing in this way is endless   and even for the
professor who professed it   it would not yield a decision   not
a real decision   and the professor   who was really a very
intelligent man   and might have known this   was just
otherwise oriented   and said to him "what do you mean 'being is
one'   what could that possibly mean?"   being a really
reasonable man   he didnt want to hear 'being is one'   unless
you provided him with a reasonable position on 'being is one'
       and gene said "well   the ontological quality is unitary"
       they couldnt talk together   as you might have expected
       they had very little they could say to each other   and they
were both valuable people   they both were pursuing their possibilities   and we in the class   felt as hostages   to something
else   which was happening   for a moment   as if the real
world had appeared   by accident   in our midst   without
preparation   now   preparing to do something   clearly you
can imagine the virtues of preparing something   i mean i can
imagine the virtues of preparing   of becoming something that you
aim to be   of readying something that you aim to do   you
start out to do some thing   i worked very long on a novel   that
was when i was doing novels   now i dont do novels   i do other
kinds of things   but i was preparing to do something that had a
name   which was a novel   and i said to myself "im going to do
this 'novel' and the novel is going to be 'about something' "   and i
didnt have to worry what it was going to be about   that was given
       it wasnt conditioned   i knew what the novel was going to be
about   the novel was about a girl who got the stigmata or sort of
got the stigmata   and i didnt know how i came to think about this

the girl who was going to get the stigmata   but i did and i
knew other things about this girl   like she had one brown eye and
one blue eye   and i dont know how i knew she had one brown
eye and one blue eye or that she was twelve years old or 13 except
that she was having a conversation on the beach with another girl and
she was walking up toward me when she suddenly looked up and i
saw that she had one brown eye and one blue   and she was staying
in rockaway in the summer of 1945 when tokyo was being bombed
by firebombs   and earlier that year an airplane had flown into
the empire state building   leaving a great gaping hole in its side
       and all of this made some kind of sense   and she got involved
with some people   other kids slightly older   and they had a
beach party   and a slightly crippled slightly drunken older black
man came by   and began talking to them   and he was coming
on that he was a choctaw indian   while they were getting him
drunker   and they didnt believe it   they thought he was
coming on   and they kept getting him drunker and drunker
       and they kept taunting him and teasing him   about how
could he be a choctaw indian   they had never seen a choctaw
indian either   but what they really meant was "youre just an old
broken down black man with a limp   and while we dont know
what a choctaw indian would look like   he wouldnt look like
you"   but they didnt really have the nerve to say that right out
to him   in case he was maybe dangerous or something   so
they kept asking him for some signs   or some special knowledge
that would prove to them that he was really a choctaw indian
       to talk choctaw or dance an indian dance or something   and
he got madder and madder and finally he got mad enough to get up
and try to dance   and because he was pretty drunk and had a bad
leg he started stumbling around and weaving and limping   while
they laughed harder and harder   till he suddenly jumped way up
in the air   and let out a weird scream and came down dancing
and singing on his bad leg   as if there was nothing wrong with it
at all   and yelling a long and unintelligible string of syllables
that sounded like it must have been something from the way he
sang them   and if anybody knew it   it was choctaw   and
was about how the earth shook and the sun went black as a veil of
hair dropped in front of it and the moon turned blood red while the

stars fell out of the sky like fruit out of a tree shaken by a big wind
which for connoisseurs of the matter was a choctaw translation
of the book of revelation   and he collapsed in a heap and they
stuck him in a lifeguard tower with a bottle in his hand and ran
away   i had all this worked out in my mind   but the preparation   i had a series of images   but to prepare a novel   a
novel was made like flaubert   the way flaubert made life   the
way flaubert made love   flaubert made love   he went and
found a girl and then he went back home and wrote her letters
and flaubert was particularly well advised in this   the two
"lovers" corresponded and the letters became a "love life"   the
way the novels were turned out   a paragraph a day   the
notion was that you prepare the well made block   novels were
sculpture   they were carved   you went chip   chip
chip   off marble   there may be all kinds of sculpture
but what you had in mind was marble   and you could make
all kinds of sculpture   but whatever it looked like it was made
out of marble for sure   and i had five sections   and in one
section somebody had to take a train trip down to north carolina
and had to cross in a train over the chesapeake bay   and i took
a train over the chesapeake bay to find out   what the train trip
was like in order to prepare to write a novel that had very little to
do with the trip across the chesapeake bay   because what you
did with novels was you prepared them   you were always getting
ready   the idea of getting ready was based on the feeling that you
were never at the right place   that wherever you were it was not
the right place   like the whole of salammbo   whatever you
had to do   it was always going to be done in an other way
and the other way would become a way you would become
capable of   because you had arrived at an other place   the
right place   that was the right place   and you always wondered
where the right place precisely was   but that was the whole
nature of schooling   was to prepare you with the notion that
eventually there would be the right place   you would issue forth
from the last day of graduate school and suddenly find yourself in
the right place   now i had a very long undergraduate career   i
seemed to major in about eighteen different things and   i was
not prepared to be issued forth from the university   in fact i had

my sixth year program well in hand   and i forgot what i was
majoring in that year   it may have been physiological psychology
or some such thing   and i arrived with my beautiful program of
classes   which i was getting for nothing   so it didnt bother
me   city college in new york was for nothing   and i had a
very good job working as an engineer in a bubble gum factory
       designing machinery for them   and   a totally absurd job
       and i had never expected to do that either   but that wasnt
the right place and i didnt take it too seriously   because there we
were in this bubble gum factory trying to determine how it was that
a child who paid a penny   for bubble gum   would get both
parts of the joke   and they would prove to be the right parts
       so that if it would say in the first frame "why did the chicken
cross the road?"   it should say in the second "to get to the other
side"   as opposed say   to the child opening up his one cent
bubble gum and it saying "to get to the other side   who was
that lady i saw you with last night?"   because the strip came off
a continuous roll   and lo if the blade cut in the wrong place
       the child would be defrauded of at least one-half of his reward
       that is   the cavities he would get from the gum anyway
       but he wouldnt get the joke   so this was not part of my
preparation   that was subsidiary and accidental   and there was
the central career   and i walked in with my program for a physiological psychological major or whatever it was and they said to me
"you have graduated"   and i said "i have graduated?   how
could i have graduated?   i didnt take hygiene 71"   they said
"you have graduated   graduated"   and i said "graduated?"
       they said "yes   we will take   we will accept zoology 32
       as hygiene 71"   i said "but it isnt   i dont know all about
those sex practices you describe in hygiene 71   ill never know
and ill be sent out into the world   whereas all ill know about will
be the various nervous systems of the vertebrates"   and they
said "no   no   no   youve graduated"   i said "i havent
had math 61"   and they said "math 61 is elementary mathematics
       youve had the theory of complex functions   out!"   and
there i was   not that i couldnt support myself   id been supporting myself since i was sixteen   but i wasnt prepared for being
issued forth from this   preparational device   this institutional

43

preparation device   i really wasnt ready for it   i didnt know
what i was going to do   what was i going to do with my life?
      what do you mean "what was i going to do with my life?"
      i was doing it all along   and there was something bizarre
about this   i hadnt the faintest idea of what i was going to do
      and i was doing it all along   but i felt i wasnt doing it   it
was very important to realize i wasnt doing it   no matter what i
was doing was not it   and i kept saying to myself "why isnt it
it?"   because i wasnt quite sure   i wasnt sure what the "it"
was that was "it"   but i knew when it wasnt there   that is
"ill know it when i come to it" was the feeling i had of it
      "ill know it when i discover it"   it will suddenly be revealed
to me   it would be something like a calling   a friend of mine
had gone to a divinity school on a scholarship and he had not had a
calling   his sense of vocation was not there   and in those days
they took it more seriously   its not that long ago it was in the
1950s   it was when wagner college was still a lutheran school
      and they had spoken to him they didnt want to discuss it
      they wanted him to go through   "dont worry about having
a calling   it will come to you"   and he felt very sad about it
      eventually he dropped out of divinity school because he didnt
have a calling   so there was this sense that you would have a
calling and the calling would come after long training   now at
some point   i had the feeling   and i dont know why i had this
feeling   that always i had been doing everything just the same
      that all the things i had been doing i had been doing   and
that comes as a tremendous and transformational shock   that i
had not been writing novels but i had been writing something
      that i had not been making paintings but i had been making
some kind of art   i had been doing certain kinds of photographing
say and making certain kinds of sound tracks   and doing some
kinds of performances   which i had thought would be getting
me ready to do something else   and they didnt get me ready
      and then i was doing researching   and it turned out that the
researching itself was something   i had been studying things
      and the studying was itself something   for no reason
      the studying itself was interesting   and then i began to
realize i could do anything i wanted   and this was odd   because

44

id always been doing everything i wanted   nobody had ever
   stopped me from doing everything i wanted since high school
        which had in fact been a prison   im sure that it was a prison
high school was such a prison that nobody did what he wanted
        the high school system of america as i remember it was a penal
institution   and i went to a very good one   it was a boys high
   school in new york called brooklyn technical high school   which
   had 5800 boys   which is a very large number of boys and really
rather foolish to arrange that way   probably because in those
days they thought only boys would become engineers   most of
   the boys who went through it didnt become engineers   thats
fairly sure   and most of the people there walked around in a
   state of walls   that is they had the feeling there were always
walls around them   so much so that i remember seeing a situation
in that school   because the rules were very mad   i remember
   seeing a situation in the lunchroom   where a fierce quarrel broke
out   you know   boys schools are always very buggy   probably because there are no girls there   among other things   but
also because of the rules   and there was this fierce hostility that
   developed between these two guys   and one guy   unable to
   contain himself dropped his tray and hit the other one   and the
   the other   who was not afraid of him   looked at the first
   one and said   "not here"   where then?   outside   after
school   behind in the park   because there was a rule in the
   school   the school had created its rule   so much so that his
   survival itself was affected by his sense that this was not the right
   place   and this inability to take things seriously   this strange
sense that you cant take seriously anything that is at hand   is one
of the great weaknesses of the theory of preparation   now i dont
   believe that you never have to prepare things   it may be that
you have to prepare things   maybe you do   because i can
   think of cases where not preparing things   or the lack of time you
   have for preparation can become a disaster   i had a friend
        who was writing   he was in college with me   a man
named john molle   and he was trying to write   i wont say
   novels   ill say about human experience   why call it a novel?
        lets get simpler   he was trying to talk about human experi-
ence   writing is a form of fossilized talking   which gets put

45

inside of a can   called a book   and i respect that can   its a
    means of preservation   or maybe we should say in a frozen food
container called a book   but on the other hand if you dont know
how to handle that frozen food container that icy block will never
    turn back into talking   and if it will never turn back into talking
it will never be of any use to you again   so lets not call it a novel
      lets say he wanted to do some kind of talking about human
experience   and there he was he was thinking about human experience and he came down with a disease   and the disease he came
    down with he came down with some tumor in his leg   and he
dropped out of school   and the state of pain that he was in made
it very difficult for him to think about human experience
      except the experience of pain   which was really a rather
special experience even if it was universal   besides which it was
not the experience he had started out by being interested in   and
he had the leg amputated   and he had disappeared from our lives
      and i remember   we were in touch with him   friends of
mine and i   we were in touch with him but it was a difficult kind
of "in touch"   he was in a hospital and   then he was at home
in new jersey   and we were in new york   and we went out to
visit him on several occasions   and i remember at one point
      visiting him in his home   and he started to talk to us
      about   life   about what he thought life was   and he
only had the life he had   and he was enshrouded by very heavy
    pain   and sometimes drugs   and he was inhibited   he
couldnt get around much   he didnt walk around much
      because he was on crutches when he was able to walk at all
      and he was overridden by a kind of   he was only nineteen
and he had this kind of walled-in sexiness   and pain   that was
all there together   and he started telling us this long story   now
what was this long story he was telling us?   he told us about
how he had been reading this novel by arthur koestler   and hed
been trying to read it and in the book there was this man who became
a prisoner and hed had this girl friend   and how their lovemaking
was built on a kind of intense mechanical conditioning   and how
lovingly they went over the details of their physical preparations
      and how when he   the lover   lying on top of his girl
friend and holding her under the arms pressed with his thumb on her

46

nipple she came   and john was fascinated with this and said how
 it made him think about how nobody ever talked about the real
experience   of masturbation   and we all felt uncomfortable
       not because we thought there was anything that was such a big
 deal about masturbation   and he kept talking about it   in this
great physical detail   he said "no one has ever described   the
subtle transformation of feeling   the casual brushing of
       maybe some alien surface   against the tender skin of the
penis   and from this   diffuse pleasure   about as interesting
as an itch   with the hand coming back to stroke   like a lover
       the interested part   and how this will shift from a gentle
aura   where its always still possible to turn back   with a flush
of pleasure to a fierce and growing concentration pointed by the
intense and systematic stroking by the fingers of the distended and
 trembling crown   then the release"   and we
all got very nervous   we said "yeah"   and there was a wall of
 silence   we had nothing to say   and it was a real experience
             it was a human experience   it was just   very walled in
       he was in the right place   that is   he was in the only
place he was   now what was he going to do?   write about it as
 a way of living?   is there a way of writing about it or talking
about it   i dont know   i dont know what there is to talk
 about that will get beyond the wall of that small room   maybe
it will maybe it wouldnt   i dont know   "will" is not the issue
       because in the end he didnt write it   in the end there was a
combination of eroticism and morphine   and then we got a black
card in the mail that he had died and we went to his funeral   and
 i remember going to his funeral   i remember driving out there
with   a wagnerian *heldentenor* named friedrich bonhoffer
       who was a friend of his   and i went out there and another
friend went out there   and we drove out to this bleak italian
funeral in new jersey   where i remember all the elderly ladies in
 black dresses with those funny shoes   and john molle had evaporated   it was totally impossible to recognize where john molle
 was in this sicilian funeral   and there it was   a grouping
around a kind of   evaporated grave   and on the way back
       i remember   for a while everybody was very quiet because
we had nothing we could say   and suddenly bonhoffer who was

47

driving   this immense *heldentenor* who was driving this tiny
broken down volkswagen that was being held together like with
    rubber bands and chewing gum started singing   and at first he
started singing somewhat gently   but in his full bellowing voice
        these swelling wagnerian arias   and in the beginning we were
nervous but then we also started to sing with him   and as we
began to run out of wagner we somehow started in on a series of silly
filthy german songs   bonhoffer roaring at the top of his lungs
    tears were rolling down this huge germans face as he bellowed
out *"amanda mach' die beine breit   der kaiser braucht soldaten"*
    then in bonhoffers house   we were eating this goddam vile
german cheese   a brown reeking cheese   a foul smelling oily
marvelous tasting cheese   as bonhoffer sat in this easy chair reading to us from a book that he had somehow picked up   it was a
book written by alfred de musset   a lunatic genteel book about
    making out with nuns in a monastery   and that was also a place
        and it was closer to johns place   that we had somehow been
unable to find   it was how somehow we couldnt find the right
place   and pornography is all about inauspiciousness and preparation also   one of the main things about pornography is that its
    involved with finding the right place   with preparations and
    litanies   you recite litanies   you know a pornographic movie
is something like the recitation of a text   there is a naming of
parts   and a naming of acts   and the recitation itself becomes
a kind of incantation in order to arrive at some place   which is in
fact called "coming"   the point is that youre arriving   the
    aim is   arrival   now i can understand places that are not
considered   the place   and the necessity for a litany   the
    necessity for a litany is based on the recognition   of unprepared-
ness   and the need for preparation   that has sometimes a
justification   the inauspiciousness of being unprepared   as
one may be unprepared or insufficiently prepared   i can imagine
being unprepared for many things   it may be though   that
    the litany doesnt get you better prepared at all   it just takes
you to a different place   and it may be the characteristic of being
an artist   and maybe that means of being human   though im
not sure about that   maybe it is that the characteristic of an
artist is the gift of being ready to do something for which youre not

prepared   i have never been ready for anything i have ever done
at all   ive never had the sense of being adequately prepared for it
     its always arrived too early   it should have arrived later
     or then it comes late   and you were lucky   you werent
preparing for it and something else happened   and you decided
     that that was it   the decision that what has happened by accident
might be it   is a decision that winds up being made by artists all
     the time   how do you know when youre through with some-
thing?   you know because the phone rang   as somebody once
     pointed out   and then you cant ever get back to it again and its
     as ready as it will ever be   because theres no reason to go on
          the telephone rang   why not?   now i might say   of
this particular discourse   that theres no place at which i can end
     it   without producing a kind of profoundly pornographic poetic
effect   which i assure you i can do   i could produce a vast
symphonic conclusion   and you might walk out feeling benefited
     but i wont do it

*the next day   at the philadelphia art museum   i
respected duchamps right to silence   i spoke for an
hour and a half without once mentioning his name*

i had to stop in new york to talk to the people at the
acquavella gallery who were putting on a matisse show and
wanted to borrow a little still-life from the ucsd collection
on my way down madison avenue i ran into max
kozloff who i hadnt seen for over a year and since it was
about one oclock we went into one of those steak-n-brew
places to sit and talk over lunch   max   who is one
of the most serious art critics i know   was concerned
about the way my new work was going   he was afraid
that by putting my critical concerns in an art context and
"becoming an artist" i was going to lose any chance i had
to have a serious effect on peoples minds   he was
more familiar with my art critical writing than my poetry
and hed recently published one of the talk-pieces in art
forum so he may have had a better chance to collect feed-
back   but what bothered him most was that the usual
effect of estheticizing a discourse was to neutralize it
and i agreed that this was a danger   all you had to
do to confirm this was to consider the ease with which

the most menacing art discourses are converted into
pleasant commodities   id been thinking about that in
philadelphia and i started to tell max how at the philadelphia art museum   in the context of the duchamp
retrospective   i had tried out the idea of the artist as
obstacle   how perhaps instead of giving a more precise
or glamourous form to the platitudes of the culture
      the artist might propose himself as a sort of impedi-
ment   like sticking out a foot in a corridor and changing the direction of traffic   max said that was exactly
what most contemporary artists were doing and the
more extreme they became the faster the rest of the art
world rushed in to admire it as a kind of "far-out trip"
      he wanted to know why that wasnt the artist as
just plain ripoff   i answered that the effect of an
obstacle depends on its placement and the direction of
traffic   i told him about my friend howie who every
couple of years   whenever it got necessary   would
      go down to an island separating the traffic on the lower
east side drive take off his clothes and meditate   which
      was hardly a ripoff but was perhaps not too effective
because they always took him off to bellevue   but i
could think of other cases   like converting a deserted
      lot into a playground for children in berkeley or
publishing the real estate holdings of the trustees of the
guggenheim museum or looking for a job through an
employment agency and covering your job interview with
your camera   or merely asking questions about justice
and virtue in athens   and when they arrest you and
condemn you to death   but leave the door open for
      you to make your escape   refusing and insist on

drinking the hemlock instead   id also heard from a
student at cal arts   an art school in valencia that had
gone through a phase of curriculum that featured mush-
room hunting self realization seminars and cocounseling
and the year before had made a big thing out of nude
swimming at the coeducational swimming pool   that
there was this guy kozloff who used to come decorously
dressed to the swimming pool and used to hold his classes
in a darkened room where he flashed slides of pictures
on the wall and talked about what they could mean
which the kid said was a trip that was really far out

talking at the boundaries

when i agreed to come here   to indiana   barry alpert didnt
have a title for what i was going to talk about   i think maybe he
  forgot to ask me   which was   i suppose   just as well
        because he had an idea   i had given it to him   of the
kind of thing i was now doing   and i had an idea too   of going
places to talk to people   i was seeking an occasion   for the
  kind of talking i want to do   which would of course modify the
  kind of talking i wanted to do   and how i was no longer   so
  clearly a poet   a linguist   an art critic   all of which i had
so clearly been   and how my work was therefore no longer so
clearly a poem a criticism an investigation but somehow   lying
between them   or on their borders   and then it came to me
  on a voucher i had to sign   to collect my check   barry had
to tell the various people who had sponsored me   a department
  of english a department of art   and a library   what i was
going to do   so that i could get paid   or so theyd have some
idea of what i was going to do   and there it was on a voucher
        my subject   it said "talking at the boundaries"   and i
had to sign it and i signed it in the wrong place and the same voucher
came back to me in the mail   and i considered it a great piece of
good fortune   to encounter my subject on a voucher   and
  sign for it   making me responsible   it seemed a good title
because it made sense   in terms of the place and my reasons for

going to places   to improvise something   because as a poet i
    was getting extremely tired of   what i considered an unnatural
    language act   going into a closet   so to speak   sitting in
front of a typewriter   because   anything is possible in a closet
in front of a typewriter and nothing is necessary   a closet is no
    place to address anybody   or anything   and its so unnatural
        sitting in front of a typewriter   that you dont address any-
one   what you do is you sit at the typewriter and you bang out
the anticipated in front of the unanticipated   people   who
may be of any sort   short   round   blue   though
usually not so marked   being a general figure you talk to so
    generally   that you dont have to anticipate   his answers
        you see   why not her answers   it just came up second
    it might as well be her answers or their answers   there might
have been a lot of them   it was a big group   or a small group
        youre hopeless   you have no occasion for speaking   in
fact the whole trouble   or rather the trouble with the whole
        and i say this with due apology for the fact that were here in a
library   the whole problem of our literate and literal culture has
been   to some extent   the problem of the totally dislocated
occasion   that is in this case the book   which goes out into a
    distributional system unknown to us   with salesmen carting
them around to bookstores   which sell them to unknown people
for unknown reasons   with birthday cards   and you have
this unlikely situation   what will these people in duquesne say
        if this book we are talking about reaches duquesne   if you
have that kind of distributor   i have a publisher for thoughts and
    my publisher of thoughts told me that he had two salesmen in the
    middle west and i recoiled in shock   because i hadnt thought
    about what it was going to be in fort wayne that i should address
        or how   so i ask him "do they go to fort wayne?"   and
he says "no   how should i know if they go to fort wayne?"
        so i say well i wont worry about fort wayne this time   but i
realized   because id been through fort wayne once and it would
have had to be different to go through fort wayne   but its ok
        were in bloomington   not in fort wayne   and its because
of this   and because this talk was sponsored by a library an art
department and an english department were on a boundary   or at

the intersection of three boundaries   so there is no opportunity
for shop talk   now it is true that i go to some places that are like
     trade journals   and my talk has been put in art journals   and
in literary journals   though ive never been put in a library journal
          but ive been put in a lot of specialized journals   and when
im in one of those special places i can do something special   i can
     talk shoptalk   and talking shop is very consoling   because
the thing about talking shop is that the people youre talking shop
to know almost everything youre going to say and they already either
     agree with it or disagree with it   and to that extent the conver-
sation is elliptical   because you only have to deal with their mis-
taken expectations   youre not only speakers of the same language
     and dialect   youre practically sitting in each others laps   and
its not exactly a reasonable human situation   for adults to spend
so much time sitting in each others laps   which suggests that its a
     little more reasonable to go out   where you cant talk shop
          so that if were at a boundary theres not going to be any capacity
to talk shop   but theres a problem at a boundary   lets assume
that theres a boundary here   maybe the intersection of three
     states   there are some places in the united states where you can
     stand on the borders of three states   and you are at the inter-
section of three states and the three states speak different languages
          at least two of them probably do   now let us suppose
          those of you who are not from the state called art   i mean
what is usually called visual art or plastic art   or whatever
          imagine there is this state right across from you called art and
there is somebody doing something there in that state near the border
     and you look over the boundary and you see him sitting there
     or standing   and hes painting a picture you see   you
know hes painting a picture because this canvas is on an easel and the
canvas is on a stretcher   anyway hes painting and you see that
the way that hes painting seems strange   because hes got what
     appears to be a photograph   the photograph is in an opaque
enlarger   and hes projecting the photograph onto the surface of
the canvas and painting it on   now you say "hes got a photograph?   why does he have to paint it?   what kind of thing is
he doing?"   hes got this picture and hes enlarged it and hes got a
grid marked out up there on the canvas and he carefully marks out the

areas he wants to paint in   now youre from the other state neigh-
boring his and you can go up to him   or rather you go up to the
   edge of his territory and say "excuse me   is it ok if i come into
your state?"   and he opens the door to his studio state and says
   "sure"   youve been speaking through the half-open door
            now you come in and you say "why do you want to paint the
picture if you already have the picture?"   then what happens
depends on his attitude to foreigners   what he says   because
youre in his state   and he says "well   im not painting a picture
im painting a painting"   "thats what i said   why are you painting a picture when youve already got a picture?"   the difficulties
arise quickly and it depends upon how he feels about being an
ambassador for his country to the people of your country   what he
   does   if he starts receiving people its going to be like the united
nations   the talk will be difficult it may never end   but
another day comes and youre in your state and somebody comes in
from the other state   and for some unlikely reason   maybe of a
   low probability   youre talking out loud and youre holding
something that you keep looking at   from time to time   and
now and then you turn a sheet while youre talking   and hes very
   observant   this foreigner   he looks over your shoulder and
sees that youre talking the talking that somebody has put on that
sheet   and he looks at you while you continue this talking
            looking into nowhere while a number of other people are sitting
around looking at you   watching you but not the way they might
   be watching somebody that was talking to them while you continue
talking the talking that somebody has obviously already said   and
he thinks youre very strange   so he says "excuse me   im
from the other state across the way   art   and id like to know
   why it is that you want to keep saying something that somebody
   has already said and want to keep saying it so much in the way
that he said it   that you have to hold this   package in front
of you   with what he said so you can keep saying it"   you
say "wait a minute" and finish up what youre doing   which by
the way happens to mean that youre saying something very wild and
exciting and it sounds as if it should be very disturbing   this
thing that the other guy had been saying that youre now re-saying
      but the people all around are not distressed at all   i mean

58

there are people dying and things are falling all around the guy whos
   talking   but nobody runs to help the talking man   because
hes not there   because youre the only one whos there talking and
its plain that nothings happening to you   and there is this container of past utterances   and the man who was talking might as
well be dead   and the man from the other state   the state of
   art doesnt know whats going on with all these people raptly listening to the reminiscence of somebodys speech   the painter thinks
this is wild   that this is a terrific country with weird customs and
   he rushes back to his country and says "you know what they do
   over there?   they make believe theyre talking   but theyre
really only repeating somebody else's talking   in the same words
      and the words sound funny and unnatural the way they repeat
them   as if they werent really sure how to pronounce them
      and then the people whove been sitting around listening to this
talking   instead of answering the man whos been talking   they
   applaud"   its like painting from photographs   now he really
   doesnt know what youre doing and you dont really know what hes
   doing   and he doesnt have to and you dont have to as long as all
you do is skate back and forth across the boundary   because after
   all   theyre open boundaries and youre just a tourist   and
   there are no heavy duties to pay and you can cross pretty rapidly
      and you are continually observing the customs of the indigenous
people   the aborigines of the other state   but while you can
talk about their quaint customs   at some point you really cant
   penetrate them   unless   you do what?   i mean in order
to be able to have some real apprehension of what these others are
   doing   youll have to behave as they do   which is to say that
   you cant learn anybody elses language without speaking it   so
that if you go to paris you have a choice   you can watch the way
the people speak french or you can learn to speak french   if you
really learn how to speak french you speak so much french that
when other people come over they say "look   hes talking french
   he must be a frenchman" and if you dont do that youre talking
english and making random raids into french   youre talking a
   kind of pigeon french   which frenchman with some knowledge
of english or foreigners in general   may or may not have the
   politeness to try and understand   and in the back of your mind

you have a funny feeling about learning french too well   which
   may be why most people who dont learn to talk french when theyre
   children dont ever learn to speak french very well   they feel
   somehow disloyal   to english say   as if they understood
   without knowing it the french proverb   or is it italian
      traduction est trahison   that translation is treason   and
while it may feel odd to say outright that translation is treason you
can see how it might be   how the people in the art state might
   think it was unserious for one of their own   to go out to the
   other state and come back and imitate that queer imitation of
talking   all the while he was looking at them without expecting
an answer   unserious and pushy   while the people from that
queer talking state wouldnt really trust the way that art man was
   simulating what they were doing   as if he was doing it without
      conviction   just as the people in the simulated talking state
would not really trust one of their own   if he started to copy a
   photograph say of a newspaper text   but since you live in different states this may not be a grievous problem   if you dont travel
   a lot   but even in the same state   there are people who dont
   paint from photographs but they paint nevertheless   some of
   these people dont even paint on a canvas   they just paint anywhere   like on a wall or a floor   and the people who paint
from photographs   on a canvas on a stretcher have a lot of trouble
   talking to these other people   they think theyre unmannerly
      they may not even think theyre painters   but the other
people feel quite comfortable as painters   because as far as theyre
   concerned painting means covering something with paint   and
   there may yet be a third group of people here who have yet a different idea of where they can paint   they only paint on people
      though they may not care overly much what you paint on them
         now all of these people live in the same country but they speak
different dialects   which may make it difficult for them to talk
   to each other or nearly impossible   because they distrust each
others motives and habits   and dont like the way the other uses
   what seems to be similar words   now you cant be everything in
   the world   because one of the inherent limitations of being
anything is that it prevents you   at that time   from being
everything else   for while there may be some range to the anything

you happen to have chosen to be it is something like looking in a
given direction   which because you only have eyes in the front
   of your face will prevent you from looking behind   which is
   almost as banal as saying that if you are standing some place you
cannot also stand in the place where youre not standing   which
   if you try it will betray the place that you were standing as you
try to accomodate to another place   so there is this justifiable
xenophobia of stance   justifiable to the extent that you can only
stand in the place where youre standing   and this feeling
      suspicion   led people like the apache   who were really
rather splendid people   but there are no people so splendid that
they dont have to pay for their splendidness with some kind of mean-
ness   and it led people like the apache or the cheyenne to the
conclusion that they were the only people and that nobody else
was a people   and nearly every indian group had this concen-
trated wisdom of stance   in accordance with which they conceived of themselves as   the people   and called themselves
   that the people   and everybody else were the others   which
sometimes led the people to do terrible things to these other people
that they didnt live with   or habitually talk to   so that these
noble people   who were quite as good as most other people
      were capable of inflicting horrible tortures on those other
people because they werent people   and this was one of the
   defects of the wisdom of this great american indian culture   that
it had a very poor grasp of the worth or the right to live of anything
   living outside the group of their people   and this defect has been
shared by many other civilizations that have felt themselves more
   generous and grand   there have always been some people that
   the people never thought of as people   but even if its understandable how you can come to feel this way   as soon as you
know that you feel this way you begin to forget how to understand
   how you feel this way   i remember a situation   and this is a
good place to remember this situation because this is the university
of indiana   and the university of indiana is one of the great places
in anthropological linguistics   and this situation i recall   the
   writing of a distinguished anthropologist   a man named warner
      william warner   who was living with   and learning how
to live with a group of australian aborigines   how they lived

and he made a friend   a close friend of an australian   a
man   a native   that is he lived there   and warner lived with
these people and it was in the '30s and warner was with them and a
quarrel broke out   at a meeting there was this kind of a general
festival of sorts when all the groups came together   people who
generally only considered each other as marginally people   but
in this large festival they considered each other people   for a
while   until they got mad and each group which considered the
other group to be less people than they considered themselves would
eventually wind up killing some of these others who were not so
much people when things got bad   and then there would be
whats called a war   that is there would be a council   you see
at first people would just kill others   thats just killing   but a
war is an institutional form   conducted only by say tribal groups
and nations   people only kill each other   wars are formal
        you have to have councils and make arrangements and you do
everything in a different way   so they had this council   and
warner   who was at the council   listened to the whole discussion and they discussed the pros and cons of having a big meeting in
which all of the people who only marginally considered each other
as people would come together and fight it out in a sportful way
        once and for all   to sort of settle it so that whatever killing
was going to take place would take place at once   that is   instead of random killings and murder they were going to have a formal
war   which would be a war to end all wars   and when warner
heard them say that   he heard an echo in it of something he had
heard before   you see this was 1930 something and it wasnt so
far away from 1917 and it made him nervous   here he was sitting
on a log among australian aborigines and listening to reasonable men
talk in a language that was not his own   and he heard when he
translated what he heard into his own language   this will be a
war to end all wars   a battle to end all battles   a fight to end
all fighting   and the man who was his friend and who was an
aborigine said he didnt like this plan   he said to him   "i dont
like this plan"   he said to him "i dont like this plan"   and
warner said "you dont like this plan?   why not?"   you see
the anthropologist comes out here   and his friend says "ive heard
this plan before"   he says "ive heard it before   a lot of times"

he says "at first a few people kill each other   one kills another person and its bad   because the relatives of the other person
kill the first person or some of his relatives or friends and thats bad
     not many people get killed" he says   "then they hold a
council in order to end this killing and everybody comes together
and they kill lots and lots of people and nothing stops   its
happened four or five times that i remember"   he says "it doesnt
seem to me that if we kill more people that we will stop killing
people"   now this discourse between warner and his friend is on
the margin   the frontier if you like between people in two different places   it is on a kind of frontier and this conversation is
between frontier people who are sitting on the boundary between
one country   people   and another   i mean warner is an
anthropologist and he has come away from his people to live with
another kind of people   to see how they live   and his friend
the australian   whose name i dont remember because i dont
speak that australian language and it is difficult to remember a name
in a language you dont speak   his friend is also something of an
anthropologist or a man of the world   because you see part of his
life he had lived with another people some distance away from his
own people   he went with them for some reason i dont remember
when he was fairly young and he lived with them for some time
and they grew to like him and he grew to like them   and he
finally got used to their ways   of living and talking   and they
wanted to give him a wife because they liked him and considered
him one of the people   and now he was back with his own people
after living abroad and i dont think he had forgotten it   and he
was able to speak to warner i think in warners language   and this
cultivated man sitting in a council of his own people with a foreigner
says to the foreigner   who is his friend   "ive heard this plan
before   a lot of times   it doesnt seem to me that by killing
many people you will stop killing people"   and now it seems to
me that this is very much of a discourse on the margin   and it is
where the margin may be necessary   because it is very close to
treason   this translation to a foreigner   this man from outside   who was visiting the people   now i know that he had
been adopted   warner was an adopted people   and that
happens generally   if you come from outside to visit the people

and they let you stay they will adopt you as a matter of course and
you become a member of some clan and then youre also a people
        so to speak   of course you could extend that habit to all
people in all directions that you could conceivably reach and then
everybody would be a relative   but the limitation of distance is
significant   and the point is that for such a discourse to take
place at all you need an act of translation   the fact is that for
these two people to talk to each other you need some kind of translation   and translation is a much used word   lots of people
talk about translation   "ive translated homer"   "ive translated a business letter"   you know i was a translator for years
        i was the scientific director of a large publishing company that
specialized in translating scientific and technical material and in my
early career i translated all sorts of things   italian annulment
papers   the history of a leather company   the transactions of
an american bakery that was trying to buy chocolate filled easter
eggs from a german candy maker which transmitted them in large
shells filled with chocolate   and the letters went back and forth
between the two companies and they were rather odd because the
letters from the americans must have been rather angry letters
        though i never saw them   but they seem all to have ex-
pressed the very grave concern that all of the easter eggs should be
exactly the same size and weight   and they didnt understand the
meaning of the german letters that came to them   and they said
to me what do they say?   and i said well   they say that the
easter eggs cant be all the same size and weight   and they said
"why not?"   and i said "because the eggs come from a nearby
eggnog factory which has explained that the size of the eggs is the
responsibility of the swedish cocks   from whom they receive the
eggs   by means of the hens   and that it is impossible to
guarantee that all the eggs will be equivalent in size   even in weight
        because they dont all have the same capacity or volume   'this
is a defect in the hens   we understand'   now you have one
other question   that is 'what does the rest of the letter say?'"
        "well the rest of the letter deals with another matter   did
you really ask them to arrange for all the eggs to be capable of
standing up?"   they had apparently wanted every egg to be
capable of standing on its narrow side   erect   so that they

could sell them more easily   this wholesale bakery   and the
germans had replied   and i was not really able to translate the
reply exactly   because what they said in german was that *"eier
werden hingelegt   und stehen nicht auf"*   which is to say
that "eggs are layed (down)   and they dont stand up"   which
is not exactly the full effect of the german   but somehow
german and english have a slight difference and there is a difficulty
in getting precisely from one place to the other   and i sort of
said it to them and i waited to find out what they would respond
        but all this had to be said in letters you see   i mean i didnt
talk to this guy   i wrote a letter and it was a sort of insanity as i
sat in the middle   as the translator   and i felt as they must
have felt very often those people sitting between the arabs and the
spaniards somewhere around toledo trying to explain to one and
the other what the other one had going on   and it was   very
complicated   when one said this and you tried to translate it
into what the other one meant   and there was a grave problem
because   ultimately it isnt clear whether a translator is someone
who converts one language into another or really an instructor to
both those people   and this is now a very devious relationship
        i mean im placing it at the level of an anecdote but its not the
only way   i mean you could imagine a language   lets be
theoretical   you could imagine a language as a container for
utterances   i mean as a notion   you can imagine that a
language is a higher order form   an envelope with as it were a
higher capacity for shapedness than the utterances that are its parts
        so lets imagine a language and you have this language   and a
language has a shape   it has a structure that has some order some
form   and i dont mean the kind of form people impose on it in
high schools but i mean what you might call the form of the language   so this language has a shape   for the moment lets say
it has the shape   of an ellipse   if it has the shape of an ellipse
it is a two dimensional form   so lets suppose that all the utter-
ences that can be formed within it are only one dimensional   and
they happen to be lines   straight lines okay?   so every sentence
in the ellipse language has to be a straight line   you can imagine
that   now you can imagine that there is another language that
lives next door   which otherwise is not very unlike this language

except   unfortunately it is not shaped like an ellipse its shaped
like a hexagon   the shape of the language is hexagonal   now
because it has different lexical fields different vocabulary different
verb systems you can imagine that the difference between the two of
them can be analogized to the difference in shape between a hexagon and an ellipse   and it happens that utterances in the hexagon
language   have to be curved lines   all the sentences in the
hexagon language are small curved lines   and all the sentences
in the ellipse language are small straight lines   how do you translate?   how do you translate a sentence in the ellipse language into
a sentence in the hexagon language   dont despair its not impossible   imagine a simple situation   a discourse in the ellipse
language   you have the ellipse and in the ellipse you have this
discourse consisting of three sentences   that is   three straight
lines   and because this is a simple situation by accident   a
lucky accident   they intersect to form a triangle   a triangle
that happens to be contained within the ellipse   its not inscribed
in the ellipse but floating somewhere inside the ellipse   in the
hexagon now   somebody said to a hexagon man   you say to
him "translator translate   what that man said in the ellipse
language   the man who said that triangle"   and you are the
translator and you say "you may not really believe this"   and
you have to make a theory fast as to what constitutes a true translation   so you say   "well   a triangle?   is it an isoceles
triangle?"   in this case its an equilateral triangle   all three sides
are the same length   and the lines join to make a closed convex
form   its a closed convex form with three equal sides and what
you do is you measure off lines of the same length intersecting at
equivalent angles within the hexagon   only these line lengths
are measured along trajectories that are subjected to some appropriate
principle of curvature   as they might be if the area within the
hexagon was imagined as some portion of the surface of a sphere of
some particular magnitude   so what you say is "thats what ill do
ill turn this ordinary equilateral triangle of the ellipse language
into a spherical equilateral triangle in the hexagon language"   by
what you may call hopefully   the principle of appropriate deformation   and this is your translation   now you say "wait a
minute"   thats true what youve said   its a true translation

66

in a sense   its a line for line translation   you took a straight
line of a particular length and turned it into a curved line of the same
length   and youve arranged the lines at more or less equivalent
angles   to the extent that you can speak of the angles between
curved lines as equivalent to the angles between straight lines
       and furthermore youve arranged the whole group of lines   in
the same way   to get a similar talk triangle and hopefully youve
situated it   but i didnt say that   hopefully you situated it
swimming in somewhat the same way in its language container
       now i didnt say that because i dont know exactly how you
would do that   i mean supposing these reservoir languages are
large   and these triangle talks were floating inside them how
would you estimate where to put them   i didnt suppose that
you drew a pair of axes through the ellipse and the hexagon and
marked off the appropriate distances of these triangles from their
walls because it would be very hard to do   does a translator say
when he sets out to translate something from one language into
another what is the shape of that language and this? or now i am
going to find the middle of the other language and find out how much
off the middle of the other language the discourse was?   then
find the middle of this language and displace the discourse appropriately?   he doesnt do that   so in truth were in trouble so to
speak   there is at least some trouble   another trouble is that
the principle of congruence is being applied only to the inner form
       that is we are imagining that if we took the triangle and applied
to it the given principle of curvature and deformation   appropriate
perhaps to all utterances say within the hexagon language or appropriate to some class of them   the talk triangles would be equivalent
       but we didnt take up one other issue   an unfortunate one
       that the hexagon is quite different in the type of its configu-
ration from an ellipse   in the type of its symmetry so to speak
       the ellipse has a certain kind of bidirectionality   there are
two distinct axes that would give you two very different looking ways
of cutting the figure in half   while the hexagon has a sort of
radial symmetry so that the differences between these two languages
is very great and could be a real problem   if say the significance
of a group of utterances in a language was not only a consequence
of their relation to each other   but a consequence also of their

relation to the walls of their container   which are the limits of
  their language   in this case you maybe would want to frame
another theory of translation   to preserve the distances between
  the utterances and the perimeter of the language   or perhaps
the area between the utterances and the limits of the language
       now all this shape formalism sounds very abstract but its really a
simple issue   if you have an ellipse and a triangle inside it the
area of the ellipse that remains after you subtract the area of the
triangle may be the most significant aspect of the triangle discourse
       or maybe since that is inconceivable in any exact sense   may-
be some native commonsense intuition about the degree of pinched-
ness or openness of the space between the sides of the triangle and
  your image of the perimeter of the ellipse say   will be required
       and your idea of congruence can no longer be based merely on
an idea of the approximate congruence of the two contained triangles
or their superposability   but on an idea of the approximate equivalence of the areas between these triangles and their language
  containers   its quite possible that thats the problem and then
  youll have to work out an entirely different way of translating
       and the normal line for line translation will be up the creek
       and you say "will this kind of translation be adequate?"   the
question of adequacy will come up   it will be a question of
  adequacy not of "correctness" or "truth" say   and the answer
will depend on what you need it for   because it is an issue of
  adequacy with respect to some intention or purpose   i mean
what do you want to do?   a language user has some purpose
       or is at least engaged in some role   which one tends to forget
when one studies linguistics   which i remember because i studied
linguistics   i did my graduate work in linguistics and i realize that
  the more one studies linguistics   or the more one used to study
linguistics the more one tends to forget that one function of language
is to discourse   in some manner or other to produce utterances
  that are related to human beings   i mean one forgets this all the
  time   its the easiest thing in the world to forget because you can
get dazzled by grammar   which is a great system whose greatness
was but lately discovered   just as in the past in the 19th century
  you got dazzled by etymology   you know the career of the
indo-european hypothesis   so now you get dazzled by depth

grammar and its transformations into surface grammars   but you
still dont know how to map one persons utterances into anothers
      and youre faced with the issue of conformability   and you
have to talk about something like congruence   or degrees of
congruence   and if youre talking about translation   and the
   understanding of anyone elses discourse   or even any discourse
at all   this may force you to talk about translation   you will
be driven to ideas of congruence degrees of congruence   the congruence of two utterances within one language   the degree to
   which they "say the same thing"   or two utterances in different
   languages   and it may be that in principle no two utterances "say
the same thing"   if theyre laid edge to edge in the same space
      at the same time   and thats a problem but not insuperable
      even if its so   because the degree of congruence you get may
be quite sufficient for the purposes of some speaker or group of
   speakers at some particular time   for the purposes of their discourse situation   for which they are willing to give something up
      because youre always going to give some things up   im going
to give some things up   for a price   im going to tell you a
   story about something that happened to me a few days ago in
philadelphia because it was an issue of explanation   which is very
   close to translation   i was in philadelphia and i got into a conversation with a cab driver   and for reasons completely escaping
   me he suddenly started to talk and told me a large part of his life
story   or his image of his life story   and it was not an uninter-
esting story   i forget why   somehow we got to talking about
the inflation   thats why   we were talking about the inflation
      somehow i think nixon had not delivered the tapes that day and
   from nixon not delivering the tapes that day we got to the inflation
that is   i offered a theory of the inflation   a nixon theory of
   inflation   i mean this inflation was special because of the recent
remarkable increase in the price of necessities   food in particular
      and i believe i suggested that nixon was purposefully raising the
price of food to stop the inflation   you know as a kind of
approach to solving americas economic problem by removing money
from the poor instead of merely putting them out of work   that
is   what would happen is that food prices would gradually rise
till the lower income groups gradually paid 50 to 60% of their

income for food   which would effectively redistribute resources
  in such a way as to remove these groups as consumers from the rest
of the market because if they spent 60 to 70% of their income on
food   which they could hardly stop buying   and there are
many more poor people than rich people   there are many more
  people who make less than ten thousand dollars a year than people
who make more   this is an axiom right there   that there are
many more people who make less than ten thousand dollars a year
  than there are people who make more   for the people who make
less than ten thousand dollars a year it will be much quicker for them
to arrive at the point at which they spend 60 to 70% of their money
  on food   clearly long before the people who make twenty or
thirty thousand dollars a year   and if one had a policy like this
       which i proposed to him because i wanted to see what he would
say about it   if there was a policy you could imagine that there
was a mind behind it and it had a name   though it doesnt matter
  what name because it is a mind and it works and its intention is to
do this   if this was its intention it would put someone in charge
of the agriculture department who would see to it that food prices
were going up   and then as the food prices went up the people
  who would be most affected   because food prices are low in
the sense that the cost of a meal is low in proportion to an annual
  income but you have to eat lots of meals in a year   and there is
a limit to how little you can eat   you would gradually reach a
point where steak gets to be fifteen dollars a pound or hamburger
  seven dollars and fifty cents a pound   where families of four
with lets say two children and a husband who makes 8000 dollars a
  year and a wife who has to stay home to take care of the children
are paying over 50% of their money for food   one could imagine
that and one would then say they cant buy the new toaster right?
  not only cant they buy the new toaster but you   whose
policy it is   can thereby control the part of the economy that
you cant control in a capitalist economy by law and convention
       i said this would be   if somebody had the mentality to figure
this out   this would be an exceedingly interesting and cruel way
in which to redistribute the situation   "so anyhow i dont know
  if its true   what do you think of it?" i said to the cab driver
       since he had started talking to me at great length about all sorts

70

of other things   he said "well"   "well" he said to me "things
arent so bad" he said "theyre not so bad   you think theyre bad
now" he said "theyre not so bad   theyre not so bad at all" he
said   "i remember the thirties" he said   "look" he says "now-
adays   so what? it takes one day of your week to make enough
to survive   so itll take two   so itll take three days of your
week but at least youve got money in your pocket" he said   i
said "some money   some pockets"   he said "in the thirties
you didnt have anything in your pocket"   and there was a truth
in what he said   he said "look   back in the depression   i
had one little girl   it was before your time   she was born in
1933 and she was about 4 years old   and she was playing with
some other little friends in the playground and i was sitting on a
bench and watching   and this guy used to come around to the
playground with a little ice cream wagon   a little handtruck with
bells on it that rang when you pushed it   and my little girl came
over to me and said 'daddy can i have an ice cream?'   in those
days an ice cream cost a nickel"   it was a depression in which
food prices were low   "and i said 'yes dear but not now
youll have to wait till we go home'   and i took my little girl
by the hand and we walked away from the playground   and
when we got outside i said to her 'look honey do you know why i
said to you you cant have the ice cream now?' and she shook her
head and i said 'because your daddy had only one nickel in his
pocket and you were playing with all your little friends   and if i
buy you an ice cream it wouldnt be nice if i didnt buy them ice
cream too   and i didnt have any money and your daddy would
have been embarrassed   so wait till we get home and then well
get you the ice cream'"   he said "thats what things were like
then   its not like that now"   "now" he said "everybodys got
money   i dont have money but everybodys got money   my
children have money   so much money" he told me "they sent
me to israel for my vacation"   i said "it sounds dangerous"
he said "well   dangerous" he said "you know they said to
me 'what do you want?   you want to go to the islands   well
send you anywhere you want   you want a vacation in the
islands?   you want to go to miami?   whatever you want'"
i been to the islands i been to miami   ill go to israel   so

i went to israel"   i said "did you go for long?   did you get a
good look at it?   what was it like?"   he said "i really saw it
     the whole thing   i was there five days   it was one of those
tours you go to athens and rome and then you go to israel"   i
said "thats great   did you stay in one place for the five days?"
     he said "no   we went all around its a very interesting place
but its so expensive you can hardly breathe   its unbelievable" he
says "you wont believe it youre in israel and i went in to get a meal
     and it cost me twenty seven dollars   to get a meal   and the
waiter says 'twenty seven dollars' and i said 'look id be glad to give
you a hundred if you came at me with a gun   but is this a meal
or a holdup?'   but the waiter says 'come on   youre an american   all americans have money'   so what could i say 'my
children sent me to israel for my anniversary i dont have any money'
     so i paid him twenty seven dollars and i said thank you   be-
cause its true   if i dont have money what am i doing there?   all
americans have money   but i got to see a great deal   i went all
around the place   i even got to the wailing wall" he said "it was
a very interesting place   the wailing wall i went to the wailing
wall i even went to a mosque" he said "at the wailing wall my wife
took along this camera and she was taking a picture of it and" he
said "suddenly you know all these old men with beards and long
side locks came rushing up toward her and right away i took the
camera away from her and stepped in front of her   i said to her
'give it to me' you know and the old men came up and i held up
my hand and i said 'stop' "   and now i have to translate because
he suddenly burst into yiddish   and he said to them   this is
the english of it 'its not her fault its my fault   shes only a dishrag
     shes just a reformed jew   im an orthodox jew   and she
doesnt know any better'   and i said "what?   does your wife
understand yiddish?"   he said "yeah   sure"   and i said
to myself "wait a minute   what did he say for her?"   i could
have sworn i heard him say "its not her fault its my fault shes just a
dishrag"   and i said "wait a minute"   now let me go over
what he said   i dont speak yiddish very well and im afraid its
going to sound more like german but ill try for the yiddish
     which i do understand very well   he said   and im trying
to remember just how he said it   *siz nit ihr die shuld   siz*

mir die shuld   ziz nur a shmatta"   "the guilt is not hers   the
    guilt is mine   shes only ..."   now for those of you who know
something of yiddish   you can recognize that im saying something
    he said   imitating it   in yiddish   or my imitation of yid-
dish   sticking to his words and word order in my more or less
    german accent   but when i translated i said "shes just a dishrag"
        and youll know that the word "shmatta"   doesnt mean a
"dishrag"   it simply means a "rag"   now why did i say shes
just a dishrag when he said shes just a rag   well   in english
    when you say you can walk over somebody you say hes just a
    dishrag   if you said someone was just a rag   which is what he
    said   you wouldnt get anywhere   "its not her fault its my
fault shes just a rag"   it somehow doesnt sound right does it?
        well the reason it doesnt sound right is that the word "rag" in
english doesnt carry the strong suggestion of that passivity that
incapacity   because a "rag" in english is more suggestive of the
    kind of tearing and fragmenting and shredding that brought it to its
present condition   i mean youre more likely to think of its shred-
dedness all other things being equal   than its complete lack of
    rigidity   you dont immediately think of it lying on the floor
and being tromped on   but somehow you see a dishrag as something capable of being wrung out and not resisting   now if english
    has the property of being a language whose shape is such that a
    dishrag is something that you can exert your will upon freely
        "walk over" so to speak   and yiddish is a language that has
a shape such that a rag can be bent to your will   then by mis-
    translating in one sense   a rag into a dishrag   i was capable
of translating correctly an important aspect of what he said   and
    this is all very easy and very cool   i mean every translator thats
        ever faced translation problems can do that and its not a big deal
        but lets take up the problem of translating in another situation
where it becomes more important   where we want to talk to
each other badly and   if you remember   we are sitting at the
    boundaries   a telephone rings and im sitting with my cousin and
he receives a call from his neighbor   were not at his house
        and the caller says youre mothers flipped out again   we get
up go down and get a cab   his mother is lying in the middle of
the living room floor   and he walks in and sees her lying there

73

he walks over to her and says "mother why dont you get up?"
she says "ohhhh"   he says "well help you well carry you
to bed"   she says "go away   im going to lie here on the floor"
there are several possibilities   obviously   you can decide
that shes chosen to live her life on the floor   lets say that we dont
translate this   shes on the other side of the boundary shes decided to live her life on the floor   leave her alone walk over her
you know   go about your life   when it comes breakfast
time if youre the one whose making the breakfast you make the
coffee you put the coffee on the floor   you know you put the
coffee on the floor you squeeze out some juice you bring her a glass
of juice you go about your business   in the evening shes still on
the floor you come in you say "hi mom" you go into the other room
you dont do that   you know   because thats also a
translation   that was your decision that she chose to live her life
on the floor and for the next six months you assumed that everything would be conducted on the floor   now theres a problem
if she doesnt get up to go to the john   theres going to be a
great problem on that floor you know   and its not a joke because
shes determinedly lying on that floor as at a crisis point   shes not
going to leave that floor and you know it   so you have an
alternative   shes lying on the floor because shes sick   that is
to say she suffers from a disease   a mental disease and she needs
help   help means you can pick her up and take her away   so
you say then "we must take her to the hospital"   we call the
doctor   my cousin gets on the phone and he says "doctor   my
mother   my mother has broken down again   shes sick"   the
doctor says bring her immediately   right away he knows exactly
what we mean   we want to ship her off   so we have to call a
taxi downstairs and pick up her loose and unresisting but uncooper-
ating flesh and translate her body out of the room   on the basis
of our translation of the meaning of her decision to lie down
that is we decided that she was ill because there was a condition
she was not fulfilling   like realizing the value of standing up
or going to her bed   which is where people lie down who
have to lie down   and perhaps we imagined   in this translation
that there was something that could be done for her to help her
fulfill the condition   of realizing she should stand up   you

74

know something like taking an aspirin for a headache and it would go
away   so the desire to lie down in the living room would go away
     i mean we would take her away to a place where they would
make her better   they would put electrodes on her strap her
down or give her an injection that would throw her into some kind
of convulsion   i mean you shake have spasmodic shock and after
a number of such salutary treatments you have been effectively
helped   by having been deprived of a certain amount of neural
tissue you know and persuaded that you should stand erect in the
living room   or at most sit down   and when you return to
the house you no longer lie on the floor probably for another year
     and for this change of altitude we have provided a therapeutic
vocabulary   now the alternative   or one of the alternatives
was to leave her on the floor   assuming that she had decided to
live her life on the floor   and wait for the crisis point at which
the department of sanitation would have to handle the living room
     i mean clearly that was an alternative translation   according
to which you would have a different explanation   you would
say "my mother has become idiosyncratic in respect of architectural
functions and she regards the living room as a combined bedroom
bathroom kitchen   my mother just has a different view of the
living room and i dont want to live with her but its her home   as
long as she pays the rent   im moving into the next apartment
     this is her apartment   this is her apartment and her life"
     you could do that   if you translate one way you send her
to the funny farm and if you translate the other way you move out
of the apartment   and both of these are translations   and
both of them have things to recommend themselves   that is
     they recommend themselves for different reasons clearly
     and theyre not complex   because they result in very direct
action   i mean they dont take great elegance to distinguish
     theres a clear choice between one and the other   and there
are even validation procedures of a relatively obvious type   i
mean if you send her to the hospital you have the crude but
obvious validation that she will likely come back and be erect when
she returns   because they wont let her out until she walks upright
     i mean you know that because it has happened before   in
other cases anyway   and there are also consequences if you move

into the next apartment and wait for what happens   because at
    some point she will either get up from the floor and reconduct her
    life or become a public nuisance of such an order that they will
    remove her as a public nuisance   and this is also a clearly validat-
able hypothesis   i mean the translation will be tested over time
    and each translation will come at a cost   okay   but here
theres a clearcut distinction and its not always so clearcut   i have a
proliferation of aunts   its not my fault it was my grandfathers
fault   and there was another aunt who was a nurse   and this
    nurse had never had a bad word to say to anyone   aunt sylvia
    never said anything bad to anybody at all in her life   she really
    didnt   and when someone said something angrily to her   "its
    stupid   sylvia"   she immediately developed big black and
blue marks   large black and blue marks   real hemorrhaging of
blood cells under the skin   and it was really rather surprising
    people generally walked on eggshells around sylvia because they
felt at any moment   she might hemorrhage   and on top of
    that she had the disease or disorder of the bourbon kings   because
if she started to bleed   hemophilia   she would continue   to
bleed and it would be difficult to get her to stop bleeding   and
    this was a strange life   i mean she was a rather generous person
    in the sense that the word generosity is ordinarily used   in
terms of all the external properties and acts of her life   she
helped people   she helped people for little or no money   she
    often worked as a nurse for people who didnt have money   on
occasion   and she was a professional   you know she was a
very useful member of the community in certain respects   she
certainly earned her living when she worked and when she didnt she
    didnt cost anybody anything   and she contributed a great deal
to the welfare of the people she worked for or merely helped
    but she was very peculiar   she was so peculiar that some-
body could easily have said that she was crazy   they could have
said she was a hysteric of some sort or another   they could have
said that she had bodily symptoms of some mental disorder   that
she was converting her social and psychological   her mental life
    problems into things like the stigmata   you know   the way
those people did who believed that they were destined for sainthood
and experience the crucifixion in their hands or some other parts of

76

their body   but my aunt had not appeared at such a crisis and
people were not ready to offer her sainthood   which is a kind of
translation   or a sanatorium   which is another translation
       but they felt that things were wrong with her life   and they
felt that her benevolence itself was   ill conceived in many ways
       that the things that she did were too much   that she didnt
take care of herself   that the things that she did for herself were
not enough   and she was a victim she was a very easy victim for
people   people who could tell her a story that she would immediately believe   and when people told her the right kind of story
she believed it immediately   she had a boyfriend named charles
       he used to come and see her once every two weeks and then he
would disappear for long periods of time on mysterious errands
       i dont know how but for some reason i met her once with him
and she said to me "charles   this is charles"   and he was a
very dark handsome man   and she said to me "this is charles
       charles is a basketball expert   hes an adviser to basketball
coaches"   and i said "oh"   and she said "yes   you know
those trips he takes i told you about   well he advises basketball
coaches in south america   all over south america"   and i
said "oh   well   what does he advise them about?" and she
said "plays   how to devise plays   complex american plays
for south american basketball teams"   and i said "well thats
great   he travels back and forth all the time doing that?"
       and she said "yes   how did you know?"   and i said
"well   it seemed likely" and she said later "what do you think?"
       and i said "i think its a good job" it seemed to me a very reason-
able job   i mean it keeps you travelling if you like to travel and
she said "oh yes he has very complicated plays he showed me
       with arrows and lines in all directions and its all very wonderful"
       and i said i thought that was great and i didnt know anything
about basketball but it sounded very interesting   and i didnt
know too much about basketball and at that moment i didnt want to
know much about basketball and i had the feeling that the less i
knew about basketball the better i would feel   but everybody
else was very mean to her when they heard that story   theyd tell
her he doesnt go to south america on basketball trips   hes lying
to you   and i dont know how they knew that because they knew

less about basketball than i did and even less about south america
but they were willing to tell her what they knew and every time
they told her something like that she got big black and blue marks
as you might have supposed   now at one point   charles
disappeared   apparently he went on a permanent basketball trip
to some south american place with a permanent need for advice
and my aunt collapsed   or more exactly   one day she walked
out of an elevator in the hospital in which she worked she caught
her heel between the edge of the elevator and the landing and fell
down   aside from some more black and blue marks there was no
discernible injury   but she couldnt get up and they took her to
the doctors   and the doctors were her friends and they looked
at her and they couldnt find anything that was seriously the matter
with her   but she said "i cant see straight"   and they gave
her some tests and they said you can see straight   its just nerves
but she said "i cant see straight"   and she said "im in pain"
and they gave her something to take and they told her to take
it but they said "it will go away because youre not in real pain
because theres nothing to cause you pain"   she said "i feel pressures in my head" and they said theres nothing to cause you to feel
pressures in your head   but she insisted and she went home
and because she insisted she was receiving disability insurance
while she was lying on her couch at home   and she was unable to
get up except to go down for groceries and come back and maybe
tidy up the house once in a while   and she lived her life at home
in retirement   watching her favorite television shows from her
couch all day until she got up to go to bed at night and receiving the
income she receives for her disability and from her nurses insurance
which was adequate for her life as she was living it   only
she lived it lying down watching television and getting up only when
people called her on the telephone and telling them "please dont
bother me im a very sick person and i have to lie down" and hanging
up   now a strange thing happened   all of my relatives called
each other up and then they called me up one night and said we
must have sylvia hospitalized   i said "why do you want to have
her hospitalized?"   they said shes lying down   i said "well
so shes lying down   i mean you know lots of people lie
down"   they said well she wont get up   i said so what

how does that hurt you if she doesnt get up?   i said is she
dying? and they said no but shes very sick   i said does she go
  down for her groceries   they said yes   i said does she watch
television   they said yes   i said so what do you care?   leave
her alone   what do you think shell be better in a hospital?
  they said theyll help her   i said thats what you think leave
her alone   i said dont bother her let her lie on her couch she has
  enough money to lie on her couch   there are many people who
  for no better reason lie on a yacht in the caribbean and you wouldnt
say they were crazy   all they do is lie on a yacht and they dont
do anything and they lie on this yacht and maybe they do lots of
  people damage when they pick up the telephone   she doesnt do
  anybody damage and she doesnt talk to you on the phone   you
  know youll never hear from her again if you leave her alone except
if you go in and say hello to her   i mean dont worry about it shes
  not hurting anyone she lives alone she doesnt bother anybody
          they said no we have to send her to a hospital   i said what
are they going to do for her in the hospital? theyre going to give
  her shots and her body is going to jump or theyll give her drugs
  theyll do some terrible things to her and shes not hurting anybody
what do you want from her?   they said its a terrible thing   you
  dont know what youre doing by refusing to come down and talk to
  the doctors   i said why should i talk to the doctors?   they
said because theyll listen to you   i said i dont want them to
listen to me i want them to leave her alone   now i wasnt going to
  translate   i mean it had occurred to me   i could have translated something to them but i didnt know whether i should translate
to them   from her body dialect   or whether it would be
  right if i translated   or what kind of purpose it would serve
          i mean i could have tried to translate   i could have supposed
she had a body dialect or a body language of some sort and that she
was saying something in that language   that what she was doing
or not doing were some kinds of utterances in this language   and
  what she was doing or saying   was not an assault upon anybody
else   though it was not entirely clear to me what it was about
          this discourse of hers   i mean as an art critic i might have
been tempted to say that i understood it   that her body had
become a terrain in which were made manifest the things that she

thought and felt and was appalled by   i could imagine it   i
   have no great conviction in this translation   as i say it i offer it
to you as talk   one of the reasons im talking rather than reading
is that i dont want to carry any more weight than talk   that is
      this is as true or as important as it is and as it sounds   and
its no truer and its not any heavier   if i put in paragraphs it
wouldnt become truer or more important   it would look truer
      and its not a lie what im saying   i assure you to the extent
that i can assure you   im not lying   but the extent of my
   assurance is not that its going to be true   because whether
what im saying is true or not depends on whether im right   and i
   have no assurance of that   all i can say is that i can see how she
may have converted her body into a terrain for representation
      like a kind of painting or sculpture   she was a kind of body
artist   only she was a body artist of consummate ability   she
could turn her body into a painting with red and purple marks
      in all sorts of places that could respond to the most astonishing
heterodox stimuli   and i dont know if i approve of it   this
art form employing this language   or even my understanding of
   it   and i wasnt disposed to explain it to them my relatives
because   supposing i told them   this aunt who called me
      and theyd say "youre crazy   why should she do that?"
and i would say because if she were to tell you in words what
   bothers her and her attitude to what bothers her   youd find her
with attitudes expressed in her mouth that would be incomprehensible
      and perhaps offensive   to you and to her   because any-
thing she would say that would depict her image of the world she
   would find appalling   and she would not like to hold any of
these attitudes   or the parts of this image   in her mouth
      by not telling them to you shes not doing you any harm
      you dont have to listen to her utterances   i mean shes lying
on her couch shes not even going down into the street   shes not
running into the street divesting herself of her clothes and showing
   her stigmata   i mean shes not going outside and saying look at
   my wounds   she isnt saying the world did this to me you did
this to me to anybody   shes saying this is being done to me
im being wounded   destroyed   by an accident   because it
   was an accident that her heel caught in the space between the

elevator and the landing and she fell as she came out into the hall
        and it was not apparent to anyone   not to you or to all of
her friends   who were doctors and spoke for medical science
   how deeply she was wounded by this trivial accident in the normal
    course of her life   now im translating again   im telling what
i think shes saying   its like slipping on a banana peel   her heel
caught in the elevator shaft on the way to doing her job helping
   other people more visibly injured   because when she fell down
   there was no apparent injury   no apparent serious injury
         nothing that anybody could see   especially medical science
         except it was clear that she was hurt   that is   she was
   clear that she was hurt   that there was something wrong with her
   head   there was pressure on it   and something wrong with
her vision   she couldnt see straight no matter how hard she tried
        and she was modestly letting everybody know   in a whisper
         that she was very ill as a consequence of bad luck   now
supposing i called up all my other aunts   theyd been calling me
up and it was only fair that in return i call each one up and tell this
   to them   do this number with them   they would call another
   conference and say davids sick   hes been working too hard
         hes sick   people dont behave like that   now people
behave in all sorts of ways that other people say people cant behave
   like and i was tempted to do this   but i really dont think i can
explain my aunt   i cant explain my aunt to them or to you
         because i dont think i understand my aunt and i dont think you
should understand my aunt   and i think its important for you not
to understand my aunt so i better tell you something else that may
cast light upon your not understanding my aunt   because it is a
   habit of mine   maybe a bad habit of mine to believe sometimes
   in the value of not understanding something   or being sure im
right   though as often as not ill argue for what i believe to be true
         i met a guy in a plane a few days ago   i seem to meet people
on public conveyances a lot   ive been travelling a lot lately
         and he was sitting next to me on the plane and he was wearing
the green uniform of a marine   a thin frail looking kid with a
   small face and hair almost as close cropped as mine   and he was
   wearing that rough textured green uniform   not the full dress
affair   and his black leather shoes and the visor of his hat were

so brilliantly shined you could see your face in them   but as he
was sitting there looking pretty much straight ahead of him   every
once in a while he would polish the visor of his hat all over again
and i had been reading but i couldnt help noticing the way he
kept shining the visor of his hat that already looked like a mirror
and i couldnt resist saying to him "it looks pretty shiny to me"
he said "yeah   but it loses it very fast"   and i agreed that
that was probably true but if that was the case i didnt see why he
would care   and he told me that that was what they called a spit
shine and it wasnt that he cared about the shine   it was just that
you could get out of the habit   that he bet i thought it was easy
but it wasnt   there were guys that spent hours at it and there
was a knack to it   and you had to work it up with a lot of real
polishing first and then you kind of like breathed on it and gave it
the delicate last touches   which was why they called it a spit
shine   and he showed me how you finished it off   but that
it wouldnt work at all unless you put in all the preliminary effort
and then we were talking   he had been at boot camp at
pendleton and this was his first real leave outside of a weekend pass
and he was on his way home   which was somewhere near
worcester   and we sat there quietly for a while without talking
and then he said to me "i bet you heard a lot of bad things about
pendleton   about brutality   about them hitting you and
things huh?   i guess they talk a lot about that huh" and i
shrugged   "its not true   maybe they did but not anymore
our sergeant was all psychological   you find out how you
all have to work together because one fuckup can spoil it for the
whole group   so you learn to help each other out for the groups
sake   like say maybe somebody really cant get a bed ready for
an inspection but maybe he does something else better   and
you all pitch in and do it for him   because its better for you all
in the long run" he said "its not so bad   it works out pretty well
in the long run"   i said "you mean nobody has any trouble?
you mean nobody just freaks out or fucks up so bad nobody
wants to help him   or if they do help him they get very bugged
with him because hes always fucking up and lean on him badly"
he said "yeah   we had a couple like that   one guy was
always like sneaking out after chicks   another one who was

82

good for absolutely nothing and his old man was a marine colonel
and you know he only got through because we all pulled him
through   but when it was time to get out he was such a fuckup
that the drillmaster told his father when he came for the ceremonies
and the old man flattened him with one punch"   i said "oh
tell me how long has it been since you been home?"   "a long
time" he said and he looked at me   "you teach?" he looked at
my book and i shook my head yeah   he said "college?"   i
said "yeah"   he said "i went to college for a while" and he named
a college in michigan near kalamazoo i think   "its supposed to
be a good school   it had a good rating" he said "i dont know
it wasnt for me"   he looked at me closely "what do you
teach?"   "art" i said   "i had art   from the egyptians to
the present   it was thorough"   i said was it interesting?
he said no   he said i studied humanities too   i said well
was it interesting?   he said not very   i said what did you do
in the humanities   he said we did the great books we had to read
all the great books   i said thats rough and he said yeah it was a
hard course   but i passed   "so why did you drop out?"
"it didnt make any sense i wasnt getting anywhere i was just
drifting   i was like lost"   i said "well are you found?"   he
said "no kidding   look at me   i didnt always look like this"
so i said "what did you look like?"   he pointed to his
shoulders and said "i looked like everybody else   my hair was
down to here   i was smoking grass and boozing on the weekend
i mean i wasnt strung out but there wasnt much to do and i was
just cruising   going to the movies sitting in a bar   and i dont
even like to drink   but it was a shithole of a town with a main
street that was all whores and pimps and beer joints and the two
local movies and they emptied out early   and if you were smart
you went back to the dorms on the early bus cause after twelve it
turned into a riot scene   i know cause i got stuck there once
after i missed a bus and i went into a place to drink and when i came
out this bunch of black cats chased us for twenty blocks to the bus
depot"   and he looked at me with a look of weary disgust "and i
hate all that dumb violence   the place was a shithole"   and we
sat there a while quietly again and then i asked him "so what made
you join the marines?" and he said "my life had no form   it

83

was all loose and there was nothing holding it together giving it a
shape   and i figured id join the service because it had an order"
      "okay" i said "but why the marines?"   he said "well they
seemed firm   and they looked like the best deal because i had a
lot of debts"   now thats the way i remember this   although i
dont remember his exact words   but it was like he was thinking
of himself as some kind of soft animal   thats held together from
outside by a shell   something like a lobster   only he would
have to take his soft flesh and put it into someone elses hands that
would present him with the shell   which was not merely a shell
but a fully articulate skeleton that would determine his way of
living and hold his soft life together and make it firm   .   and there
was no doubt that it had worked for him   his shoes were shined
he got up regularly in the morning and he did some kind of real
work   and "you know what" he said to me "you know why im
going home?   .   i want to see what they think of me"   "who?
      your folks?"   "no" he said "my buddies   the ones that
are the way i used to be"   i said "you mean the ones with long
hair?"   he said "yeah"   i said "well what do you think
theyre going to think?"   "theyre going to think i look funny"
      i said "i dont know if youre going to look funny to them
      but what if you do look strange to them   what are you
going to tell them?"   he said "im not going to tell them nothing
      im going to ask them whether i look funny"   i said "well
what if theyre noncommittal   i mean they were like your friends
      what if they dont want to hurt your feelings and they dont say
anything?"   and he said "well i dont know"   so i said "tell
me what if they dont tell you you look funny but they ask you a
question   about whats going to happen?   what if they dont
ask about the way you look   what if they ask you if something
terrible happens whats going to be the outcome?"   i said "you
know youre in the marines   how many years are you in for?"   .
      he said "a bit"   i said "look   supposing some terrible
thing happens in this country   like we get a bad   an unrepre-
sentative government"   i said "you know   suppose some
undemocratic government was to take over you know   suppose
some man in office   unfairly and unwisely   were to send
troops into some place we shouldnt be"   i said "supposing the

84

united states decides that it very much needs oil and a country say
      like saudi arabia   for reasons unknown to us decided they
wouldnt sell us their oil"   i said   "what would happen if this
  president   i understand that its not likely   but what if the
president sent you   as part of our contingent of military forces
      to see that we got the oil?"   he said "i guess id have to go"
      i said "well what would happen if the people of that country
felt that we   the americans   who were coming for the oil
were treating their country unfairly and resisted?   that is
      these people felt that they were being invaded   and say they
didnt have any arms they just stood in the streets and jeered at you
      you know   and some of them started throwing rocks at
you   what would happen?"   he says "i dont know   i really
wouldnt want to shoot them"   he said "i really wouldnt want to
  shoot them   i dont like the idea of shooting anybody"   and
i believed him but i said "but you enlisted in an armed service and
  youve got a gun   its the role of the armed service to obey its
orders   and youve got a gun   youre holding a gun   now
im not saying anybody is going to tell you to shoot anybody   i
mean the officer in charge may tell you to fire over everybodys
      head   but supposing the crowd freaks out and keeps throwing
  rocks and they do tell you to shoot somebody   they tell you to
shoot into the crowd   you told me before you hated violence
      that you dont want to have to kill anybody"   and i believed
him   "but they order you to fire   what happens?"   and he
  looked at me and said "i dont know"   and ill tell you something
      im sure he didnt know   and while you could guess or i
could guess what he might do   we really dont know   because
he doesnt know   what he knew was that he had taken the matter
of his life   grey amorphous and soft as an oyster   but still
  pulsating   ticking with life   and placed it in some other
hands   so that they would put it into some kind of container
  that would shape it for him   hold it together   this ticking
thing   and placing it in this container and holding this container
  containing his life   those hands holding it may be moving
      may be certain or uncertain   variously stable or unstable
      until they arrive at a situation which is itself unsettling
      causing things to shake and those hands to tremble that have

translated his life to this place   maybe dropping this ticking container   which may result in his shooting into the crowd or
shooting his officer or running away or just staring openmouthed
   watching things happen   treasonous and terrible   that may
   result not from translation   but from his necessity   and
failure   to translate

i was tired of riding on planes so i decided to take the
bus to south bend   where i was going to be talking at
notre dame   it was a very slow bus that stopped at
every town between bloomington and south bend
      at places like kokomo wabash milford and kosciusko
      and traveled over a large empty highway that theyd
run right through the old farmland   there was one
place where a stubborn farmer seemed to have held out
against the state because theyd had to run the highway
right around the farmhouse so that the farmhouse stuck
out on a small island separating the roadway with the
      southbound traffic passing by its rear door and the
northbound traffic at its front   i wondered how they
got out of the house when the traffic got heavy

on the bus i shared a seat with a high school kid whod
spent the weekend with his sister at the university where
she was studying to be a dietitian   he said he hoped
to go to the university also when he graduated if his
marks were good enough   now he was on his way
back to indianapolis where his parents were coming to
meet him and drive him home   i asked where home
was and he named a town i wasnt familiar with   so i
asked him where it was   he said he didnt know
         you just take the bus to indianapolis and your parents
come in a car and take you home

i had an hour stopover in indianapolis and a change of
buses so i checked my bag and decided to walk around
the city a little   there was a chill in the air and the
city was getting ready for winter   the department
stores were displaying fur trimmed coats and hats and
heavy sweaters and scarves and gloves   the kind of
clothing you dont see much of in southern california and
i was beginning to feel nostalgic for the east   the bus
terminal was in the downtown area and the cafeteria
where i went in for a cup of coffee was a hangout for
some hip looking black hustlers with flashy clothes and
snappy hair styles   the rest of the clientele were
mostly pale and drab with faintly pained expressions on
their faces that looked out of line with the hard rock
and heavy soul music on the jukebox   more in line
with the watery vegetables the gravy covered meat and
soft white rolls accompanied by little pats of butter
       when i reboarded the bus it was still fairly empty
       a few older people travelling to some of the smaller
towns to the north several college kids and one very
heavily made up girl looking like a gogo dancer   one
of the college kids   a young girl probably a freshman
or sophomore making her farewells through an open
window to a group of people i couldnt see on the other
side of the bus   at first she seemed to be talking to a
whole group but then she seemed to be exchanging some
slightly more intimate conversation with a particular
friend   trying to get in a last few words before parting
       while the bus driver was getting himself ready to go
       the driver got off to pick up some last minute
papers   and during this short interval the girl tried to

persuade her friend to try to come up to the school on
the weekend so they could spend it together but failing
in that she suggested he call her so they could have a
long conversation by phone   shed run out of her
allowance and wasnt going to be able to make any lengthy
long distance calls but since it would be his birthday
maybe he could call on his folks phone   the conver-
sation went on for a long time while the bus was filling
up   people were starting to sit down near her and her
baggage   which wasnt up in the rack yet   was
getting in peoples way but she kept on talking with her
head out the window   when the driver came back she
suggested that they follow after the bus part of the way
in their car before turning off the highway for home
*   before closing the window she got very sentimental*
"tell your folks" she said " 'thanks for having me' "
*   which i thought was a touching way of telling your*
boyfriend that youre glad he was born   but when
the bus pulled out i saw shed been talking to a girl

*it was dark when we came to south bend and raining   i
had to catch a cab out to the university and the cabby
was complaining how everything was changing out there
       all the kids were coming in with long hair they were
starting to let in girls and they were even talking about
cutting out the football team   he blamed it on the times
and the war in vietnam   i was staying at the campus
motor inn   a big holiday inn type place overlooking
the golf course that the school had built to accommodate
the conventions and class reunions and the crowds that
came down for the weekend games   id been there for
a week in 1968 as a "critic and artist" in residence with
the art department and it was during the student uprising
at columbia   i remembered sitting in the dining room
watching it on television surrounded by tractor salesmen
from duluth and ball bearing distributors from lansing
and their girl friends   the men mostly middle aged big
and fair haired or greying and overweight   looking on
uncomprehendingly at the events unfolding on the
screen   the women younger and brightly made-up
tense and violent   i remembered one woman   a
handsome platinum blonde pointing to the screen where a
cop was hitting a kid with a billy club   digging her nails
into her escorts arm and screaming "i saw him i saw him
he had it coming   he gave the cop the finger"
       things looked changed at least so far that the dining
room was nearly empty   a young priest having drinks
with a couple of friends on the lower level   a family
       two parents and their son   having dinner a table
away from me   i ordered a bloody mary and there was
no change there it was awful as before   peppery and*

tasteless and came accompanied by those dried up little
bread sticks and crackers packed in cellophane   i wondered whether it was doctrinal and they considered a
"bloody mary" something of a blasphemy   across from
me the father was talking to the son quite forcefully
     the son listening with no particular expression
nibbling his filet   i tried to make out what they were
saying but close as they were i couldnt make out a word
     they were an interesting group and hard to place
     the son could have been new york and jewish   he
was maybe seventeen or eighteen large and overweight
with glasses looking like a stuyvesant science kid dressed
old ivy league in button down shirt repp tie sport jacket
and cordovan shoes   but the father looked like a
working man whod made it   an energetic stocky little
man with polished fingernails and gleaming black hair
     could have been an italian contractor moved to mt
vernon   but the mother i couldnt place at all   a
sultry beauty with bright lipstick and heavy eyeshadow
with the old fashioned look of her expensive clothes
     spike heels and black nylons she might have been a
nightclub singer at las vegas   right now she was trying
with what looked like uncharacteristic humor to intervene
between the father and the son   to divert them with
     light chatter   i strained to catch what she was saying
and realized the conversation was in spanish

remembering
recording
representing

before coming here i stopped at a number of places   ive been
   travelling a lot   im beginning to feel a little travel shock at this
   point   ive gone east from california to philadelphia   from
   philadelphia to new york   from new york to bloomington
      and now im here from bloomington   and when i was in
   bloomington i was introduced to a painter   a very good
      skilfull painter   in the positive sense of that term   a
figure painter and he was working   on a large painting   on a
      diptych   i guess   maybe eight feet high   and each
part of it   maybe four feet wide   and the painting was very
   formally devised   with borders painted around both sections in
the manner of a medieval painting   and in one part of the diptych
there was a woman seated   and in the other part a man   standing   and they were   each of them   in a house that looked
   like it would have been one house joined across the two panels
      except that the borders of both panels split them from each
   other   and outside of the great window or windows of the room
      or rooms   housing them were landscape elements   and
the two   landscapes were somewhat   disjunctively chosen
      looking through the window on the womans side there was a
section of a freeway that began and ended without going anywhere
      that began abruptly in the midst of some countryside and
   terminated as suddenly   and on the other side   the mans

93

there was what seemed like a more   rural landscape   and this
felt confusing   somehow as if on the womans side you were
looking into a room in italy out onto an american countryside
      while on the other side it seemed you were looking from an
american room into italy   and this seemed so because   the
woman on the left hand side was clearly an italian woman   or
she was dressed as an italian woman   in a stylized black italian
dress   the kind of chic black low-necked dress that a fashionable
european woman might wear or might have worn several years ago
      and she was hunched over a table   it might have been the
kind of severe black dress worn by an unfashionable female member
of a family of impoverished country gentry or wealthier peasants
      anyway she was hunched over this table and it looked as if she
was drawing   lemons   or something of that order   that is
she was looking away from the man and down at a piece of paper
      and making a drawing on the far side of her section of the painting
      and the drawing was projecting over the border on that side of
the diptych in the manner of certain 15th century paintings
      which might have somebody pursuing something say   inside
the painting   and the prey passing over the border of the painting
      which is a painted border   and there is this ambiguity about
where the painting ends and the world begins   now in this other
part of the painting the man was holding up his hand   i think
      and looking it seemed somewhat in the direction of the woman
      now there were things about this painting i didnt understand
      in some sense it looked very low pressure   the way a lot of
painting looks in america   that is it looked as if it was not urgent
      about anything   painting is embarrassed to be about anything
      its been embarrassed for a long time   theres a grave sense of
embarrassment before the possibility of being about in painting
      which they call being literary   and literary is a bad term for
a painter because everyone knows that if you paint a painting of anything it shouldnt be about anything but painting   so that a
figurative painting must be an abstract painting in disguise   so
      that if you were to ask someone   a painter   about a woman
in his painting say he would probably tell you it was a figure not a
woman   maybe   or maybe even just a pattern he needed
there in that color or those colors to support his plastic values   i

mean "who is that woman?"   what a thing to say   if you said
that in 1953 the painter probably wouldnt have answered you at all
    but this is 1973 and im brave   so i ask the painter "who is
that woman?" and he answers   nervously "i like to think of that
as my wife"   actually i didnt ask him anything of the sort   he
volunteered   kind of playfully   that he liked to think of the
woman in the painting as his wife   and i said "oh?" or something
    noncommittal and he said yes   "we have a place in italy   in
fiesole   and i spend half the year here and half the year there
    my wife stays there all year round and then we join each other
in the spring"   having some image of what it is to live with someone or to be married and have a wife   the half year seemed rather
difficult to sustain   i know people have sustained longer intervals
but it seemed to impose some character on the painting that made
me wonder whether we were dealing with an abstract painting or not
    the separation of the two parts of the diptych interested me and
i wasnt sure that i could say anything to him about it because he was
very nervous   yet he had said "of course i like to think that this
is like my wife and this is me" he said later   and then he said
"and i like to think thats italy and thats america   but of course
thats for me   i wouldnt want anybody to think its important"
    and so i pretended i didnt think it was important i said of course
drank some wine and ate some peanuts and i looked at the painting
    there were a lot of objects in the painting   quotes i mean
from oh trompe loeil paintings from herculaneum and pompeii
    and other things that were floating around in the painting
looking   reminiscent   and they made the painting look less
important   more like other paintings   for example   you
couldnt see what the woman looked like   she was looking down
and the painter had in a rather characteristically chic manner
deformed her shoulder   hes an extraordinarily competent painter
and he always deforms his people   usually people who are painting
representational paintings which they suppose to be partial abstrac-
tions impose a signal upon the painting so that you will recognize
that it is not a painting of something   but rather a painting
    so what they tend to impose is what you could call the art
deformation upon the picture   so that you wont be inclined to
say "what is that a picture of?" but "what does that painting mean?"

95

perhaps   well she had this sort of hunched back and i knew of
course that that didnt mean that his wife had a hunchback   in
fact i was pretty certain his wife didnt have a hunchback   and
the man in the painting looked peculiar too   he was standing
very stiff   looking as if he had been stylized   as if the painter
had realized that paintings should be done in certain ways not intended to make his figure too much like a man   but let me take
that back   he made it look as much like a man as any painter
might   but he also made it as wooden as any kind of man he
could conceivably make while still having you recognize that it
looked like a man   though this was not a "picture" of a man that
you were looking at but a "painting" in which there was a reference
to a man and a reference to a woman   you might call this kind of
stylization lexical   which is to say that it was the kind of image
you might see in certain kinds of indian painting of the 18th and 19th
centuries   there is this style which tells you how to shape images
of things   and you reach for each image like out of some bag
and you pull out a "cow" and a "man" and you put them
together   you sort of make simple sentences with these images
you make "cow" "man" landscapes   "the man follows the
cow up the hill" say   for which you need an image also of a "hill"
and an order   in which the cow and the man face toward the hill
with the cow "higher up"   for which you need a conventional
sign indicating "higher up"   like placing the cow higher up on
the paper say   and you need to put one foot in front of the other
so someone will read "walking"   but while the painting   this
painting   had the kind of lexical stylization of this kind of sentence building painting it didnt read like that   i mean this was
not the ramayana you realize   for while everything in the
painting seemed to say just "read this"   it wasnt at all clear what
you were supposed to read or whether there was anything for you
to read there at all   while the purpose of such a style   in indian
painting say   is just to tell you to concentrate on reading and
then to give you the sentences they want you to read   so if this
wasnt the ramayana   or some other story   which the painter
had assured me it wasnt   why were these things looking this way?
i wasnt entirely clear   yet i did know   that when one has
considered the whole issue of representing in this culture   how i

96

feel and others   i think that the 20th century that i grew up in
   has come to feel   and maybe for a lot longer time than that
      that the true reproduction of reality   visual reality   is
conveyed by the photograph   and you may say thats not true
      or not entirely true   but i think i can satisfy you on that
score   suppose a man is accused of committing adultery with a
certain woman and the court is presented with a photograph of the
two of them sitting on a bed   it will probably be admitted as
evidence   whereas a drawing will not   and i think you will
   agree with me that there is something of value in the agreement of
   the society to the high value of the photograph as testimony
      that places the photograph somewhat in the position   of an
absolute validation principle   that is   a drawing clearly breaks
off somewhere else   now why do you suppose thats the case?
      there are a lot of reasons   its true that you cant get a photo-
graph of a person unless you   holding the camera   are standing
in that space   to take a photograph the camera has to be there
      i mean that seems to be true   though there are ranges of
reliability for this truth   it is quite possible after all   to produce a faked photograph   in which two people will appear in a
   space that they never ever inhabited   because of what you do in
   the darkroom   but this   fake   is not really a photograph
      it merely looks like a photograph   and it may look exactly
like a photograph while it is really three photographs   with some
marks that were not from any photograph   printed to look like
one real photograph   nevertheless you have the feeling when
you look at a photograph that it is a testimonial to the fact that a
   man held a camera in a particular place and thats what he saw
      now you say "thats what he saw"   well at the low level of
validating that somebody was somewhere holding the camera
      that the camera was somewhere   its clear what the photo-
graph is a testimony to   whether "thats what he saw" is something else again   what did he see?   what did the camera see?
      i dont know how clearly youre aware of the history of photo-
graphy   the history of photography is very old   its very old if
   you remember that the history of photography is the history of the
   camera as well as the history of the film   because the camera is
very old   it probably goes back to ancient greece   though the

evidence is uncertain   it seems fairly reasonable to conclude that
aristotle was describing   in one of his books   a camera oscura
     that he had devised in order to observe a solar eclipse   he
had set it up in such a manner to "see" the eclipse   you say "why
did he need a camera to see the eclipse?" and you say "how was
that seeing the eclipse?"   well the first question is easier to answer
because you cant look directly into the sun without burning your
eye out   though i suppose he didnt strictly need a camera oscura
     he could have oiled a piece of paper or something   to shield
his eyes with   used some translucent material   cloth
     whatever to mitigate the intensity of the sun   but thats not
what he did   what he did was inspect an image of the sun during
an eclipse   which is not exactly the sun unless you have a notion
about images that makes you suppose them to be like seeing the
sun   look   the notion of a camera oscura goes far beyond
shielding your eyes   it supposes a relation between the sun and
a small disc on the wall of a darkened room   a relation that holds
between your eye and the sun   you see i said "eye" not "eyes"
     the camera oscura has only one "eye" or hole and that eye col-
lects an image thats upside down   though if you turn a regular
disc upside down i dont suppose it will make any difference   at
least not in the case of the sun   so you project this disc on the
wall   and watch it go through its number so to speak and its
wonderful and it doesnt matter that its upside down   and you
can even make marks on the wall tracing the course of the eclipse
     which you couldnt do with your eye   so what youre doing
is what the eye does   seeing   only more so   and the idea
of this connection   between   the camera   the dark chamber and the eye is very old   there is   if the aristotle is unclear
     an eleventh century treatise   an arabic treatise on optics by
al haithami or alhazen as he got to be known in the west   on the
eye and seeing   and it is the usual arabic kind of work on the eye
     they couldnt for religious reasons   undertake dissections of
the eye   but there is this diagram   with the eye shown in
cross-section as a kind of dark chamber   terrifically symmetrical
and all that   with the crystalline lens in the center of the eye
     which is not where it happens to be   as the world tends to
be less perfectly symmetrical than the mind likes to think it   and

this lens   taken together with the vitreous humor   which together al haithami called the glacial sphere   this body was supposed to receive   passively   the image of the world on its
screen   because   al haithami says   definitively
     "seeing"   "the act of vision is accomplished by rays coming
from external objects and entering the visual organ   it is not
accomplished by means of rays sent out from the eye"   and in
this same manuscript al haithami describes   clearly and in similar
terms a camera oscura   that he must have used for   recording
eclipses of the sun and the moon   since the arabs were not very
original in this   and seem to have gotten most of their information   including their mistakes from the greeks   it seems likely
that the greeks also had the camera oscura   and also connected
it with the human eye   so closely   i would say they invented
the camera to imitate what they thought was the eye   or at least
what some thought was the eye   because there was another
theory   a competing theory   that the eye sent out a ray
     some emanation of your personality   into the world   and
it met with another ray   an emanation from the personality of
an object   these married   and the fruit of this union   its
child so to speak   a new ray combining features of the object
and the seeing subject   returned to the onlooker as the image
     while there were many things that were attractive about it it
was not a theory that lent itself to empirical validation   you
couldnt build a camera with it   and there was this other view
     a less interactive view   that the eye consisted of a small
aperture and a screen   upon which images   the reflections
of objects were thrown   yet   for someone interested in these
objects   there were certain   deficiencies   problems in
the eyes capacities   everyone knows that accuracy of vision is
relative   there are people with better or worse eyes   at different distances   eyes can be clouded or confused   aristotles eyes
might have teared trying to look into the sun   on the analogy
with mirrors there were dark and light ones   and then these
images were fleeting   now sometime in the renaissance
     somewhere in the 16th century perhaps and certainly by the
17th   this great respect for objects   for mastery of objects
     and their truth   reached a head   and it expressed itself

at times   in a vast enthusiasm for ingenuity and competence
in manipulating them   mechanics   now many of you have
read vasaris lives of the artists   its a very funny and loveable
book   and in it   three times he tells a story   there is a
road and a child sitting by the roadside drawing on a stone   and
each time   it happens that a famous man   some great artist
is travelling on this road   well he passes by the little boy and by
chance observes what the child is drawing   it happens to be a
perfect circle   the great artist gets off his horse stares in admira-
tion at the perfect roundness of the circle and says "you must be
giotto!"   or andrea del sarto or whoever the great artist is whos
drawing the perfect circle   now theres nothing to drawing a
perfect circle   for a renaissance man   he knows from euclid or
somebodys version of euclid that a circle is the locus of all points
equidistant from a given point in a single plane   so all he needs
is a flat surface a piece of string   a piece of chalk and some kind
of peg   though even his finger will do   he merely takes the
chalk ties it to the string fixes the other end of the string to the
intended center on his flat surface   and if he holds the string
rigidly enough he swings a perfect circle   right?   it is a perfect simple little machine   so whats so impressive about making
a perfect circle?   well the famous little boy   giotto or whoever else he happens to be   is not using a string   hes drawing
this perfect circle freehand   the mark of his mastery consists of
his ability to simulate a simple machine   now i take this to be
symptomatic of two fundamental ideas in our european   techno-
logical career   two ideas that need not and often are not
related   look   the idea of a circle   a perfect circle
is not visible   strictly speaking a perfect circle is not visible
it is metrical   that is there is an idea of perfectly regular
relations between any point on some line   the perimeter   and
one point not on that line   but lying in a plane determined by
the center and any two points on that line   the truth of a perfect
circle   is a pure idea   of relations   the notion of drawing
a perfect circle is the notion of imposing a pure idea on the physical
world   and strictly speaking you could only do it with a perfect
machine   in which the string is of an ideal tension the surface
ideally flat and the chalk and the peg are ideally fine points that

travel perfectly without friction or wear in their orbits   the idea
of imposing these pure relations on a flat stone is a kind of white
    magic   a triumph of mind over material   but supposing you
had such a perfect machine   how would you know that you had
it?   you would need a perfect measuring machine to apprehend
the perfect circle drawn by the perfect machine   so the idea of
    drawing a perfect circle is two triumphs instead of one   a triumph
of handling and a triumph of seeing   the two parts of the techno-
logical dream   mastery and the knowledge of mastery   the
dream of power and the dream of truth   now you can see why
    you would want photography   just as you might have wanted
        did want   to overcome the ebb and flow of concentrated
directed power that is the outcome of the physiology of muscle
    of living tissue itself   you can suppose a perfect seeing
    that would take all the images of the real   as if let us say
that the real consisted of some finite number of objects of which you
    could imagine taking the true images   and that you could assemble
these true images in a great museum of the world of man or of culture   put them on the wall so to speak and exhibit the truth
        this is the neutral view of things discovered neutrally   without
the clouding effect say of that fluid emitted from your eye in the old
    platonic thory that went out and married the world object   and
changed it say by diluting it or pushing it   or maybe in some way
    dissolving it   what you wanted at best   was not to bug the
world and yet to have it in a little package   smaller than usual
        maybe uncolored   maybe two dimensional   but so correct
        now people believed that people saw something like this great
camera only not so well   a distinguished scientist in the 17th
century   giambattista della porta tried to show that an eye was
    like a camera oscura   he snuck up on the back of an oxs eye
        after having killed the ox removed its eye in the manner of
science   and he tried to see if he could observe the images formed
    upon the screen of the oxs eye when he flashed images at it   but
the cow   not being alive saw nothing and della porta didnt see anything either   but della porta had forgotten   wanted to forget
        the cautious suggestion that we see through the eye or with the
eye   that the eye doesnt "see"   he had   along with others
    reinvented the eye as the camera that was invented to be like

the eye   and was now just like the eye they had supposed at the
   start   so they forgot platos suggestion   which he made without too much hard information   just a good deal of common
sense   and it has taken contemporary computer science and
technology combined with a different kind of psychology to break
   down the notion of the eye as a passive receptor screen like a mirror
or camera   with maybe a little help from an understanding of
   video technology   because what we seem to have now is an eye
thats always travelling   doesnt sit still at all waiting for an "image"
      but makes rapid passes   scanning   because it seems we
dont have a whole retinal screen available for sharp focus viewing
      that only at around a small area   the fovea   is there a
dense enough packing of receptor cells for sharp discriminations
      that will give us 2 or 3 degrees of real acuity out in the real
world   now at anything like a reasonable distance   two or
   three degrees of clear reception will not give you anything like what
you usually think of as a whole image   i mean at about a distance
of six feet you should get a circle of acute reception about three or
four inches in diameter   when youre focussed there   not what
   youd usually call a real image at all   outside of that circle youd
receive less precise information   which you would only recognize
as information when its distinctive   or more precisely   what
i mean is you may receive all sorts of light reflections   but what
   you seem to   register   react to   are sharp discontinuities
between fields of light and dark   and it appears you mainly react
   to them   register them   as they move across your field of
view   the eye is always moving   roving   hunting   it
   tracks discontinuities in light and dark   which it will register
      if it is moving relative to them   this shifting or movement
of light to dark or dark to light seems   intrinsic to seeing
      because if there is no movement of the lights and darks across
your eyes receptor field you wont see anything   because someone
tried it   attached a clever device to the eye of a human observer
   which presented an "image" to the observer   but by deriv-
ing a signal from his eye movements   which it analyzed for dis-
placements of position   it moved the image precisely the same
   distance in the same direction   so that relative to the motion of
   the eye the image didnt move at all   and the observer saw

   102

nothing   which kind of makes sense   from the point of view
of survival   because it seems the eye makes passes over the field
and registers somewhere in the mind the passage of distinctive light
and shadow contrasts that it crosses or that cross it   and is alerted
somehow sometimes   to seek more information   contrasts
here   whips back to scan the problematic site again   this one
and another   perhaps takes movement bearings to estimate the
distance from problem site to problem site   while the mind is
guessing how to put the pieces together into an image of enemy or
friend   on the basis of what you want to find there   expect
to   hope or fear   plato may have had it right   something
goes out from the observer to the world and something from the
world comes back to meet it   but what is an image?   i mean
we had this dream   of truth   the truth of things maybe
in a photograph   and we look at a photograph and the
photograph is a very real meaningful thing   i dont want by any
means to knock photographs   one of the things about them
that is so meaningful is the total conviction of truth we tend to find
in them   which is maybe not the same as finding the truth in
them   but it is not entirely different either   possibly because
of something about the idea of truth   and the idea of an image
now in a very personal sense   i think i have some understanding of this   when i was a very little boy my father died   i was
very young   i think about two   and i have only two images
of his existence   or only two that i can remember   i remember seeing him from the end of a corridor i was passing through
i could see him through the open door of the bathroom and he
had one foot up on the bathtub   i think he was shining his shoes
now that i think of it maybe there was another   he was
passing in front of a window   i mean these are not what you tend
to think of as a loaded image   theyre not the sort you think of
as describing   as a rich experience   they have   the first
one anyway   because its the one i remember most clearly   the
transient quality of fact   a child passing through a corridor catch-
ing a glimpse of his father doing some neutral thing   by some
accident remembered   shining his shoes one foot up on a bathtub   i say a neutral thing because i detest the vulgarity of mind
the imperialism of that psychology that would unmotivatedly

103

provide some trivial to me psychological need that would pretend
    aggressively   to explain the remembrance of this scene
        because i can believe in this unfunctional scanning   a kind
of casual registration of the world   having no need i can now
understand   i also have no memory of the child   i call it me
only because i assume if i have the image   can call it up   i had
to be there to perceive it   and i   the child walking past the
    corridor   taking whatever interest or pleasure he took in the
casual appearance of his father doing something ordinary   like
    shining his shoes   had no knowledge then that would make this
image valuable   a prized possession   that might bias it into
    fantasy   not knowing then his father was soon to die at twenty-
seven of a sore throat and medical science   which made the par-
donable mistake of treating what they probably should have left
    alone   to nature   painting his throat somewhat excessively
with a dangerous disinfectant a silver compound that poisoned him
    and not having foreknowledge of this the image remains
    neutral   uncontaminated   surrounded by no drama
        a man seen down the end of a long corridor shining his shoes on
the bathtub   now there is another image a larger richer image that
is more detailed than this   it is an image i have of being taken
somewhere   to my fathers place of business it was a factory of
sorts where there was a shipping room   cage   because the
room was fashioned of cage-like walls   where they showed me
how i could make cardboard boxes by folding   which i did
        and i think they took me to the window   from which i could
look down onto the street   and see the people and the cars that
    now looked very small   after that my father took me out on the
fire escape   where he held me on his lap while someone took a
picture of us there   i think i remember how warm and secure his
    arm felt holding me   now i say i think i remember this whole
scene   the cardboard boxes   the people and the cars below
        how warm his arm felt   i even remember that i was holding
some small stick   and yet now that i think of it   for years my
mother had on her dresser a silver framed photograph of a man with
a serious gentle oval face his hair peaked at the brow   holding in
his arm a small boy who was sitting on his lap holding a stick
        and this photograph was clearly taken on a fire escape in an

104

industrial neighborhood   how do i know that what i remember
was the scene and not the photograph?   besides how do i know
that the man in the photograph was my father and not my uncle
julius   who looked exactly like him because he happened to be
his identical twin   i have no detailed image of my fathers face
down the end of the long corridor   he was far away and backlit
by the bathroom window   besides at that distance you cant make
out a persons face   now my uncle continued in that same business   in which he and my father had been partners   and had
many times taken me to his place and let me make cardboard boxes
and stare at the people in the street below   besides   years
later i worked in a similar business and was quite familiar with the
look of the shipping cage its tables and twine   besides i have no
recollection of that child   slightly pudgy with a ring of blond
curls around his head   as you can see i dont have any hair now
but when i did have hair   till i was about eighteen   it
was black and wavy not golden and curled and i have to take my
mothers word that the child in the picture was me her word also that
the man holding the child was my father and not my uncle   now
my mother had not been there when the photograph was taken
so i have to rely on her word that she could distinguish from a
photograph my father from my uncle who was his identical twin and
looked so much like my father that according to other members of
my family they sometimes played jokes on people who knew them
well   my father pretending to be my uncle or my uncle pretending to be my father   and nobody could tell them apart   except
my mother   she said   because she said she could always tell
because my father was more sensitive more serious than my uncle
and in this   that my father was the serious one   the
intellectual one   my mother had agreement from my uncle
who was a slightly foolish figure   a selfconstructed buffoon
telling ridiculous jokes he knew to be ridiculous of the order of
"you know whos in the hospital?"   "who?"   "sick people"
always uncomfortable with what he took to be a "serious"
consideration   reciting some sentimental poem of pushkin and
laughing at himself for doing it   and he agreed decisively that my
father had been the serious one   and they both   my mother
and my uncle received support here from another uncle   abe

105

who had been a close boyhood friend of both my father and my
uncle   now i had studied the picture many times   trying to
decide if i could recognize in that photograph any difference between
the man sitting there and my uncle   and i think i had decided
that the face in the photograph was a more serious sensitive face
      and later seeing him in another photograph with friends that
must have been taken around 1927 or 28 i was struck by how much
the whole group looked like a gathering of dada poets in paris
      though im not sure on what basis beside the style of their clothes
and sensibly   i doubted the whole business   my uncle
was a self deprecating man   as self-made buffoons must always be
      caught alone in any moment of repose he could have looked
exactly like the man in the photograph   though i had never seen
him look like that   but sitting facing into an afternoon sun with
a two year old child on your lap is less likely to provoke the clown-
ishness of an uncertain man than a boy of five or ten might   i also
      distrusted my other uncle   who was a doctor dying of a self
inflicted kidney disease   said to have been the result of an ill
conceived experiment born out of his unrequited love for experimental science   for which he had been the subject   i distrusted
him also because in his kind and scornful way   he lived in rego
      park and treated the poor   meaning negroes and italians   in
his patronizing way for nearly nothing   giving them advice with
every medication   probably like the advice he gave to me on the
occasion that he told me about my father   it was during the
korean war and it seemed i was going to be drafted and what he
advised me to do   if i was sent to the front   was to "surrender
immediately"   because the north koreans were communists and
it was the rational thing to do   and because he was an old communist and sitting there   swollen to a round bubble by his
poisoned liquids of which the hospital drained him monthly   he
was scornful of nearly everything   except russia   experimental
science and the dead   which were all remote   i remember he
told me with scientific assurance how he knew that alger hiss was
innocent and whittaker chambers lying because all the time
chambers testified he kept stroking his long cigarette holder   a
certain indication of his homosexuality   which rejected by hiss
      had provoked this revenge   as for my mother   i had reason

to doubt her also   because every time she left her second husband
        and it happened three or four times that i remember   she
wrote her autobiography and showed it to all of us and it was always
different   not about the child   there were other pictures of
this same blond curled baby   some of which she was in   so i
could connect this child with the dark haired child in that other
photograph   still slightly soft faced but with a smoldering look
of the four year old in the photographers studio who she assured
me was on the point of throwing his toy truck at the photographer
for his insulting instruction to "look at the birdie"   an intention
with which i could   at least in principle   identify   but
what i couldnt accept with certainty was her identification of my
father   she was so sure of it her ability to distinguish them
        and they were so playful with their identicality   so slightly
malicious   that i could imagine they had deliberately   if lightly
        told her that to trick her   said my uncle was my father
knowing that she really couldnt separate their closeness   and
        then my father died   and what had merely been a casual trick
became a memento   the bereaved womans emotion-loaded relic
        and it would have been too cruel to set it straight   and now
i have it all in all this dubiousness and richness   this image
        oddly entangled with a photograph   oddly because we dont
normally think of a photograph this way   surrounded by all this
        talk   this questionable narrative   and there are these two
images   the one   isolated and momentary at the end of a long
        corridor   fixed like a photograph   and it was not   a man
shining his shoes on a bathtub   and it has all the character of
        certainty and clarity   that i still prefer to associate with the idea
of a fact or of truth   while the other has all the slipperiness of
human discourse   and in this preference   prejudice   i have
        the historical precedent of most western thinking   which i can
        still sympathize with   while doubting its force   the idea of
a fact   of truth   is as the idea of a thing in itself as a pure
object taken in its correct projection   as those silhouettes
        which up until the 1940s you could still get made in amusement
parks   are the pure projection of a profile drawn by the light on
        a wall   the idea of the "pencil of nature"   which in a photo-
graph   as the sun is truly disinterested and the silver halide equally

responsive to the reflections from a thimble or an execution
        approaches the notion of real knowledge   of truth   of
fact as the manifestation of pure presence   and so i can understand my preference for that neutral image of the man at the end of
the corridor   as if the hand of the eye was unshaken   by
interest or emotion   by anxiety or love   and its also easy for
   me to understand how it came about   that this respect for the
integrity of the pure presence of that other   the object   would
engender this distrust of human intrusions   of the shaking hand
or the moist eye   and i can see how a respect for the notion of a
pure apprehension of this thing in itself   which was the idea of
   fact   could give rise to notions of a pure mode for representation
of this fact   leading to a taste for a "style of fact" that presented
        convincingly   "matter of fact"   but about this photo-
graph   its true that it fixes an image in something that approximates an instant of time in a definite locus of space   and of course
this is not true for an image seen through the eye i mean look   i
have an image of this room im standing in and while im talking i
think i see tom fern over there   hes part of my image of this room
        but as i say this i realize i cant really "see" tom fern from the
corner of my eye   though when i turn in his direction   where
a moment previously i saw only the shadow of his sport jacket
        theres tom sitting reliably over there waiting   and had he
walked away and been gone when i turned to focus on him i would
   have been surprised   but suppose hed walked away and i had
never turned to focus on him again   i would always have registered
the presence of tom fern sitting there in the corner of my image of
this room   you see my image of this room is based on my point
of view   which includes not only what is within my range of
view at any moment   but my memory of what was within my
   range of view some moments previously and my expectations of
what will be there some moments in the future that i include within
the duration of that present within which i conceive my image
        my experience of this whole space encloses my image of it
        it includes those prints of albers on the wall   the ones in
back of me as well as those in front   that is   my image of this
   room is that im in a room filled with albers   and ive barely
looked at them   yet i recognize them   ive seen so many albers

by now it would be hard for me not to recognize an albers   to be
    puzzled by an albers   think that i was seeing something strange
that seemed to bear some family relation to albers that would require
    looking at   yet i might go home and talk casually about the
albers that id seen thinking id seen it   as indeed i have   in my
    image of this room   now this kind of image is not quite the
same as that other image that was a dream of truth   not like the
sun standing for aristotle upside down on the wall of his room or
    the man shining his shoes on the bathtub   photography was
going to freeze the truth   now if you freeze life   its like frozen
    food   frozen life bears no more relation to life than frozen food
bears to food   frozen food approximates food   it translates
food into something that will not spoil at the same rate that real
    food will and is several degrees colder   and when you translate
something it changes   if you bite into a birdseye frozen pea before
    unfreezing it youll find out   and when you translate it back its
not the same or not quite the same   as anybody knows whos
    tried to close his eyes on an airliner and guess what vegetable hes
eating   now this great fact-freezing machine   this camera
        became something of an image of science   for it certainly
was not an image of art   now imagine this great world camera
        that would take the perfect the undistorted   the true world
picture   the world fact   now you understand it would have to
    be a complex fact   consisting of multiple images   because
each image must be the result of a camera focussed at a particular
    place   a camera is only in focus at one particular place   unlike
    the eye which is not really focussed at any particular place for the
taking of an image   and to be focussed in this particular place it
    would have to be situated in some particular place   facing in
    some particular direction   excluding by its frame some partic-
ularly large segment of the world fact   because the world picture
would have to be a complex assemblage of subsidiary world images
        mounted perhaps on the multiple faces of some hyperprism
        with a nonfinite number of faces   that would be the sum
    of all the particular places   viewpoints   from which the
world thing was taken   because a fact   like any image   in
this case an undistorted   a true one   like any projection
requires a point of view   and the truth in this sense   in the

sense of the way it is with the world   the correct world picture of
   the thing as it is by itself   is still a projection   seen from the
point of view of what?   of a god maybe who stands everywhere
all at once   which used to be thought of oddly as the true view
rather than the viewpoint of someone who stands in too many
places   for what kind of insect eye would it take to apprehend it?
   this truth of the world from outside?   in college i had a
friend named molly roland whose father worked for some film company   warner brothers i think   and he had invented a movie
camera   or so she said   that could take moving pictures over
a range of 360 degrees   now while this is not the same thing as
   the world camera its aiming in that direction   and i remember
wondering what purpose it would serve since nobody could take in
360 degrees of vision with eyes only in the front of his head   any
truth that requires an inhuman apprehension is only an alien view
   but art as we think of it seems not to have had this problem
   this involvement with truth   because even when it was representational   and it was once fashionable to think of art as representation   it was not common to found its value on the truth or
correctness of that representation   i mean there were exceptions
   aristotle tried to make a case for poetry   dramatic poetry
   over history   by the essential truthfulness of its representation
   that is   he says it in a funny way   which is a consequence
of standing up on your feet and talking   that history tells what
has happened while poetry tells what could or should or must have
happened   and then   remembering that some tragedies tell
what has happened he reminds you that what has happened certainly
could have happened and sometimes must have could have happened
   which sounds a little funny   but what aristotle really means
to say is that the truth of historys representation is more or less accidental while the truth of dramatic poetry is essential or fundamental
   this is not an easy case to make   and i dont think anybody
tries to make it now   except for the novel maybe   and then
only by a kind of special pleading that will explain the novelist in his
   role as characteristic man induced by the frame of his task   his
genre   into a characteristic state of mind   a state of mind
   that is characteristic of his time and so a representation of it   so
what you come to even here is a claim for a different kind of truth

110

its not a truth of correct depiction   of the representation of
fact   but a claim for a characteristic depiction   characteristic
of a class of depicters and apprehenders   not characteristic of
 what theyre trying to depict or apprehend   and with painting it
has nearly always been the case that whatever meaning you attributed
 to the painting   aside from maybe an iconological program
        you referred to the artist not to the world   and this was
understandable because there was no reason to suppose that the
artist had any special aptitude for the world   i mean if a great
artist could draw a perfect circle a great machine could draw it better
 more truly   so it would be easy to imagine a great mechanic as
having a greater aptitude for the world   a great scientist so to
 speak   and it wasnt clear how freaky   say newton was
        with his primary seven colors   his color octave that no one
else could see   and it seemed reasonable to suppose that scientists
had a greater aptitude for the world   even though as late as 1898
hearst was sending artists out to draw the news   but that was
 largely an accident in the history of printing   that truly mechanical engravings   that could translate the cameras truth by mechanical means   without the touch of opinionated hands   onto
 the rotary presses   were not available just yet   but this defect
was soon corrected and the truth of newsprose soon combined with
 the truth of the photograph to give us the total truth of the newspaper   a truth that seems so clearly now a total artwork   that
 we can go back to where we started and think about drawing again
        or painting again or talking again   or even photographing
again   now that we no longer believe in the triumph of that
mechanical truth   and there are only these various instruments
 and materials that you may want to handle for some human purpose
proposed to the hand by a human mind or eye   but it seems weve
forgotten what art has to do   i mean theres no reason why anybody should want to think of painting as art   except for the way
 some people used it to make art   because it lay to hand then as
a way   though it was not an easy way   i mean it was for a
 long time   the painting   a kind of commodity   and
because of the career of commodities   their use and distribution
        there was always something demeaning and limiting about the
fact that an artist   .a painter anyway who was also an artist had

to make something that somebody would want to buy   that he
was in a business   a store so to speak   you know "would
you like this one or would you rather have a blue one?"   i know
this is an old gag   but only seven or eight years ago there was in
the marlboro gallery in new york a large exhibition of works
        collages   by one of the great 20th century artists
        schwitters   kurt schwitters who made these marvelous little
constructions out of small scraps of garbage   that you could say
        and you could say a great deal more than that   exemplified
the triumph of man over the productive machinery of germany
        because the productive machinery of germany   like the
productive machinery of most of the world   was producing garbage
at a much greater rate than it was producing anything else   and
schwitters was like a little rag picker going through the mess and
        producing these elegant little works   and there they were these
cheesy little things   organisms not more than five or six inches
in any dimension   magnificent in their fragility and crumminess
        which was barely poised against their "prettiness" and estheti-
cized arrangement   and the marlboro gallery took these works
        that were once alive and barely making it   and inserted them
into frames that were five feet high set them back eight or nine
inches behind glass   matted them with crimson velvet cambered
walls that came out to meet the glass of the frame   and it was
        under those circumstances impossible to see them   and while i
walked around the gallery   trying to reconstruct what some of
        them may have been like   i overheard a well dressed gentleman
with a pronounced southern accent in a serious conversation with
        one of the marlborough salesmen   and what he was saying with
        great seriousness was   that he really liked the collage they were
both standing before   he really liked it and thought it was first
rate   but what he really wanted was an orange one   now the
        marlborough man was not surprised and i was not surprised that he
wasnt surprised   because he was one of those young englishmen
who make a whole career out of not being surprised by anything
        which is i suppose how you used to survive in england   but
what i really wanted to find out was what the young marlborough
man was going to do   because i knew he was going to find an
"orange one" and i was very anxious to find out what an "orange

one" was going to be   but in the end it was disappointing because
all he did was walk across the vast floor of the marlborough gallery
  and come to a stop at another collage that had a spot of orange in
it and the southern gentleman was happy   but it is this relatively
  disgraceful situation that is part of the western commercial system
  that artists have had to struggle with   now many of them saw no
  disgrace in it and many of them saw no need to struggle with it
     because many of them felt that they could make their art on
top of or alongside this   commodity   and some of them
     the art they were making   had something to do with making
a decorative or a correct or a high class thing   and the artists
struggle   the real struggle for those artists whose main concerns
  were not with the decorative thing or the high class thing   was
not so much to make it acceptable or salable   it was to keep the
  salability from swallowing everything else   you know this culture
  has proved you can sell nearly anything   or even nearly nothing
for very high prices   and its doing it nearly all the time   all
the artist had to do was learn from the rest of the society how to sell
     intangibles   the way my uncle sold the "good will" of his
wholesale garage supply store   or the way the developers sold to
another uncle   the good life or gracious living   so that he
would buy a condominium on a golf course in smog choked riverside
california   the artists learned very early that it wasnt hard to sell
  what they wanted from the hand of a genius   virtually any
scrap or scribble or dropping   because what your customer was
doing was not buying a product at all   he was subscribing to a
  project   underwriting an artists life and so   participating in
the life of art   and if you were an artist all you had to do
     and it was not a trivial job   it was and is a very absorbing
career   what you had to do was convince the part of the world
  that subscribed to such schemes   the art world   that you
were a genius   and this absorbing career   which has been going
on for hundreds of years has gotten so interesting that it seems to
have swallowed almost all of the artists energy   because it takes
  nearly constant attention and energy   and now that they have
gotten rid of   or nearly gotten rid of the commodity object
     which was always a dangerous and limiting condition for art
  artists have developed a new primary product   the artists

personality   and i admit that i dont think thats all bad   not if
the invented personality is part of some meaningful theatrical production   i mean i dont see why artists shouldnt   if they want
to   shift their main attention from a kind of construction to a
kind of theater   but then the value of that art will depend upon
the meaning of those performances   of those roles within that
theater   and the meaning of that theater itself   and a lot
of artists once theyve convinced their audience that they can
occupy this role or some form of it have forgotten there was anything else to do at all   like play it   because one of the problems
of this kind of theater is that the audience is some other you may
come to feel youre fooling and grow contemptuous of and consider
fools because youre fooling it   in which case your role changes
and represents you as an imposter   who you could define as an
actor with no confidence in his audience   so you see no matter
which way we go at it theres going to be some kind of representation
and i suppose it would be worth it to consider what kinds of
representation you could conceivably want to make   if you cant
escape them   look the australian aborigine in the desert country
say   may merely lay up a cairn of stones it doesnt look like much
of anything   but it marks a place   its the mark of a sacred
place   an important place   the place his ancestors pass
through and marks   the closeness say of water   the cairn of
stones put there   is a mark   and represents or is part of an
overall representation of the important place   important in this
mans life   he has a career too   that marks him as the kind of
man he is within his life   or say on bathurst island there are
people who make drawings   paintings   marks on a bark surface   that represent things and places   now there may be some
two kinds of more or less circular marks   one kind say with a dot
in the center and the other without any dots   and these   he
may tell you   represent two kinds of yams   one of them is a
special   a poison yam   the other one an ordinary edible yam
and you couldnt have recognized this from the painting   but
these representations are of important things   that these people
care about   these poison yams are growing things that were
dangerous   because they were very like undangerous   wholesome yams   and they   these people learned   discovered

114

by some great cultural invention   a way to make these poison
yams wholesome and edible   this is a cultural triumph to turn a
poison into a food   and it is rightly thought important   and
it seems only reasonable for someones art to take up something he
finds important   related to the realities of his life   and i
think of the painter i met in indiana   who is a good painter but i
think it might have been better if all those objects in his painting
the quotes from pompeii and herculaneum   were really
quotes from his life   which would have been even more enigmatic
to me   it wouldnt have been better for me   it would have
been better for him   i think it might have given him a sense of
the urgency of his role or task   his painting   i mean hes standing there and hes his own audience   lets make believe that this man
and his wife are separated   separating   then in some sense his
life is at a dividing line   i have no such information about this
man   i know him only casually   spoke to him only twice in
the only two days i ever saw him and there may be no such relation
but it seems to me that if his life was approaching a dividing
line   that would be an excellent place to begin the task of painting   to use the painting to find out what hes thinking about   i
mean painting can be a way of thinking   interrogating yourself
asking yourself questions about yourself   this is a very
traditional idea   an idea of self-portraiture   but what kind
of idea is it?   an idea of a sort of theatrical performance in which
you take two roles   you look at yourself and make some marks
you ask someone else   who is also yourself   if thats
right   he says no or yes or maybe   or maybe asks you why
you think so   now supposing from this point of view we consider
representation all over again   from the point of view of portraits
since we started there   and you have a show of portraits here
in the other room   i mean portraiture is an imaginary task   and
the way you imagine it will cast you in a role and cast the subject of
the portrait also in a role   now the portraits you have here are
very nice   considered as paintings   but from the point of
view of portraiture what are they?   from the point of view we
were talking about before   truthfulness   or adequacy of
representation   well we cant really talk about that   but what
kind of task is portraiture?   if its the idea of a unique   or even

a significant characterization of a particular human being   some
kind of statement? an interrogation about someone?   if thats at
all possible to imagine its not the kind of portraits you have in the
next room   but maybe we should imagine this task   this work
we are supposing in a somewhat different way i mean work requires
someone to do the work   some agency   and now we are not
talking about an imaginary fact-registering machine   which we
do not suppose to exist   i mean if you look at a street photographer   i mean an artist photographer   a man who takes his
camera out into the street to make "a portrait" of the street   you
see him walking and looking or standing still for long periods of
time   without photographing anything   i mean hes stalking
the street for its portrait   he has some sort of idea that the light
and dark reflections admitted from some particular place during a
period of 1/125 of a second and recorded on a rectangular surface
the right 1/125 of a second   at the right particular place
will be the right portrait of the street   and whether this is
true or not   it places him   the photographer in a particular
role of hunter   explorer   and we all know that role   its
overly familiar from the tedious myth of the news photographer
weegee as well as stieglitz waiting in the snow for the winter
city to appear   but thats not even the only way of doing it   i
like to think of doris ullman travelling in her touring car with niles
the folk singer   her chauffeur her assistant   and friend   the
great lady with her view cameras and all of her clothes going to look
for the mountain folk   the preservers of the crafts   barrel
makers   weavers   instrument builders   how she stopped
at towns and talked to folk   how they admired her wardrobe
which she brought along for just such occasions   letting the
girls try on her dresses   how she talked to folk got them to show
her their grandaddys workclothes their grandmas dresses   how
they talked about what it was like then   the way they remembered
and how they put them on and sat before the great ladys cameras
sometimes even worked by niles   and showed how it used to
be in older times   these are also portraits   but theyre part of a
play   named "olden days" and everyone is beautiful   diane
arbus set up another play that youd call "freak street"   except
you know thats not the whole play   just the parts that are played

116

by the people in front of the camera   whats interesting   what
you really want to know   in her play   is the part she played
her theater is a kind of guessing game   you want to know
what did she tell those people to get them to look that way and
let her show those pictures?   its beginning to look clearer now
portraiture   admittedly something of a special case in art
is a kind of negotiation   a theatrical performance with two
actors   negotiating a task they share   the old daguerrotypists
knew this   even in the way they set up their props   the marble
the velvet hangings   flowers   gems   the busts of great
men   paintings   who would have dared to enter one of these
great studios without a sense of his responsibility for the task?
which sometimes weighed too heavily for the dageurrotypists
preference   we remember how matthew brady kept working to
get lincoln into what brady thought was the right role   which
would lead you to suppose   perhaps that this was less of a negotiation than you might think   and that the performance was maybe
too dominated by one actors opinions   the way we knew theyd
be when weegee went out to interrogate the street   or stieglitz
to ask himself the question   "if i was a street what kind of street
would i be?"   or what kind of cloud?   because we know exactly what kinds of clouds stieglitz thought he was or ought to be
that the clouds didnt have much of a say   but lincoln was
lots tougher than a street   or a sky   and he got slightly bugged
at brady and quipped "mr brady would like to shorten my neck"
which made everybody including brady laugh and wind up with
another kind of picture   so i can imagine a different kind of
portraiture say   suppose i take a great big view camera   you
know glass negatives   the kind of camera thats almost too big
for anyone sensible to carry   and i throw it over my shoulder and
walk around the street ringing doorbells   pretty much looking
the way i am   and when someone comes to the door i say to
them "look   im trying to understand this place   this town
and youre a part of it and id like to take your picture   but i
really dont know what youre like or do   so why dont you think
about it for a while   what youre like and how you should look
like it   if you feel like doing it   and then when i come back
you pose for me   stand or sit or do whatever you feel like doing

and then ill take your picture   and when i develop and print
it ill come back and show it to you   because its not always easy
to tell what a cameras going to make you look like   and then
you tell me whether its right or not and maybe we can do it over"

or maybe i should go in with a video camera instead of a view
camera   and ask these people if they want to tell me what they
think its like   their life   and i shoot it and show it to them so
they can give me their second thoughts about it   because maybe
they think their first thoughts werent right   it seems to me
most people would want to take a crack at that   making their
own self portrait   especially if they arent worried about their
lack of readiness or competence and have a chance for second thoughts
except perhaps in that part of the art world where no one has
second thoughts about his life   because you cant have second
thoughts where there are no first ones

a week later i went up to berkeley to do a performance at
the university   the arrangements had been made by
leonard michaels and morton paley   who with some
help from jo miles were trying to keep a sense of life in the
literature department up there   both morton and
lenny were old new yorkers   lenny thin as a splinter
a sombre dandy   an east coast intellectual now a
writer of freaky bleak stories   morton a poet id gone
to city college with   still a poet and a great blake
scholar   always gentle   if anything softer now with
a small brush moustache that reminded me of my old
classics professor   a gentle humourous man   who
had quietly resigned after a radio columnist reported a
rumor that a known communist was a member of the
city college classics department   it was the fifties then
as i remembered it   with its loyalty oaths and air raid
drills   as i remembered one day outside the greek
class the six students who were taking the language waiting casually outside the classroom while the air raid

*alarms sounded   because thats what you were supposed
to do   when the professor   who was a slightly
portly man appeared with his briefcase from the stairwell
at the other end of the corridor   who at the unex-
pected sight of his class assembled at the classroom door
began to jog slowly briefcase in hand down the long hall
        the class watching all the while   and arriving
slightly breathless murmured "thank god i got here in
time to save you all"*

the invention of fact

i wanted to talk about something that happened a long time ago
     an idea that came to be a kind of   obsession   that there
was a way of talking   that was more responsible than another
  kind of talking   and that it paid its dues to truth more seriously
than other ways did   and i think that its not important what day
  this happened but that it had been happening for a long time
     it had been happening   people came to believe that there
were some ways of talking   that were more responsible
    people didnt always seem to be worried about responsibility
  when they talked   no more than the responsibility than
    lets say than the group demanded that was talking   or than
the talking demanded   and the romans   when they wrote
  about talking   when they talked about talking   they assumed
that everybody understood that   and when they talked about
  talking they didnt expect a great deal of truth or demand it   no
more truth than you would expect from a man who had something
  at stake   as they supposed that a man who was talking always
had something at stake   so the men who talked about talking
  talked about how you could talk and be persuasive   they talked
  of a talking that could   convince people to agree with you
     or of the worth of your talking   and there were many such
talkings about talking that got taken down in books and these were
called books of rhetoric   and these books were not especially

concerned with fact or truth   though they were sometimes concerned with a way of talking   a style that would persuade
         people to agree to accept what you said as if it was fact or
   truth   now there were always people who were concerned about
   truth   they had always been concerned with truth   to some
   degree   there are plenty of reasons for being concerned with
   truth   and some of them are human   where something has
happened say and somebody   to whom it has not happened
         wants to know what has happened   or whether it happened
      or how   something might hang on it or somebody might
hang because of it   somebody might go to war because of it
         truth is not entirely trivial   but the idea that something is
true or not true   is a very narrow concern though very weighted
         somebody did something to someone and that someone is dead
say   somebody killed him and the man wasnt looking and they
   attacked him from ambush   and they killed him   he was
killed and thats serious   because it might lead you to want to do
something   not trivial   if thats what happened   if its a
fact   but whether its a fact or not hangs on a number of things
and an order of things   and whether a way of talking about this
order of things is true   "that man was killed"   well first is the
   man dead? thats usually easy to establish   with a kind of evidence   there are a couple of kinds of evidence that everybody
recognizes   reports and things   probably the only two kinds
   of evidence there are   things and a way of talking about things
and what happens to things   and everybody supposes he knows
   what things are   because you can look at a thing and feel a thing
or smell it   but it isnt quite so clear what happenings are
         though they seem to involve an order of things and changes in
   things   that are no longer the things that they were or the places
   they happened to be   according to reports   but the evidence
of things consists of the things that you can associate with reports
      and the reports   now somebody died means theres a corpse
      which is a thing   something that was alive is now dead
         and its lying there   and you go and corroborate it its lying
   in the street   well thats easy to do its dead it looks like a human
being it has a face it probably had a name   so that from all you
   can tell it was once the kind of thing that was alive and now it doesnt

   122

move and it isnt likely to ever move again and its dead   so that
  now the kind of thing that was probably once alive is now the kind
of thing that isnt alive and will never be alive again   thats not
much of a problem   but what happened how it came to be dead
  is not so easily determined as that a dead thing was once a live
thing   then there are reports   and in the report somebody
said "we saw someone and he came out of there   and he attacked
that man   when he wasnt looking   and the attackers
     there were seven of them and they overpowered him   and
killed him"   thats a report   and thats either true   or its not
true   or it has some relation to being true   because that has
to do with what that other man   who was parking his car say
     saw that was happening   saw them come out of the alley
  or whether he saw them lying in wait   whether they signaled
or didnt   whether they seemed to be waiting for that man   all
these considerations are based on this mans way of talking about his
way of seeing   theres no way around it   a report is a report
  it has the problem of adequacy   its not only a question of
whether the report is true but whether its adequate   whether his
way of talking is an adequate way of   representing his way of
seeing   and whether his way of seeing is   an adequate way of
  representing the way   something is happening   he was parking his car and saw one person in the alleyway and there were maybe
  seven but he didnt see them   or he saw a bunch of them but
they werent together   on purpose   four of them bumped into
  the other three   who got scared and ran out into the street
     where they collided with that other one who died   he thought
they were attacking him and pulled out a gun they killed him and ran
off   pursued by the other four   this is all very familiar
     this problem of reports   whether theyre adequate   this
has been a good year for reports   weve had a lot of reports lately
     everybodys been watching watergate this year   and the
watergate has been filled with reports   more and less adequate
     before the committee   a young white collar gentleman
  named strachan was asked a question   about the destruction
of certain documents in the files and he said i received instructions
  from mr haldeman   mr haldeman said to "make sure that our
files are clean" and strachan shredded the documents   since he

123

supposed that was what mr haldeman had wanted him to do   now
what we have here is a report about something that was happening
       and one of the things that was happening was a way of talking
that would lead to a way of doing making something happen   so
that this way of talking was itself a way of doing and not just idle
chatter   but in order to report this way of talking young mr
strachan had to report a way of saying of speaking that had to
represent the way of talking that he wanted to report   now, what
was this way of speaking?   according to strachan   because
mr haldeman seems not to have remembered his way of speaking or
even the occasion of speaking   according to strachan it was
"make sure that our files are clean"   which mr strachan took to
be the same as "see that our files are clean"   or "clean out our
files"   all of which are slightly different ways of saying and
speaking   though they might very well be exactly the same way
of talking   of telling somebody what to do   because   you
see "clean out the files" would appear to direct mr strachan to remove from the files anything that would be considered "unclean"
while "see that our files are clean" could be telling mr strachan to
go down to the files and bring back to mr haldeman the assurance
       of which he was already fairly confident   that the files were
"clean"   which might leave room for mr strachan to return
bearing the surprisingly bad news that the files were not in fact "clean"
or completely "clean"   which would still leave up in the air the
problem of what to do then   and mr haldeman could certainly
say that at the least he had no idea of what to do then   because
he had never expected to find anything unclean   and at the most
he could say he would have made a clean breast of it and proclaimed
loudly his surprise and dismay   though you might not have
believed him   because   while its not entirely clear what precise
kind of talking a particular way of speaking will imply   its very
clear that the kind of talking a way of speaking will imply will depend
upon the kind of agreements in speaking and doing there are among
       the people who do a lot of it together   and you could believe
that because young mr strachan had worked for mr haldeman and
       listened to a lot of talking from mr haldeman and performed to
his satisfaction   that he understood satisfactorily mr haldemans
way of speaking as a way of talking and doing   and it seems clear

124

enough now that no way of speaking   is clear   as a way of
   talking aside from an agreement among the people who do their
speaking and talking together   and that agreeing in talking is not
   the same thing as agreeing on the words with which you happen to
be talking   because you could use the same words for very different kinds of talking or   different words for the same kind of
   talking   and you could have different kinds of agreements
   about the amount of agreement or kind of agreement you had for
   different kinds of talking together   still for all of those people
who were very concerned about truth and fact   which is a special
   kind of agreement about talking   about things and whats happening to things   for people who are very concerned with whats
   happening   it seemed important and desirable to fix the ways of
   speaking or saying things so that people would always say the
   same things in the same way with the same words   so that the
   people who were talking would always be party to the same agreement and say   so many things in so many words   so that they
   could get on with   finding out about these things   and
because they were anxious to get on with finding out about things
   they began to organize into societies that were very solicitous of an
agreement about the manner of speaking of their members   and
   in the words of thomas sprat   who was the first historian of the
royal society of england   the society exacted of its members "a
close natural and naked way of talking"   and rejected "all the
amplifications digressions and swellings of style" in order to "return
   back to a primitive purity and shortness"   wherein men said so
   many things in so many words   well what is a close natural naked
   way of talking?   that will return back to a primitive purity and
   shortness   it turns out to require a kind of "mathematical plain-
ness"   if you happen to think of mathematical discourse as a
kind of plain talking   "plain" because you may think it lies so
close to thought itself that it is   maybe   not so much talking
   at all   not even plain talking   but plain thinking   said
straight out without any roundabout manners of speaking   figures
of speaking to deck out or clothe   this naked thinking   which
is to say that this kind of talking is a kind of clear or transparent
   talking   through which you can "see" the naked thought as
through some vinyl clothing   which wouldnt hide it   not the

125

way a figured speech might   now what this would require   as
they thought   would be one word for each thing   no more
no less   and one word for each relation of each thing to each
and every other thing   and one word for each group of things
  you admitted   because of their relation   and one word for
each operation that could change the relations among any of the
  things or groups of things   or even among the relations among
the things   so that such a language would seem to require very
many words or a world with very few things   like arithmetic
    still hugh blair thought that the many figures of speech in natural
languages arose from a correctable deficit of terms and an understanding perhaps insufficiently developed to apprehend truth
directly   and the truth of the natural world was a matter   let
  us say   of a space-time manifold   a man standing on a particular corner at a particular time   who was run down by a trolley
car   you have a convention for determining time   arithmetical
maybe   an agreement about a way of   a convention for
determining location in space   perhaps thats also arithmetical
    you have a map say   and an agreement about a way of talking
about certain relations of things   in time and space   and an
agreement about a way of talking about certain changes in the relations of things   you have a map and a calendar and a wristwatch
  and a measuring tape   you know what a man is and what a
  trolley car is and you can identify them in a crowd   and now
the man is no longer a man and hes under the trolley car   right?
    take a war   1709 say thats the time   its as good a time
as any as good as 1708 so why not?   get a newspaper   the
  newspaper will report happenings   thats news   its important
for a newspaper to report things that happen   because thats how
  a newspaper gets readers   you see a newspaper is a kind of
marketplace where things get bought and sold   it sells reports to
its readers and it sells its readers to its advertisers   and the advertisers pay the bills   now the way you get readers to sell to the
advertisers is by telling the readers what they want to know about
    the things they want to know about   well one of the things
the readers wanted to know about was what was happening   in a
  lot of places where they hadnt been and in the normal course of
events wouldnt know what was happening   in some other city

say   in france or constantinople   and the only way you could
know something about what was happening there   was if you got
  a message from somebody who happened to be there and sent you
  a report   so the newspapers or what served as newspapers
published letters   messages that one supposed had come from
  these places where those things were happening that you wanted to
know about   like a war   because maybe it would have an
effect on something you cared about that affected you   like the
price of linen say   and you got this message   together with
the advertisements   which maybe you didnt care about   but
  what i said was you got this message or report when i suppose i
should have said you got this letter   because a letter comes from
someone and goes to someone   and talks in a particular way
  because thats the way this person talks   about the particular
things he happens to talk about   or at least when he talks to the
particular person to whom hes sending this kind of letter   but
thats not what happens or happened in a newspaper   a newspaper
  is to anyone   so that a letter in a newspaper is not a letter to
anyone in particular but to anyone in general   but more important than that   after a while its not a letter from anyone in
particular   because if you get a letter from a particular person
you may become concerned about how his particular interests or
concerns   or even his abilities   may limit his manner of talking
  to you or the things hes talking about or what he has to say about
them   now what was happening in 1709 was a war   of the
  english with the french say   and you were in england and there
were things involved in this war   like prices say   or maybe
merely idle curiousity because you just wanted to know what was
going on in your name that your country was fighting a war for and
  you got this letter in a newspaper   which told you about the
consequences of your own blockade of the french and the dutch
      which according to the reports of these newspapers you were
able to carry out because you had a powerful navy   and your
navy   according to the report of some letter   had cut off
the ability of the french to obtain certain types of food and bread
was going for sixpence a loaf in paris   and that was pretty high
      and according to this same report which shows up in the news-
paper the crowd in paris was outraged at this price for bread

which they probably couldnt afford   and the mob   the
people who couldnt afford sixpence a loaf   rioted   for bread
        stormed saint germain and plundered the shops   and when
the kings guards came out they pushed them away   but the kings
        guards grabbed two people and brought them before the magistrate
and the magistrate sentenced them to prison   well then four people
came from the crowd   before the magistrate   and threatened
him   saying he would have to answer for what had happened to
        their friends   and the captain of the kings guards   who saw
this happen and was apparently aware of other things that might
happen then went back to the crowd and said out of pity for your
plight i have interceded for you and your friends and your friends
        will be pardoned   and thats what was happening in paris in
        1709   according to a letter that was published in the tatler
        which you could believe or not believe depending on what you
thought of the mail and who might have sent it or what you thought
of the tatler and who printed it and why   though this might not
have occurred to you since it seemed so much more like a report
than a letter in a newspaper   which also said that at the siege of
namur   in the company of one captain pincent   in the regi-
ment of frederick w hamilton   there had been two men   one
a corporal   unnion by name and the other a mere sentinel named
valentine   and the two fell to quarreling once   over a love
        affair most likely   and valentine   the sentinel got the worst
of it most likely   from the corporal   unnion   who made
        his life quite miserable   giving him the worst details   even
beating him occasionally   and valentine   the sentinel com-
plained and grumbled all the while   and threatened all sorts of
revenge and in this state of affairs the siege of namur began   the
attack on the castle was ordered and unnion got a bullet in his thigh
        and fell down and cried out for help how can you leave me here
        valentine?   who seeing the french about to trample him
        quickly picked up the fallen corporal threw him over his
shoulders and dragged him out of the french charge and brought
him as far as the abbey of salsine   where a cannonball blew off
        valentines head and he fell under the weight of the corporal he
was carrying   now unnion   who was himself not in very
good shape at this time   got up looked at the body of his former

enemy and forgot his own wounds and tearing his hair cried out oh
valentine was it for me who have so barbarously used thee that
thou hast died? i will not live after thee   and he threw himself
upon the bleeding carcass and was not to be separated from the
body but had to be removed with it bleeding in his arms to the
hospital where his wounds had to be dressed by force   later in the
hospital he tore off his bandages and died lamenting how badly he
had treated valentine   which report furnishes richard steele
     the publisher of the newspaper and the report   with the
opportunity to observe that when we see spirits like these in a people
to what heights may we not suppose their glory may rise?   and
which report in its close details   though perhaps not so natural
or naked language   that specifies captain pincents company
     colonel frederick hamiltons regiment   unnions corporalship
     valentines sentinelship   the abbey of salsine   may lead
us to ask which figure of speech we are listening to   and to
answer   history   from which i can tell you another story
     its called the "truman doctrine"   which has to do with
another war called "the cold war" and this was in 1947   which
is a lot closer than 1709 but still some distance from 1973   well
the truman doctrine got its name from what was proposed to congress and the american people by president truman on march 12
1947   and what he proposed was to "defend free peoples everywhere"   by which he meant free countries   countries that
were free in respect of certain institutions like national elections and
     certain kinds of publications and certain types of owning of prop-
erty and things like that   he proposed that in general   in
particular he proposed to support   with money and force the
national governments of greece and turkey   which were not so
notably free   apparently on the grounds that if we supported
them they wouldnt become less free and that other governments
     which were perhaps more free in respect of these institutions
     would remain so   now this was a long time ago and may
seem a little difficult to understand   so lets get in for a closer
     look   this country had come to the end of a great war   and
there was a new president   who was not an elected president
but a vice-president who became president after the elected president
     who had been a very popular president and had remained

129

president for a very long time   grew sick and died toward the end
of this war   which had been a very great war and had been fought
for a very long time   but very far away   in europe and asia
and the united states had been in this war for four years
though it had gone on much longer for the people of europe
and asia   and because it had been fought far away and for a long
time most of the people of the united states wanted to forget about
it   this war that they now thought they had fought for the
people of europe and asia   and they wanted to go back to whatever they thought was their ordinary way of life   but the new
president   who had been president for two years but was still
new as presidents go   was now telling the congress and the american people that they couldnt just forget the whole thing and go back
to their ordinary way of life and that they would have to go on
thinking about it   europe and the near east anyway   and
they would have to do something about it and maybe keep on doing
something about it   and this was the doctrine called the truman
doctrine   now how did this happen that president truman
decided to say this and congress decided to do it   well   according to the story   or one of the stories   for there are several
stories about it   it began on a sleepy gray afternoon one friday
february 21 1947   in the old state department building on
17th street and pennsylvania avenue in washington   the secretary
of state had left early that afternoon   he was a new secretary
of state   george marshall   hed been an important general in
the great war and he had been secretary of state for just about one
month   and now he was on his way to princeton to deliver his
first public address as secretary of state and then he was going on to
north carolina for the weekend   and the telephone rang   with
an urgent message from the office of the british ambassador request-
ing an immediate appointment with the secretary of state   who
had just left for the weekend   well the new secretary of state
had a very experienced undersecretary   an accomplished lawyer
a state department professional named dean acheson   and
acheson took the call and persuaded the english ambassador to send
over a copy of the document   which he would take charge of
in case any preliminary preparations were necessary   and
brief the secretary of state for a meeting with the ambassador early

monday morning   and since   according to acheson   this
was what would have happened anyway   the english ambassador
agreed and sent copies of the documents over to the state department
building with the first secretary of the british embassy   documents   because there were two not one   and what they said
was surprising   or somewhat surprising   and when loy henderson   who was the state departments chief of the division of near
eastern affairs   read through them   because he was the man
who received the visit of the first secretary of the british embassy
he said not a word about it to mr sichel   the first secretary
who also remained pretty silent   because they were both
professionals   and then he went down the hall to the office of
john hickerson   the chief of the division of european affairs
another professional   who also found them surprising
and the two of them went down the stairs to lay the facts before
dean acheson   and they were these   the british government
was going to get out of greece and turkey within six weeks   now
what was surprising was this   greece was having a guerrilla war
going on   a civil war   and the british government had been
supporting for some time what we could call   the greek government   a de facto   royalist   right wing government
that england had helped make the government and was now
supporting with money and troops   now england says were tired
and were getting out   in six weeks   and were getting out of
turkey too   what was mainly surprising was the speed   so
acheson says this is very grave and he takes the first action in this
series of events   he calls a number of meetings   to decide
what they should do   now the first meeting he calls   or
orders called   because he has henderson and hickerson call it
is a high level staff meeting   to lay out the facts of the
situation   and this meeting took place that evening   on friday
february twenty-first 1947   and that meeting was chaired by
george kennan   a russian specialist who was then lecturing at
the war college   and henderson was there and hickerson and the
senior members of their offices and a few others   and they drew
up a paper in which they all agreed that the united states would
have to step in to help out greece with money and arms   while
the problem of turkey seemed less urgent and got passed over

131

and they were all pretty excited about the new role the united
states was going to take in world affairs   george kennan remembers driving home   with a sense of having taken part in a historic
decision   and with a sense of great developments impending
this much is history   which sets forth what has happened
unlike poetry which according to francis bacon is history at
pleasure   and according to aristotle too   who was standing
up one day talking about poetry and history and said history sets
forth what has happened   while poetry sets forth what should
have happened or could have happened   or must have happened
and then thinking of poetry and remembering poems   said
of course there are poems that set forth what has happened   but
what has happened could have happened   or it wouldnt have
happened would it?   so sometimes that happens   history and
poetry overlap   but poetry is somehow more essential than
history and less precise   and for our purposes history is a story
that is more precise   more arbitrary and absolute in its detail
well then there is more detail   more meetings   on saturday
february 22nd hickerson and henderson met with admiral sherman
and general norstad of the departments of war and of the navy
acheson phoned the president and secretary of state and informed them of what had happened and what had been done   the
near eastern affairs staff in constant contact with acheson by phone
worked all that day drawing up a final   revised expanded and
refined version of the paper they had all drawn up hastily friday
night   and sunday afternoon henderson drove over to achesons
georgetown home with the final version   and he asked acheson
whether they were still working toward making a decision or
executing one   to which acheson answered   "the latter" and
they drank a martini "to the confusion of their enemies"   monday
morning lord inverchapel   the english ambassador formally
delivered the documents to general marshall   marshall met with
president truman to tell him what had happened and what the state
department had done and was doing   the secretary then met
with secretaries of war and of the navy   and then the cabinet
secretaries and their military advisers and henderson and hickerson
all met in achesons office   where they agreed   in achesons
summary   that it was vital to the security of the united states

for the governments of greece and turkey to be supported   that
only the united states could provide the necessary support   and
that the president would have to ask congress for the money and
authority to do this   on tuesday february 25th acheson laid out
the situation to the subordinate state department staff and took up
the rest of the day writing with henderson and the near eastern affairs
staff the final paper called the "position and recommendations of
the department of state regarding immediate aid to greece and
turkey"   on wednesday february 26th acheson met to discuss
this with the secretaries of state war and the navy   who endorsed
it   then acheson and marshall met with the president   who
needed no convincing   and called a meeting for the very next
day   february 27   with the leaders of congress   because
these were the people who were going to have to help him explain to
congress and the people of the united states why they couldnt just
forget about europe and asia and go back to their ordinary life and
why they would have to do something about it like sending millions
of dollars and maybe troops to help support the governments of
greece and turkey   and this wasnt going to be easy to do   so
they invited the leaders of the senate and house   vandenberg and
martin and rayburn and charles eaton and styles bridges and tom
connally and sol bloom and john taber   who couldnt make it
and the only one they forgot was senator taft but they made
that up by inviting him the next time   and they met that next
morning in the white house and   at the request of the president
secretary marshall led off in the presentation of the problem
and he blew it   in dry and economical terms the general
explained the facts   how england was going to get out of greece
and turkey and how much that would weaken them   make
them vulnerable to soviet domination   and he explained what he
thought we should do about it   and the reaction of the congres-
sional leaders was bad   they wanted to know why this wasnt all
trivial and why we were pulling british chestnuts out of the fire
and they wanted to know what we were letting ourselves in for
and how much it would cost   and the answers to these
questions only took things further off the main track   things
were going very badly indeed   when acheson leaned over to
secretary marshall   who was sitting next to him   and asked in

a low voice "is this a private fight or can anyone get in?"   so the
   general asked permission for acheson to speak   which was
   granted   and he stood up and made a rousing speech   in the
   past 18 months soviet pressure had mounted   on the dardanelles
on iran and on greece   this mounting pressure could open up
   three continents to soviet domination   if they broke through
turkey they could extend their control over greece and iran   if
   they broke through greece turkey would sooner or later fall with
iran and the rest of the middle east   from there they could push
   on through egypt into africa and they could push through greece
to italy and france and the rest of europe   only two great powers
remained in the world   the united states and the soviet union
   not since rome and carthage had there been such a polarization
of power on this earth   and these two powers were separated by
   an unbridgeable ideological chasm   for us   freedom
   democracy and individual liberty   for them dictatorship and
   absolute conformity   for the united states to take steps to strengthen these countries threatened by soviet aggression and communist
   subversion was not to pull british chestnuts out of the fire   for
if the soviet union succeeded in extending its control over 2/3 of the
   worlds surface and 3/4 of its population there could be no security
for the united states   we had to act to protect freedom itself and
   we had the choice of "acting or losing by default"   when acheson
   finished there was a profound silence that lasted for about 10 seconds   then senator vandenberg got up slowly and with gravity
   said   how greatly he had been impressed   shaken   by
what he had heard   it was clear this country was faced by an
   extremely serious situation   in which help for greece and turkey
   were important   but only part of an overall situation   . and he
told the president that if he was going to ask for the money and
authority to help greece and turkey he would have to lay all of the
   grim facts before the american people   lay the whole situation
   on the line   and thats how it happened that the presidents
advisers prepared the message that the president delivered to congress
   and the american people on march 12, 1947 that got to be known
as the "truman doctrine"   and thats history   which is the
   account of what happened   only   as it happens   there
are three accounts   each of them given by somebody who was

there for part of what happened that led up to the event were calling
the truman doctrine   and the first account is by a man named
joseph jones   who was one of the state department staff who
helped write the speech the president finally delivered on march 12
and the first meeting he was at was on friday february 28th
when dean acheson announced to the rest of the state department staff what was going to happen   right after the president
and the secretary of state and mr acheson had met with the con-
gressional leaders on thursday the 27th   and he wrote his account
by 1955   now george kennan also gives an account of what
happened in his autobiography   which is a kind of intellectual
history of his life   and he took part in that first staff meeting
in the state department the evening of the english ambassadors call
and his account was written by 1967   and dean acheson
who took part in almost all of these happenings   gives his
account in his autobiography   which was written by 1969
and they all seem to agree   in general   that thats what
happened   and george kennan   when he gives his account of
what happened   commends jones account for its great and faith-
ful detail and encourages interested readers to consult this book
      the fifteen weeks   published by harcourt brace and company
in 1955   which he cites in a footnote   which is a wonderfully
precise detail that we are accustomed to in history   only joseph
jones book was not published by harcourt brace in 1955   it
happens that i had this book in front of me only a week ago and it
was published by viking press   now this is not a very important
detail   and could easily have been the outcome of a trivial error
made by somebody who was copying down george kennans
account of what happened   but its not the only detail on which
kennan and joseph jones dont agree   when kennan gives his account
of that first meeting which he was at in the state department building
with loy henderson and jack hickerson   he says that loy henderson chaired the meeting that joseph jones says kennan chaired
and then kennan describes this meeting   which was to lay
out the facts of the situation and decide what to do   that took
place on february 24th 1947   which was not the evening of that
gray friday on which lord inverchapel called for a meeting with the
secretary of state and for which the secretary of state was not there

which was the evening of february 21st   and dean acheson
in his memoirs   in his account of the story of what happened
when he gets to that meeting   he doesnt mention kennan
at all   though he locates the meeting on friday february 21
now this is still a small point of detail   though if kennans
memory was right   and the meeting took place on february 24th
which was monday   it would   according to both joseph
jones and dean acheson   have occurred hours after the secretary
of state had met with the english ambassador and with the president
and after the secretaries of state war and the navy and their
advisers had met with dean acheson and agreed that the president
would have to go to congress for money and the authority to act
and one whole day after dean acheson and loy henderson in
georgetown drank their respective martinis to the confusion of their
enemies   its hard to see what historic decision kennan could have
played a part in   which we could suppose   that kennan
played no historic part in this historic decision   because kennan
who gives his account of the meeting   is not so insistent on
his own memory of the importance of that meeting   which is
what he remembers   but he also gives loy hendersons account
of that meeting   or rather he gives his account of loy hendersons
memory of that meeting   according to which   the meeting
arrived at no historic decision   because all the decisions had been
arrived at by dean acheson and himself over the preceding weekend
and the purpose of the meeting was merely to outline this
course of action in greater detail and make suggestions about how
to explain this to congress and justify this course of action to the
american people   and kennan gives this account   as well as
his own   and this account would not conflict with a meeting
that took place on monday february 24th   and it would be
tempting to accept this account   which we should remember is
kennans account of loy hendersons account   except that it
places an enormous amount of authority in the hands of an undersecretary of state and his chief of near eastern affairs   which
kennan explains with yet another detail   that the secretary of
state   george marshall was then in moscow and dean acheson
was acting secretary of state   but this disagrees with all other
accounts everywhere   so were back where we started   with

136

the first disagreement of detail   either kennan was at a meeting
   on friday night   which might have contributed to a decision
   about what to do   or he was at a meeting on monday night
which couldnt have contributed to that decision   or he was at a
   meeting on friday night which seemed as if it could have contributed to the decision   seemed so to kennan   because of the
   kind of discussion it was or because of the kind of man george
kennan was   and didnt seem so to loy henderson   because of
   the kind of man loy henderson was and the kind of man dean acheson was   or because of the kind of man loy henderson thought
   dean acheson was   and all of these things are important in
understanding accounts   even historical accounts   because
   accounts are by people   even written accounts that are written
down soon after the events   and as it happens there is no written
   account in the archives of the state department of that meeting
         which either took place on friday evening or on monday eve-
ning on february twenty-first or twenty-fourth   and if that meeting
was to decide what was to be done   there might have been a
significant difference if george kennan was there on friday night
   rather than monday night   because george kennan was the russian
   expert   and as we learn from kennan in his memoirs he didnt
think the security of the united states or freedom itself   depended
   on our helping greece and turkey   as he tells us   he didnt
think much would be lost at all if greece fell to its rebels and he
thought it might even work out as a disadvantage to the communists
      who would then have had to face all of greeces economic prob-
lems   and he didnt think turkey was in any danger at all   still
   he remembers supporting aid to greece   without any sense of
urgency   and he remembers being opposed to any special aid for
   turkey at all   so its hard to see what part he played in this
historic occasion   though its possible to imagine that he did play
   a part   which was subsequently erased by later events   like
the situation in which dean acheson confronted the leaders of congress
      who wanted to know why this wasnt all trivial or merely pulling
british chestnuts out of the fire   and what we were letting ourselves in for   and how much it was going to cost   and what
acheson had to do in this situation   what acheson did and said in
   this situation could have erased the part that george kennan played

in this historic decision of the truman doctrine   if george kennan
played any part in it at all   so it becomes a matter of some interest   if we are going to establish the facts   to determine just
what dean acheson said at this meeting on february 27th 1947
      well he said it was rome against carthage   he spoke of a
geopolitical chessgame   in which pressures were mounting   on
the balkans on the turkish straits on iran   with the map of the
world as a chessboard and two players   making moves   towards
conquest   toward annihilation of each others power   *delenda
carthago*   the voice of cato the elder   invoked with latin 5
      is there any doubt who is rome?   who carthage?   thats
the account the way joseph jones gives it   only he wasnt there
      acheson tells it a little differently   there is still pressure
      soviet pressure mounting on the straits on iran and the balkans
      threatening a breakthrough   which is the geopolitical chess-
game with the board of nations   but then it is the danger of one
rotten apple in a barrel infecting all the others   by contact   the
infection would spread from greece to iran   to all of the east
      to africa through asia minor and egypt   and to europe through
france and italy   a homespun contagion theory   while for
  senator vandenberg who was also there and happened to be a
member of the senates atomic energy committee   "the fall of
greece   the collapse of turkey   threatened a nuclear chain
reaction"   though it was not till april 8th that the senator came
to this view of the situation   and as late as march 5th was
"waiting for all of the facts"   and when we go to his private
papers for his account of the february 27th meeting there is no
mention of dean acheson at all   just a summary according to
which   general marshall had briefed the legislators on the global
  pressure pattern   that senator vandenberg had known nothing
about till that very moment   and the general had concluded
  with the pithy aphorism "the choice is between acting with energy
or losing by default"   which the senator later paraphrased for
  the senate as "an ounce of prevention is worth a pound of cure"
and "one stitch in time saves nine"   so that if this is history where
are we?   are these the facts?   or if it is poetry which poetry
is it?   the poetry of the prep school latin class?   the chessgame
of diplomacy?   the folk wisdom of the general store?   or

138

popular science?   and what does it have to do with the "facts"
senator vandenberg was always wanting to "face the facts"   "this
plan faces facts" he told the senate on april 8th 1947   about the
    truman doctrine   "we avoid war by facing facts"   well the
facts were what was happening in the grammos mountains   in
athens in ankara   in london   and in washington   well
what does this poetry   these poetries have to do with it   what
was happening or came to happen?   and who were these people?
    who understood what was happening and laid out these facts
    well   as far as we can tell it was these professionals   the
state department professionals who laid out these facts from which
the decisions had to be made   laid out these decisions that were
made   now i suppose you could say that it was the president
    president truman   who laid out the truman doctrine   but
although there may be plenty of times when a president may make
decisions this doesnt seem to have been one of them   here he
    seems   as far as all the stories go   to have the facts laid out
for him   and the decisions he could make   and   he seems
    to have been offered only one   and he agreed   and while it
was quite possible in principle for him to have not agreed   if you
    look at the facts he was presented with its not easy to see how in
practice he could not have agreed   it would have taken an awful
    lot of confidence to deny the facts   that had been gotten for
him by the professionals in the state department   now the secretary of state was not a professional   not a state department professional   he was a professional soldier   with the virtues of a
good professional soldier   the most important of which was he
    thought quite precisely and not over much   he had a motto
about that "dont fight problems   solve them"   and he liked
to have all the facts in front of him but not the unnecessary details
    he liked clear lines of authority and wanted his experts to
provide him with the facts of a situation   and the policy alternatives   so that leaves us with the professionals   the experts
who understood the situation   in this case dean acheson and
    george kennan   now who were these professionals?   these
experts who understood russia and the middle east   and what
    was this understanding based on?   well   they had reports
and they had opinions   and since they had the same reports and

139

what might pass for different opinions   the opinions would
seem to be more important   and the question i want to ask is
how did they come to their opinions?   who were these men?
     well george kennan was a russian expert   an emigre intellec-
tual   from milwaukee   who was an emigre at princeton
     when he went there from a military academy in milwaukee
     after reading f scott fitzgeralds *this side of paradise*   which
     when he got there   didnt seem quite like fitzgeralds prince-
ton   and somehow he went through princeton   as he says
     inconspicuously   and he went on to enter the foreign
service   mainly because   as he says he couldnt think of anything else to do   and thats where he says he found himself
     one fourth of july in the hotel beau rivage over lake geneva as a
new vice consul resplendent in a cutaway   there on that summer
     day   with the orchestra playing on the terrace   and the
great lake shimmering beyond   sharing with the other officers
of the consulate general the duties of host   greeting and welcoming
the ever appearing guests   and realizing then for the first time
     that he had a role to play   a reputable and appointed role in
the proceedings   he was no longer a naked intruder on the human
scene   well this sense of role lasted through the summer and got
     lost after six months as vice consul in hamburg   after which he
was ready to drop out of the foreign service and maybe enter a
     graduate school   but he found out he could do that and stay
in the foreign service anyway if he was willing to take on an exotic
     language   like chinese or japanese or arabic or russian   and
he picked russian   for one reason because he had a distant relative
hed never known   also named george kennan   who back in
the 19th century had been a russian expert   and with whom this
     george kennan noted he had a lot of similarities   for they were
both born on the same day of the year   they both played the
guitar   they both loved sailboats   they both wrote a lot and
lectured a lot   became members of the national institute of arts
     and letters   both devoted large parts of their adult life to russia
and both were expelled from russia at about the same point in their
     careers   so he picked russian and the foreign service sent him to
estonia and latvia and lithuania   by way of berlin and stettin
     because the united states had no formal relations with russia

and these baltic states were the closest they could get to russia
    and he studied russian   or started to   in tallinn in estonia
  with a ukrainian teacher who spoke no other language than
ukranian and russian   and he learned it there in estonia   surrounded by estonians in tallinn   from a ukrainian   from
little childrens illustrated picture books in the old spellings that the
soviets had since reformed   learned it from fairy tales and jingles
  while working at visas and invoices and notarials at the consulate
    before going on to riga   to work in the legation chancery
and live the bachelor life of this second petersburg   in the white
nights of latvian nightclubs and drozhkis and vodka and balalaikas
    for to live in riga   as he said   was to live still in czarist
russia   and then to graduate school at the university of berlin
    where they steered him away from soviet studies   because as
he understood it the aim was to provide him   with a background
in the language and culture of a russian of the old prerevolutionary
school   thus prepared he cultivated russians   wild impractical
  people   emigres like himself   living a russian life   in
spandau a mother a son and daughter living a penniless precarious
existence   the daughter played piano the son was trying to write
    kennan himself wrote   an article   for a german magazine
    felt like a russian himself   when he went off to norway to
get married to a norwegian girl   volodya and shura come to see
him off load him down with flowers they cant afford they wave
goodbye everybody cries he loses their address   and he goes off to
riga with his norwegian bride   thats the way it is   russia is his
    passion norway his bride   and he goes off to do   economic
reporting on russia   he collects material   to write a life of
    chekhov   and when the united states opens up diplomatic rela-
tions with russia he goes along as interpreter and stays to set up the
    embassy   he gets a ringside seat at the moscow trials makes
pilgrimages into the countryside to visit orthodox churches chekhovs
    homes   later he goes to prague berlin to lisbon   and winds
up in russia again after the war   this is his expertise and its not a
    question of how much experience he gets of russia   but what
kind of experience that is   which is an experience of the russian
soul which is so incomprehensible to foreigners   specially "anglo
saxon" foreigners   of which he counts himself one   when he

141

doesnt consider himself a russian   this mysterious russian soul
      which is all contradictions and extremes   long periods of
sloth and indolence alternating with bursts of energy   excessive
bouts of cruelty and kindness   simultaneous hate and love
      the great slavic openness hiding behind a byzantine closure that
is motivated by centuries of "neurotic fear of penetration by the
west"   whatever the facts   kennan is representing an absolute
form of the romantic mistress   that he alone understands   and
it is in one of those fits of exasperation with her   probably pretty
well justified   that he sends off a violent 8000 word telegram
to the state department complaining of her bad character   and it
happened at that time   that james forrestal   an american
      businessman   was serving as secretary of the navy   and he
happened to spot it and was delighted to see someone in the state
department taking a realistic attitude to those reds   so he had
kennan brought home to lecture at the new war college for the
instruction of americas high military on his sound apprehension of
      the facts   and how to deal with her   and so forrestal brought
him to the attention of general marshall   which was how dean
      acheson came to consult him   or have his staff consult him on
the greek and turkish issue   but who was dean acheson and what
      was his expertise?   he was a gentleman and a lawyer   and
something of a dandy with a curled moustache and dry ironic tone
      a well mannered eastern professional combatant of the law
      with all the polished combativeness of the hired legal champion
      out of prep school and yale and harvard law   one of brandeis
law clerks working the national and international courts   the
corporations versus the country   one country against another
      the corporations versus the unions   the unions versus the
      corporations   all in the low key aggressiveness of eastern appel-
late argument   a confident man with a powerful sense of his own
dignity   resentful of offhand familiarities such as roosevelts first
      name habits when he served briefly in fdrs first cabinet as under-
secretary of the treasury   a man certain of his own abilities and
disdainful of others seemingly less certain   like cordell hull
under whom he served as assistant secretary of state   and what
      he couldnt stand about hull   besides his lisp and the heat in his
office   were his habits of working around and around a question

in talk   among others   because apparently it was hulls
habit to call together all of his most important assistants in his office
on sunday mornings   for long sessions in which they talked
around and around whatever was happening and what they thought
was happening and what they should do   and apparently it was
also hulls habit sometimes to take one side of a question and sometimes the exact opposite of the very same question before finally
settling for what came out sounding best   and this really drove
acheson crazy   it drives him so crazy that he tells us about it
twice   until he starts finding it funny   the idea of coming
to a decision   an important decision   by talking it out
        thinking it out in public   which he assures us is a long way
from the working methods of the best legal minds   which he
unfortunately doesnt explain   and you begin to realize   as you
go over his accounts   that the one thing you absolutely cant
explain from achesons accounts is how he ever arrives at a decision
        because he never arrives at one in public   there is something
wonderfully private and unexplained about all of his important
opinions   as though he never "arrived at them"   and they had
always been there   ready for whatever occasions to be acted on
        like the situation in greece   concerning which he advised the
president as early as august 1946 that the russians "should be resisted" there "at all costs"   while taking precisely the opposite
position on china   where a similar guerrilla war was going on
between chiang kai shek and the chinese communists at precisely
the same time   and its quite possible to imagine a presidential
adviser considering the facts and deciding to take precisely the same
position about the civil wars in china and greece   conceiving
both wars as merely a single aspect of a greater war with a single
ideological enemy   russia   or to come to that decision
about neither of them   or to decide that both were worthless
for the united states to get involved in in any case   because they
would both prove too troublesome to whoever got involved in them
        russia or the united states   or to arrive at different opinions
on each of them   but in an opposite manner   deciding that
greece was not worth trouble while the natural resources of china
made it worth infinite trouble to dominate and control   but if
its possible to imagine all of these considerations going through the

143

mind of an adviser to an american president   from acheson we
  dont get any of them   though he tells us approvingly how well
the president understood and approved his advisers opinions
    how at this meeting   in august of 1946   acheson presented
these opinions   for himself and secretaries of the navy and war
    and how general eisenhower   who was perhaps a little doubt-
ful of this phrase "at all costs" and the presidents ready compliance
with the notion of sending another aircraft carrier to the turkish
  straits   asked acheson in a whisper whether he thought the
president was sufficiently clear that this action could lead to war
    which president truman overheard and promptly drew a map of
europe from a drawer and lectured his advisers on all the strategic
  implications of the eastern mediterranean and the extent to which
they had to be prepared to go to keep it free of soviet domination
    which showed how well he understood the implications of these
recommendations   says acheson   because   in picking the
  straits and iran as points of pressure   the russians were following
the invasion routes of the barbarians against classical greece and rome
    and of the czars to warm water   "from thermopylae to the
crimea"   and if some americans had found their history rusty
    neither the british nor the president did   since chinese
history was not a regular feature of high school latin classes   we
  may suppose the pressure of the northern slav on the chinese wall
seemed less obvious in its implications   but whether we suppose
  it or not this high school poetry is the closest we ever come to a
basis in thinking for any of achesons fundamental opinions   so
  that   again   it may be too much to say that that we are
dealing with any kind of thinking at all   in this first class legal
  mind   and we should say that these decisions are *a priori*
    they have always been there   as though hed been born with
them   or inherited them the way a child of the rich inherits an
  estate   or the way a lawyer inherits a side of a dispute   along
with an opponent   so that you can see why george kennan must
have always felt   slightly abused in his presence   because all
  kennan wanted to do was ruminate about the difficulties of his
mistress   while acheson sat there with the suspicion of a smile
  playing faintly about his nearly always ironical lips   and waited
patiently for kennan to get on with it   which takes us where in

our search for fact?   in history   in poetry   to autobiography?   jean jacques rousseau wrote his autobiography   its
a nice autobiography   he calls it his confessions   and youll
see why in a moment   at one point hes in paris   and hes a
young guy and he sees some milkmaids   i dont know what
milkmaids are doing in paris   maybe its not paris maybe theyre
not milkmaids   just young girls   and he opens his fly and
exposes himself   as a flasher   and then he had to run away
because they were laughing and he feared for his life   he says
now what i would like to question is this   how do we establish the truth value   the fact value of this   confession   i
mean is it true or false   or somewhere in the middle   let us
propose that there are several possibilities for jean jacques rousseau
and his fly   jean jacques rousseau is a liar he likes to tell embarrassing stories of this kind and put himself down he never opened
his fly   all right?   thats one possibility   or jean jacques
opened his fly   now we assume he is telling the truth   in
this sense   but whether it *is*   the truth   is not clear
he opens his fly holds his cock in his hands the girls laugh
this is also true   we assume   but we dont know if they
see what hes holding in his hand or just his foolish face   or theyre
laughing at a story theyve told each other and he runs for no reason
all of which are possible within the domain of fact   because
we have now come to the point where he may not be lying yet it
may not be   an adequate representation of what happened
its quite possible that he did in fact flash they laughed and never
saw jean jacques at all   right?   now cant we assume that we
may be standing on the frontier of a lie and a truth?   its not so
easy to come to a fact   it doesnt come so fast   and then he
was traveling too fast   because he was running   see?   that
was the problem   maybe if hed stayed he could have found out
even so there would have been problems   we wouldnt be
quite clear yet what was at stake with jean jacques and the girls
its possible to imagine that this truth has to be   constructed
you dont fall heir to it so fast   even with a style   say you
come to a paper   it has a style appropriate for fact   newspapers
are places to which facts should come   right?   i mean
we all believe that   we say   newspapers "have deteriorated"

a lot lately   we turn to open the newspaper and we say   they
   dont give us the facts   we turn on the television and they dont
give us the facts at all   we cant find out the facts   we find
out say that john dean   who was vastly believed in a report about
nixon and other members of the watergate   or other possible
  members of the watergate   is vastly believed   why is john
dean believed?   aside from the possibility that he may be believ-
able and we may wish to believe it   and it may be true   john
dean read from a book   what do we know of john dean? he was
  the one witness who came with a statement one hundred and some
forty-six pages long and he read it   he read everything in that
voice in which you read written reports   and everything was
organized in relation to everything else in such a way that it seemed
  obvious   that you could turn the pages back and forth and
check every fact against every other   it was organized   in such
a way that it was difficult to believe   that a man could put together such an edifice without it being true   and then somebody
said john dean where did you meet with herbert kalmbach   and
  john dean and herbert kalmbach didnt agree   john dean said
we met in the mayflower hotel and herbert kalmbach was not in
  the mayflower hotel   on the occasion   on which they were
supposed to have met   kalmbach was staying at the john jay
  hotel   and kalmbach was able to produce a receipt showing that
he had stayed at the john jay hotel   and deans lawyer made the
suggestion that john dean had met with herbert kalmbach in the
  mayflower coffee shop of the statler hilton hotel   which dean
explained   by pointing out that he tended to confuse these two
  places   because the statler hiltons coffee shop had the same
name as the mayflower hotel   so its difficult for us to understand
what to make of this   and i dont think it has any important
  bearing on the substantial value of deans account   but whats
happened now? to the one hundred and forty-six pages of facts
      that interlocking edifice in which each fact interlocked with
each other in such a way that the whole structure could not be
knocked down   this edifice was built out of text   written
  words   and spoken aloud the way people speak writing   it
  was read   now i could have read to you tonight from a text
      and all the statements ive been making   i could have

supported them with notes   written records referring to more
   writing   the records of the reports that my report is talking
   about   and im sure you would have been more inclined to
believe what i said if i wrote it all down and read you a record of
   my report   instead of just talking to you   and if i supported
my record with a vast array of footnotes that accounted for the facts
as precisely as to state that john dean and herbert kalmbach met in
the mayflower hotel   john dean presented a record like that with
an array of footnotes in writing   and then it turned out there
was another record in writing that denied that   and when that
appeared it turned out   even more peculiarly   that john dean
no longer remembered whether the report on which his precisely
written record was based was accurate or not   and im not knocking
deans charges and i dont think theres any reason why he shouldnt
forget and confuse these two places with the same name   mayflower   the mayflower hotel and the mayflower coffee shop of
the statler hilton hotel   because after all   as far as he was
concerned   this hotel   where the message said they should
   meet   where the meeting took place   was only a coffee
shop with bad coffee and a name   and remembering is like that
   but not a record which is something else again   where you
get facts in a style that we could call   the figure of fact   in
which according to mr sprat "so many things are delivered in so
   many words"   and we know that if we were to pick up a newspaper in new york say in 1836   which was maybe before "the
   deterioration of the newspapers"   and we could hope to get the
facts   we would learn that the case of ellen jewett was on everybodys lips   everybody exclaimed "what a horrible affair!   what
a terrible catastrophe" for the personal history of ellen jewett
and her private tragedy overshadowed all other news   her real
name was of course not ellen jewett   it was dorcas dorrance and
she was a native of augusta in the state of maine   though here
   she passed under the name of ellen jewett   as in boston she had
passed under the name of helen mar   she was an orphan   her
father   mother   poor people   who died during her infancy
   and she was adopted by a respectable gentleman   judge
western by name   whose female relatives pitied the bereaved
condition of the young orphan and subsequently invited her to live

147

at the judges home   dorcas   was at that time young beautiful
innocent and ingenious   her sprightly temper and all her good
   qualities won the fond feelings of all the judges family   of which
she became the *chère amie* as companion and playmate   at an
early age   as her mind was budding   she was sent to a female
academy at coney   over the kennebec river   at school her
intellectual power shone forth with great brilliancy   but not
more so than her form and appearance   she was the pride of her
   teachers   beloved of her schoolmates was obliging   good-
tempered   intellectual and refined   after continuing at the
academy for some time   dorcas   in the summer of 1829 went
to spend the vacation at a distant relatives place at norridgewick
      a town on the kennebec river about 23 miles above augusta
   she was then 16 years of age and one of the most lovely interesting black eyed girls that ever appeared   in intellectual accom-
plishments   in the arts of conversation particularly in wit and
   repartee she was unsurpassed   but even then   at this tender
age she gave occasional indications of a wild mind   dark glints
of humor and fierce bursts of argument pointed to a mind stronger
than it was settled on fixed principle or moral knowledge   gradually her passions began to take control of her   her education only
   gave fuel to the power of her fascinations   in this town she
became acquainted with a youth by the name of h———— sp———y
      a fine young man   elegant and educated   who later
became   it is said   a cashier in one of augustas banks   soon
all was gone that constitute the honor and ornament of the female
   race   after a little while she returned to augusta   where her
situation became known to the family   a quarrel ensued and she
left her protector after having   in a fit of passion   lost all the
rules of virtue and morality   from there she retreated to portland
where she took the name of maria benson and became a regular
aspasia among the young townsmen   lawyers and merchants
      at portland her life was rather experimental   she was quite
young and still retained some traces of gentility so that she had
   some currency among the more cultivated and gentler parts of
society   but she got into trouble there   and one morning she
took the opportunity of going off to boston where she assumed
the name of helen mar   from a popular character in a young

lady's novel   she lived there for about a year and a half and left in
the company of a distinguished young man for new york   here
she took the name of ellen jewett and has lived since at several of the
houses around town   during the last winter she lived in disguise
with a kentuckian at one of our most distinguished hotels   her
way of life in new york corresponded with the degraded state of
society in this city   at such fashionable houses young men
married and single   congregate in the evening   spend
their time and money   wasting their treasures and their sensibili-
ties   and break down every moral tie that hitherto kept the
elements of social intercourse together   ellen jewett was well
known to every pedestrian on broadway   she was famous last
summer for parading up and down wall street in a green gown
often with a letter in her hand   peering boldly into the faces
of the brokers   she had a peculiar walk   something in the
style of an englishwoman   and from those who know her we
have learned that she was a fascinating woman   full of wonderful
conversation   rich in intellect and learning   but at the same
time possessed of a devil of spite and nursing a morbid hatred of
the male race   her greatest pleasure was to seduce promising
young men   especially those who at first resisted her charms and
for whose fascination she worked out a subtle campaign to enslave
and reduce them to despair   "how i despise you all" she would
say   "you are a heartless unprincipled sex and have set out to
ruin us   you have thought to ruin me so i will ruin you and
delight in your ruin"   and one of these young men split her
head open with an axe on a bad night in a whorehouse   which is
what you learn from this newspaper in 1836   as you learn that
she used to read byrons *don juan*   this fascinating woman in
the green gown who went up and down wall street staring boldly
into the faces of the brokers   and that she might have been
with more favorable fortune or a steadier moral principle
the successful housewife of a wealthy young man who visited
a whorehouse and split somebody elses head open on a bad evening
but suppose for the moment we abandon the figure of fact and
propose an allegory   allegory is a very corrupt figure   a figure
notably incapable of supporting fact   so let us propose an allegory   that will have to live on its own   lets imagine a country

its hard to imagine a country   i live in a town and know
most of its streets   but there are places in it to which ive never
been and people ive never known   its called solana beach and i
can imagine this town   but lets imagine this country   that we
live in it   that my town of solana beach is part of a state called
california and that both are part of this imaginary country   and
we go to the store and find that the prices are rising like crazy
chopped beef that we paid 49 cents a pound for has gone to 69
to 89 cents a pound   a loaf of bread that cost 33 cents last year
costs 41 cents this year and may cost 51 cents next year or 61
prices are going up and up   food prices   and other prices
of tractors and television sets and automobiles   and at the
same time businesses are closing or laying off workers and nobody is
doing anything to stop this   and you say why isnt anyone doing
anything to stop it   why are they doing this?   so let us
imagine a "mind"   and give it an "intention"   let us assign it
to a person and call him a "president" and give him a name   like
"nixon"   i realize that there is a problem in this a statistical
problem that makes it very improbable   but we will imagine a
"president" as a man with a mind that has an intention   that he
"intends" to do something and "has power" to do it   that he is
faced with an "inflation" in this hypothetical country "america"
an ever declining value of "american goods"   in terms of
"dollars" required to buy them and compared say   to the value
of other goods of other nations and the "dollars" required to buy
them   and what he proposes to do   "this president"   is to
"check this inflation"   by which he means the ever declining
value of "american goods" vis a vis "foreign goods" on an "international market"   and he proposes to do this   to check the
ever rising cost of american goods in this "foreign market" as compared to the cost of goods from other parts of this "market"
which could cause a decline in sale of american goods in this
"world market"   and he proposes   our imaginary president
to check this   this threatening decline in the sales of american goods by the great american businesses   to these other hypothetical countries   of our figurative world market   and how
does he propose to do this?   by a brilliant structural innovation
by increasing prices   he proposes to check this inflation by

150

increasing prices   and you say how is this possible   to check
an inflation by increasing prices   but im not through with my
    allegory   this fictional president will not increase all prices
        just some prices more than others   he will increase much
more than all other prices the price of small indispensible things
that people cant avoid buying   especially the cost of food and
shelter   but above all   the cost of foods   now foods are
very small things that everybody has to buy some amount of all the
time   and keep buying   no matter what the cost   and by
a poetic license you will allow me to assume that "our president"
        "nixon"   can do this   by some complex manipulation of
supply and supports cause a progressive increase in the cost of bread
and milk and wheat   now let us imagine one other thing   that
    in this country   "america"   most of the people are poorer
than the rest   that there is some large group of people
    "families"   more than half   who have to live on less than
$10000 a year   and lets say that a "man" who makes less than
$10000 a year is more typical than a "man" who makes more in
this "country"   and that there are many more of "him"   this
    typical "man" "citizen" of this "country" than there are "men"
"citizens" who make more than 12   14   20   30 thousand
dollars a year   and as this food is difficult to stop eating   and
a man who makes $8000 a year may have a "family" with four
"members"   who all depend on this $8000 a year   and they
    must eat a certain amount of this food in order not to become sick
and die   no matter what the cost   it is very apparent that as
these food prices rise continuously   at some point this food
will cost this "family" 30   40   50   60 percent of his
income   seventy percent of his income   imagine a number of
people   who live in families that make less than $10000 a year
    with continuously rising food prices they will soon attain to
that state in which they spend fifty sixty seventy percent of their
money on food   in order to survive   much sooner than the
much smaller number of people who live in families with incomes of
20   30 and 40 thousand dollars a year   its not so difficult to
imagine   with our vast experience of poetry we can imagine it
    that this "man"   with an income of less than 10 thousand
dollars a year is spending 30   40 percent of his income on shelter

and the remainder on travel   to get back and forth to his job
    and then one can say to oneself   what is there left that this
"man" can buy?   and the answer is   nothing   there is
nothing left that he can buy out of all those other products that this
imaginary economy has been producing   those toasters and wash-
ing machines and lawn mowers and mixmasters and stereos and
television sets and campers and electrical toothbrushes that this
"affluent economy" has been producing all of this time   and
    which no one in our allegory previously could control   because
we have imagined for this country an economy that is largely what
    is called a "free enterprise economy"   in which it is not possible
or politic to restrict or redirect the production and sales of variously
useful and useless commodities   some of which may be con-
veniences or luxuries or sheer uselessness   in relation to some way
of "living"   well now it is fairly apparent   that this strategy
    by consuming fifty or sixty percent of the available dollars of
this large group of people who make less than 10000 dollars a year
    will effectively reduce the value of their 10000 a year   will
depreciate their ten thousand dollars   to seven thousand dollars
    to five thousand   effective dollars in terms of their older
income   and you see they will no longer be able to buy these
other things out of that part of our "economy" that they could
not have been prevented from buying before   without the introduction of some very novel political devices into this "country"
    so that this "president" has begun to control what could not
have been controlled before   but you say thats not possible
    its very dangerous   it could cause a depression   this
sudden drop in buying could leave vast inventories of goods in the
warehouses of "american" businesses   cause severe losses and
bankruptcies throughout the "country"   but im not through with
my allegory   lets ask the question for this "country"   given
the economy we have provided for it   what part of its businesses
is it very easy for a "president" to support   which reaches in all
    directions into the busyness of the "country"   and the answer
is the military-industrial complex   in the course of things it is
    very easy for a "president" of "this country" to buy billions of
dollars of goods for "its defense"   from "aerospace" from "the
computer business" from "the steel industry"   for the largest

152

"consumer of commodities" in this country is a "consumer" controlled by the "president"   the "government"   now let us
resort to a metaphor   if we consider that the rising cost of necessities is something of a "brake" on the buying power of the country
        then governmental expenditures "for defense" will represent
something of an "accelerator"   and thus equipped our "president"
will be in a position to effect   in a somewhat malthusian manner
        a vast reorientation of our economy   to produce   effec-
tively   a multitude of poor who are nevertheless still employed
        however at a greatly reduced personal gain for themselves and
their families and a greatly increased gain for the relative few who will
profit most heavily from the government expenditures and the improved position of "our economy" vis a vis that of "other nations"
        but you say 'this is a wild allegory   because you imagined
"an intention" and "a mind" attributed it to "a president" and called
him "nixon"   this is poetic license   it is but a trivial figure of
speech that can hardly lay claim to the status of fact   moreover
your figure has structural flaws   even in your own fanciful terms
        for if there are in "this country" many people who make less
than ten thousand dollars a year   there are some   perhaps many
        who make less than eight thousand and some who make less
than six or five   and there must be also in this imaginary "nation"
        some number of the elderly and disabled   pensioners on fixed
incomes who the slower though inevitable rate of wage increase ex-
tracted by the organized labor force will never affect   these and
the young who are not yet part of that force will become part of a
larger and larger unemployed that the reduction of purchasing power
will create   and they are not counted into such a plan   these
will come to occupy the obscure fringes of this society in dark desti-
tution   where they cannot be kept from malnutrition and death
without enormous costs to the nation in always insufficient ineffective
and humiliating charity and aid   and they would send forth far
beyond their wretched enclave waves of disaffection and disease that
would ravage all parts of the nation that hoped in this way to be
saved   what you have described is an impossible elegant plan for
        an arrogant and malevolent mind   trivially contemptuous of the
arduous landscape of fact and called it a "president"   in this
corrupt figure consists the viciousness of poetry'

153

jehanne teilhet invited me to speak to a seminar of
advanced students who were considering a sociology of
primitive art   i had been rereading stanley diamonds
essay on "the search for the primitive" and i had been
thinking of his insistence that the search for the primitive
in all its problematicalness   was the attempt to
define a primary human nature   and of my own simultaneous sense of discomfort with the term primitive and
of the need somehow to discuss again our ideas of the
human and natural at this particular time   as i was
myself in these talking pieces trying to explore the possibilities of natural language genres   and it seemed
appropriate to discuss this in social terms   for if the
right handedness of a particular man may be biologically
natural   the right handedness of a society verges on the
political   bearing these things in mind and the fact that
the building i was to speak in was to have been named
after giambattista vico   this talk poem became something of a meditation on anthropology and art

the sociology of art

i assume that were all here to figure out   what a sociology of art
might be   if there was such a thing   what a sociology of primitive art might be   if there was such a thing   it would be
interesting   because its obvious that there is another kind of art
thats other in its whole social arrangement   of making and
giving and presenting and looking and reading   i mean its obvious
that there are other kinds of groups and ways of grouping   that
there are   i hate to use the word   other kinds of societies or
cultures   and that the ways of making giving and looking
     in those other kinds of groups   are sufficiently different to
justify calling them by some other name   and that the ways of
their being different   are so much a part of their ways of arranging   people into groups for the purpose of making giving looking
and receiving   to call our way of talking about this art   a
sociology   that is   a social logic of this art   now there is
something unappealing about the notion of a "primitive" art
     what i mean is there is something both repulsive and attractive
about it   because there is something inherently repulsive and
attractive about the notion of "primitive people"   it was a term
that arose   i think   out of a mixture of feelings in people
who felt that they were themselves decidedly not primitive
     primitivity is an idea that got stuck in peoples minds when they
began to feel that they had "advanced" to such a terrific degree

sometimes to the degree that they felt "decadent"   and they
looked around to find things that werent decadent   and naturally
they found these smelly little brown people   who were repulsive
and sexy   and sang and danced well   and told terrible lies
   and they called them "primitive"   and they called their lies
"myths"   a myth is the name of a terrible lie told by a smelly
little brown person to a man in a white suit with a pair of binoculars
     now you may not want to believe that   because there were
other men in white suits with field glasses   who followed the
first ones   and sometimes they were also the first ones   who
heard these lies and said "these arent lies   theyre secret truths"
     because at the back of every lie theres a truth   and it belongs
to a "primitive" culture to have a truth thats not like your truth
     and they gave these lies all kinds of values   generally allegor-
ical meanings   by which i mean they constructed an ingenious
mechanism for   converting these colorful   nearly incomprehensible and idiosyncratic lies into a series of easily comprehensible
and generally accepted platitudes   as a matter of fact   in its
earliest uses this notion of   primitive   was applied to the
greeks   to the history of the "gentile nations"

      from these first men   stupid   insensate and horrible
   beasts   all the philosophers and philologians should
have begun their investigations of the wisdom of the gentile
   nations   and they should have begun with metaphysics
      which seeks its proofs not in the external world
      but within the modifications of the mind of him who
   meditates it   in such fashion   the first men of the
gentile nations   children of nascent mankind   created things according to their own ideas   but they
         in their own robust ignorance   did it by virtue of
         a wholly corporeal imagination   and   because
it was quite corporeal   they did it with marvelous sub-
limity   such and so great that it excessively perturbed
   the very persons who by imagining did the creating
         for which they were called "poets"   which is greek
   for "creators"   hence poetic wisdom   the first wisdom   of the gentile world   must have begun with
metaphysics not rational and abstract   like that of
   learned men   but felt and imagined   as that of
   these first men must have been who   without powers

   158

of ratiocination   were all robust sense and vigorous
imagination   this metaphysics was their poetry

and the stories they knew to be lies   they called them "fables"
and "legends"   and sometimes "myths"   because myths
merely meant stories   the word myth means a story   it comes
from a greek verb   an interesting verb   *mutheomai* means to
tell   to talk   originally what it meant was   to talk
      when someone gets up and starts rapping   in an epic   by
homer   the verb that they use to describe it is *mutheomai*   he
gets up to tell a story and he mythomizes so to speak   he myths
      the truth value is not immediately called into question   that
is   it doesnt mean its a lie   but if i told you that president ·
nixon got up and "mythed" in congress   youd figure that he told
a lie   right?   if i told you he got up and mythified   "the
senator rose and mythified for several hours"   that would be the
end of that   on the other hand if i said   he told it as it was
      you wouldnt really think he was "mything"   youd think he
was doing something else   so it seems to me there are a number
of interesting distinctions   one is that the word "myth" meant
to say or tell   and nothing else   and then it got specialized
for those tellings   that people didnt believe anymore or felt
there was a problem about belief in   now whats all this got to
do with the idea of "literal" or "oral" societies   well i dont like
the word "primitive"   because its wrapped up with these terrible
lies   and this notion of little poetic beasts   who are as tal-
ented as children   or women   or criminals   or lunatics
      some animals   and all of those creatures held to be passion-
ate and stupid   by all of those other people who were either
      so content or so fatigued with being so dispassionate and wise
      now there is another use of the word "primitive" that might
be a reasonable use   but it is hypothetical   i could imagine
the use of the word "primitive" the way you use the word "atomic"
      everyone knows that there are no atoms   that is "atoms"
dont behave as "atoms" when you deal with things   as a human
being   they dont exist as things you encounter   atoms are
      hypothetical constructions invented to support a theory   and
they are in turn   and its only fair   supported by this theory

which they have just helped out   because of this its not easy
to speak about "atoms" outside of this theory   in which they are
merely operators   but for the sake of simplification and since
we know the theory   lets say that these atoms are primitive entities   primitive whole entities   and when you "break-up"
these primitive whole entities you wind up with *parts* of atoms
    which you can consider a problem of its own   the notion of
a hypothetical part of a hypothetical primitive whole   but as we
imagine a primitive physical entity in all the simplicity of its relations
and combining capacities   we might imagine   primitive
people   primitive human beings   who were   so to speak
    atomic in their humanness   as you might imagine a pheno-
menological universal   you might imagine also modifications
    perversions?   of this humanness   so you might imagine
that the idea of the "primitive" is like a kind of atomic theory of
humanity   if that was all it was   and if it could be employed
in a nontrivial way   if it was possible to form such a theory at
all   we could attempt to imagine what are "natural" feelings
what is "natural" thinking   the way you can imagine of the
body what is natural movement   now you may imagine these
hypothetical states and capacities when they are not obscured by
    responses to accidents   and become congealed as habits
under the arbitrary conditions of culture   so you try to imagine
    a cultureless entity   but how do you do that?   imagine any
group of people   two say   is it possible to believe that their
ensemble of needs and desires   demands   and satisfactions
will be perfectly matched   over any significant length of time
    given even our trivial knowledge of biological systems   it
seems unlikely   so the outcome of this small group situation will
not be entirely "natural"   this too will not be the place to encounter truly "primitive" man   probably even the situation of a
    single man alone will possess enough of the arbitrary   in his/her
relation to any given environment   no   its purely a theoretical
construct   primitive man   like the atom itself   and you
will never be able to encounter it or anything like it   and the
value of thinking of it will depend solely upon its explanatory
power   but maybe you think this is too extreme   so you
think of something less ideal   a "natural culture"   say

communist   utopian   sylvan   and you imagine these
people   clad in whatever natural people   more or less natural
    are clad in   gardening say   because the earth is filled
with fruits and vegetables   and animals that easily pop into your
hand   and from your hand they pop into your mouth   and
you imagine this primitive group of people having primitive relations
    men and women distributed at random   by casual pleasure
    one might suppose that incest is not a primitive taboo   after
all theres nothing natural about such a constraint on pairings   one
might but one might not   one might say that since some kind of
incest taboo is found everywhere incest is a primitive prohibition
    but that seems rather silly   because even if one could find
strong political   social   reasons why such a prohibition might
"strengthen or articulate" the group structure of the group that
practiced it   theres no need to assume that natural man recognized
this   or even that all kinds of groups would be "strengthened"
this way   anyway   maybe you dont want to think that political effectiveness is primitive   its probably easier   even more
attractive   to decide that the incest prohibition   or more
precisely some incest prohibition   was the first act of sophisti-
cated culture   the arbitrary   perhaps playful distinction
    quite invisible   between the suitable and the unsuitable
    but this goes nowhere except back to the trivialities of conjec-
tural history   back to the fantasies of "primitive man"
    which never got us anywhere anyway   so lets leave primitive
alone   and lets talk about something else something   that by
contrast is fairly clear   that before there was writing there
wasnt writing   that seems like a fairly minimal assumption
    before there was writing there wasnt writing   we can still find
groups of people that dont have writing   or until the anthropolo-
gists and missionaries got there   quite recently   they didnt
have writing   now before people had writing they had to get
along without it   we are going very slow   but its a radical
    assumption   once there was no writing   now if there was
no writing id like to call that culture that had no writing   for
the moment   an oral culture   because in order to transmit
    messages   or to deal with people   outside the range of an
arm and more gently than with a spear   perhaps   when you

161

couldnt push someone into a place but still wanted to bring him
there   to reach someone at the level where physical constraint
is not possible   or desirable   you use language   and in
order to contain nonpresent entities   to operate on nonpresent
entities   that is entities that are not present at a particular time
or place   if you have no way of preserving them   in your proximity   theyre not there   the yam that you ate yesterday
is no longer a yam   unless you remember it was a yam   if
you remember it was a yam   you remember it linguistically
by which i mean that you remember it by a family of features
that distinguish it from whatever else it might get confused with
and in order to talk about that yam   communicate about its
badness say   lets say it gave you indigestion and you want to
discuss that fact   that that particular kind of yam is not a good
thing   and you dont want to eat that kind of yam again
you need some way of describing that yam   some label for
that yam   or some set of instructions by which people will find
that yam   but also remember the yam that it once was   and
the class of yams it belonged to   which means that you will need
at least two categorical assignments for that yam   you will have
to have one category for the class of things you know as yams   as
opposed to other tuberous foods say   and another one for things
that make you sick   poisons say   all other yams may look
alike   but this one better look different   feel different
smell different   or live in a different place   now in
order to remember this yam you might draw a picture of the yam
though it is not easy to see how this will help you if the yam
doesnt look different from other yams   if there were no specially
marked visual features that set it apart   it wasnt greener say
or more spherical or symmetrical or whatever   besides which
this whole notion of drawing is not different from remembering
linguistically   the drawing also consists of categorical assignments
you are representing the yam among other yams and its differences from them   and the only special thing about the drawing
will be that those differences will have to be visible   but while
all this sounds logical enough   it isnt in fact the way drawings get
made by oral cultures anyway   since it would be nonsensical to
begin by making a drawing of a yam that you didnt already know to

162

be the poison yam   the important yam   or the yam in question
        you have already started with a clear memory of that particular
yam   no   drawing a picture does not replace remembering
        it is protoliterary anyway   in the sense that it articulates
        fixes or freezes an already existing memory   it commits you
in some particular way to a model   a particular model of a
memory   one particular remembering   it is therefore a literary
        activity   but talking about a yam is a bit different   talking
about a yam is not drawing a picture of a yam   and remembering
a yam is not writing a yam   and you have a different way of
communicating   because you have the problem of remembering
        and remembering is a very odd form of behavior   when its
not conducted against a model   think of the task of remembering
        the past   a past for which you have no model   im sure
youve all had lots of conversations over the past week   and im
sure that   if i asked you   to remember a conversation you had
last week   you could produce something   you would say was
        that conversation   right?   i mean if i asked you
        anybody?   you feel confident?   that you could repro-
duce the conversation you had last week?   or any part of it?
        think about it   what do you mean by "remembering" the
conversation   i can remember conversations i had when i was four
        some of them   i can remember them but i bet i cant repro-
duce them and if i could reproduce them i dont think i could be sure
that i could reproduce them   now let me describe the difference
        between reproducing something and remembering it   i did a
        piece once   i did a piece in which i asked ely   my wife   i
asked her to remember something   i told her a story   read it
        to her and i asked her to remember it   and then   the next
day i asked her to tell me what she remembered   and i recorded
        it   and then the day after   i asked her to do it again   and
then a week later   i asked her to tell the story she remembered
        and then a month later i asked her to do it again   and then a
year later i asked her to tell me the story   and finally   just
        recently   five years later   i asked her to tell me the story
once again   and she really tried very hard to remember the story

~~~~~~~~~~~~~~~~~~~~~~

the merchant of x   lived   in the town of L   and
he came to the doctor   one day   very distressed
      because   he couldnt remember   his wifes face
now i dont remember if his wife is dead or not
      couldnt remember his daughters faces either   he
used to draw very well   he knew the whole center in-
terior of the town   when hed close his eyes he could see
it before him and he could always draw it   the courthouse   the pergola?   i think   but   the
merchant of x lived in the town of L   in europe   he
came to the   analyst   in great distress because he
could no longer remember his wifes and daughters faces
      i dont recall whether they were alive or not   but
he couldnt recall them at all   he used to have a very
good memory in his business and also for   the town in
which he lived   he could recall   every building
      of the main streets   he could also in fact draw
them   he was able to   draw   geometrically
      the architectural features of the courthouse the
library and   various other buildings   and he could
quite definitely   delineate   verbally   a kind of
conceptual map in his head   he could verbalize it
      and say   and describe it   but   as far as his
family went he could no longer do that   he   also
spoke several languages   german french etcetera
      and greek and latin   it turned out that   he
could no longer speak german   though he dreamt in
french   he had a   i dont remember if it was a dream
or an experience in which he looked up and his wife
spoke to him and he didnt know it was her

*you can change your mind   if you think thats not the
formulation   try to remember*

his wife had dark hair   he knew that   but thats all
he knew   this isnt a story that   now in my head its
  wrapped up with the "little herman"   and various
things like that   i see him in his library

164

what do you remember?

    i dont think   this is not from there   "sitting in his
    library. . ." and his wife talking to him   and when he
looked up   he couldnt remember her   he no longer
could draw the principal streets of the town of L
     though he may have been able to draw the harbor
     he owned factories   or if he didnt he should have

was he getting better or worse?

well i never quite understood his problem   it was hard
    to tell what his problem was

once he had a great visual memory

    thats true he had a great visual memory   and he knew
    many languages

but after a while he lost his visual memory

yeah but i dont know

he had to train himself to go differently

oh   he had to train himself   oh yes   with great
care he memorized   the visual features   that he   .
could no longer remember   of the town perhaps
     perhaps he walked through the town again   and
tried   deliberately   to recall everything   though
    i dont know if the story   told this process   or

well didnt he come with a complaint?   *that is he came
    there he had a complaint*

    yeah but also   i dont think he spoke the same languages
anymore   i dont remember if he was melancholy
     sad   or in any kind of distress   i dont think so
     i dont think it was bothering him in his business
i just seem to remember

*you think he managed to get by in business without that
kind of memory?*

well   business   a business i guess tends to lumber
    along   never said what kind of business he was in

*he seems to have been a merchant   it said he was a
merchant*

a merchant   but i dont see why

"the merchant of x"

i dont see why his enormous memory   his former
   memory   why its loss would have interfered with
his business

   do you remember what he used to do about accounts?
      how he could remember whether he had spent or
   lost money or what his books were like?

i dont remember

   he always knew where the accounts were because he had
   a visual memory of the whole system

   oh yeah   he had a visual image of the whole page
      he could remember in his head   he could go down
   the columns   in his minds eye   and remember   i
   assume how much money such-and-such owed him or
   whatever   the details i dont remember but all the ac-
   counting pages the bookkeeping books   he could
   recall in his head   hed close his eyes and hed see it
      and he no longer saw that   but of course thats
   not necessary   that sounds like

when he lost that   what other type of memory did he
have? was he able to go any other way?

   well as i remember   he had something else   and
   he tried to go in that direction   to compensate for his
   loss   it wasnt auditory   he had to retrain himself
      to remember   all the accoutrements of his life
      and of his business   i dont think he regained his
   memory the way it had been   and i dont   i think
   he forgot latin and greek   which he had been fluent in
      and   i think   while he no longer spoke french
      he dreamt in french

   why would he have trouble with   the language?

i dont see why that should have bothered him

   why would he have trouble with the language?   what
   part of the language would he have trouble with?

   i think   in his head   he couldnt remember to

166

himself   its possible that when he spoke he could speak
it but that   in his head   he couldnt speak any of
those   languages   to himself

any of them?

   i dont know if he was swiss   or german

*now he knew modern greek as well   but it wasnt his
native language   what was the language of his childhood do you remember?*

french

   you sure?

   thats why he dreamt in french

*he spoke fluent french   was french really his native
tongue?*

   german?

*what are you remembering   you remember it as french?
and which was the language he dreamt in?*

   i remember certain noble romantic sentences

   which was the language he dreamt in?

french

and he was fluent in what languages?

   he had been fluent in   now you say it i recall modern
   day greek   latin and   i assume german

   and what had happened?   i mean what had he lost?

   i was never too clear what he lost   i was always   he
lost the ability   i remember the sentence "he lost the
   ability to..."   he lost the ability to remember   in
his mind   that visual memory that he had had   he
   lost the ability to call up all those things that he used to
   remember

including his wife

including his wife

   visually

167

visually   but maybe he could still speak   the
languages

all of them?

i assume he could speak german

*what did he finally do   what was the outcome you
remember?*

the outcome was that

                                        the outcome was
that   he had to retrain himself   to sort of   remember things i think he retrained himself to   i think
he may have forgotten what the town looked like and he
retrained   yeah as a matter of fact i think every time
he went through the town it was like coming to a foreign
place   and he didnt recognize it   and then he retrained himself to remember it   he gave himself a map
in his head   but hed have to do it   redo it   each
time   each time it was like coming to a strange place
in fact i think now   that the point of the problem
was that wherever he was it was a foreign place and he had
to   make a conscious effort   to hold it together in
his head   i guess to say to himself   "now this is the
town of L this is my town where i was born and where i
work   this is my wife with the black hair   dark
hair   this is my house"   i dont recall   if after
retraining himself   every time to do this   it may
have been that   the doctor   that is   it was suggested to him that he retrain himself   i dont recall
then if it stayed in his head or if it went away again
i dont know if he lost it   or if it stayed

*now if you had to put this whole story together now as a
single narrative   i mean if you had to remember the
whole story coherently   how would you tell me this
story?   in one piece   if you were going to try and*

168

make this back into the story that it was?

the merchant of x lived in the town of L   and he
came to a doctor   with a problem   he was very
   distressed   he had always had a superb visual memory   which helped him in business   he could close
his eyes and visually see the page that he wanted from his
books   in fact   he would go down the page with
   his eyes and scan it   perhaps with a finger in his
   minds eye   and find the information   or the data
he was looking for   he also used to draw well   and
he could draw the whole town of L   including the
harbor   and the main streets and the courthouse
   library etcetera   in fact   he could very specifically
         he could draw   the arch   that was in the
"principal"   i remember that word   building
      there was an arch   and he could draw that arch
      though is it possible he couldnt remember how it
held together?   i dont know   anyway   his
problem now was that he no longer   could remember
      his wifes face   when he closed his eyes and he
had lost his visual memory for his business books as well
      also   the language of his childhood   i dont
recall what it was   he could no longer speak   and
he had also forgotten modern greek   which he used to
know   and latin   he could still speak french
      in fact he dreamed in french   he had to retrain
himself   to recall the town   and his wifes face
      every time he entered the town   you see the
problem was that every time he entered the town it was a
   foreign place   it wasnt as if he had been born there
      and had been there all his life   and he had to
make a conscious effort to recall the streets   and the
   buildings and various landmarks   as well as   to
realize   every time he came to his house   that it
was his house   "this is my house and this is my wife
      this is *my* house and this is *my* wife"

~~~~~~~~~~~~~~~~~

169

mr x was a merchant born in vienna   he was highly
educated   master of german spanish french greek and
latin   up to a year before he read homer at sight
             virgil and horace were familiar and he knew enough
modern greek for business purposes   up to this time
he enjoyed an exceptional visual memory   no sooner
did he think of persons or things than features forms and
colors arose with the same clarity as if the objects themselves stood before him   when he tried to recall a fact
or a figure from his voluminous correspondence the
letters themselves appeared before him with their entire
content   irregularities erasures and all   in making
computations he ran his eye down the imaginary columns
of figures and performed in this manner the most varied
operations of arithmetic   he could never think of a
passage from a play without the entire scene   actors
stage and audience appearing before him   he had been
a great traveller   and being a good draftsman he used
to sketch views which pleased him   and his memory
always brought back the entire landscape exactly   if
he thought of a conversation a saying an engagement the
place the people the entire scene rose before his mind
             his auditory memory had always been deficient   a
year and a half ago an extraordinary change came over
him   after complete confusion there came a violent
change between his old and new self   everything about
him seemed new and foreign   although he saw all
things distinctly and clearly he had entirely lost his memory for forms and colors   when he realized this he
became reassured as to his sanity and he soon discovered
that he could carry on his affairs by using his memory
in an entirely different way   he can now describe
clearly the difference between his old and new states
             every time he returns to A from which place busi-
ness often calls him   he seems to himself to be
entering a strange city   he views the monuments
houses and streets   with the same surprise as if he
were seeing them for the first time   gradually however his memory returns and he finds himself at home
again   when asked to describe the principal public
place of the town he answered   i know that it is
there but it is impossible for me to imagine it and i can
tell you nothing about it   he has often drawn the
port of A   today he vainly tries to trace its principal

170

outlines   asked to draw a minaret he reflects says it is
a square tower and draws rudely four lines one for
ground one for top and two for sides   asked to draw
an arcade he says "i remember that it contains semicircu-
lar arches and that two of them meeting at an angle form
a vault but how it looks i am absolutely unable to
imagine"   the profile of a man that he drew on request
was as if drawn by a child and yet he confessed that he
had been helped to draw it by looking at the bystanders
similarly he drew a shapeless scribble for a tree
he can no more remember his wifes and childrens
faces than he can remember the town of A   even after
being with them for some time they seem unusual to him
and he forgets his own face and once spoke to his
image in the mirror taking it for a stranger   "my wife
has black hair i know but i can no more remember its
color than i can her person and features"   now when
he looks for something in his correspondence he must
rummage among the letters like other men till he finds
the passage   figures which he adds he must now whis-
per to himself   the words and expressions that he
recalls now seem to echo in his ear   an altogether
novel sensation for him   if he wishes to learn any-
thing by heart he must repeat it several times aloud to
impress it on his ear   when later he repeats the thing
in question the sensation of inward hearing precedes
articulation   this feeling was formerly unknown to
him   he speaks french fluently but affirms he can no
longer think in french   he must get his french words
by translating them from spanish or german the lan-
guages of his childhood he dreams no more in visual
terms   only in words   usually spanish words
he is troubled by the greek alphabet

~~~~~~~~~~~~~~~~~~~~~~~~~~~~

and the only way i could tell that she couldnt remember the story
   as it had been   or more precisely   the only way i could tell
   the difference between her story   the story that she remembered
   and the story that she was trying to remember   was that i

171

happened to have a tape recorder and take it down   now surely
you can imagine a time when there were no tape recorders and there
were no texts   i mean if i had an extremely efficient and "exact"
kind of shorthand   thats sort of paradoxical   but if i had i
suppose i could have taken it down   but as ive said   if i had
done that   writing it down   i would have had the story
     a telling of a story   stored in a space   which is again
something like drawing   but if i just told you a story   and i
asked you to tell it back to me   i might think i knew whether
you were being accurate   right away   though i would have
only my confidence to rely upon   but a year later   how do i
know that the story you tell me isnt the right story?   it is something of a problem   if the differences seem important   if i
were to tell each of you a story   now   and then one year
later ask you to tell me the story again   and its not on tape
     we may have to resort to an argument to decide whether its
the same story   i may think its not the story   but i sure dont
have any way of proving that the story you told me is not the story
     though i may find certain inconsistencies and improbabilities
in the story   then we could argue it out but in the end there
would be no absolute model against which we could check the
story   thats a very odd characteristic of places   that dont
have what i would call   literal reproductive capacities   a
nonliteral society cant check against an absolute   now this is a
construction   this oral society weve invented   because theres
no society in the world that doesnt have some possibility of absolute
reference   but there may be   the possibility of absolute reference and there may not be   the habit of using it   for example
     you live in a place   and you have to get somewhere
     regularly   and you have to go into places that are   confus-
ingly similar   say you live at the edge of a forest   and you
have to enter that forest and then come out of it   to get home
     its a simplified situation   but close enough to a reality
     now when you get to where you were going   and youve
finished gathering something or other   you have to get back
     and presumably you have to remember where back is   there are
a number of ways you could do it   at least we could imagine a
number of ways you might be able to do it   but if you didnt

172

get back to the right place   your memory wasnt too good   and
this is one situation where you have a fairly clear test of your
powers of memory   because if at the end of your wandering you
dont arrive at a familiar village and the hut on the right doesnt
contain the woman who was there when you set out   you may
regard this as an improvement but it is clear that your memory
has let you down   since it is obvious that most hunting or for-
aging expeditions do not result in the founding of new villages   or
rounds of wife trading or life trading   it seems at first that this
fact   that you can get back to the place that you started from
is a fundamental challenge to our notion of the instability of memory   though i dont think that it is   but let us see why we
would suppose that   to begin with there is   the difference
between the place that youre leaving and the place into which you
must go   your home   your starting place   camp   hut
village   is   a human construction   is humanly devised
or arranged   even if it is a temporary station   you will have
adapted to a human order   the place that youre going into is
not humanly arranged   it is the forest   the desert   a kind of
chaos   or at least its order is "natural"   rather than "human"
when you go into it   you can become "lost"   which
means that   you cannot apprehend its order   or relate its
order to your human order   so what do you do?   you seek
its regularities   you make a map   the sun rises regularly
more or less regularly   in the east   this is the order of
nature   and it sets in the west   if you face it   the rising
sun   your left hand points north and your right hand south
this axis is the order of culture   the human order   now
you lay out the space   with your home at the center   or at
the northern end or whatever   and you place in your mental
chart all the landmarks you encounter   you know how long it
takes   walking swiftly   more or less   to reach the two tall
rocks   or the waterhole   and when you know all this   and
you mark off proportionate distances in your picture   you have
a map   now anytime you are in the forest   if you are confused   all you have to do is find out where you are in your map
to do this you look for the sun   you put yourself in position
find your left and right hands   and try to remember how long

you walked to the right or the left   or forward or backward
        and that tells you where you are and how to get back   now
i dont doubt that any society   any group of human beings has
   this capacity   to devise a whole spatial representation   a
literal space chart that they can stand outside of long enough to draw
        and oversee completely as a formal configuration   in which
they themselves must be represented by some formal double   a
   dot or a cross   "thats me standing by this tree"   i dont
     doubt it because its been done by some societies   and if some
   men can do it im sure all men can do it   the question is whether
they do do it   or whether its the only way to do it   or even
   the most reasonable   sensible?   way to do it   but you
   may not really appreciate how freaky a thing theyve done   to
     do this   what theyve done is to isolate a space   outside of
   the one theyre in   they have in some sense to alienate
        themselves and their world   which they have always been
   inside of   to put it "over there"   some other place   to
   create a "double"   for themselves and for "it"   now you
may say they have to do that even if they merely tell a story about
what happened to them   they have to isolate themselves from a
   series of events   which was up to the moment of the "telling"
        with them all the time   as part of a continuous   a dura-
tive   present   now they have to cut it off and push it away
   as the past   and while there is some truth in this   it isnt
much   because a "story" is never present all at once   its
   beginning and end cant be surveyed at the same time   so that
it never has the isolated and bounded content of a drawing or map
        it is never an "object" to be handled   at its most alienated
        it is "material" that passes through your hand   moreover
        when you tell a story   if you think of the great tellings
        there is a progressive act of memory   you gradually approach
a past   you begin in the present   outside it say   remembering only its name   and you call on it and try to find your way
   to it   till at some point you are "in it"   and it is then present
        if only for a while   and then you move out of it again
        and there is a way of finding a place   thats quite a bit more
like remembering the past than like referring to a map   about a
   month ago   i had to go to encino   which is the name of a

174

"town" not far from los angeles   or more particularly i had to go
   to an art gallery   that people described as being "in encino"
      i had been there before   to the art gallery   i had no
notion   and still have no notion of what encino looks like as a
space   or where it is on a map   or in a picture   that would
   also show los angeles   san diego   pasadena   or the pacific
ocean   now i live in solana beach   and i have a very adequate
grasp of what solana beach "looks like"   though i dont have a
configural or aerial view of it   though i could make one   ive
walked out of my house and all around the town of solana beach
   or more particularly that part of solana beach that is on the
ocean side of the old highway   i also know how to get from
solana beach   from my house   to places in san diego
      now how did i get to encino   the gallery in encino   i
walked out of my house   and got into my car which i took in
the direction i had been facing when i left the house   which by
the way was away from the ocean   i went past the old highway
up a hill past a shopping center called "the place of the seven flags"
   to a bigger road   and turned onto it going left   i stayed
on this road for a long time   how long?   i didnt look at my
   watch   but at some point i was passing an empty stretch with
   no developments   a few palms and some chaparral   that
was camp pendleton   sometimes you see tanks and troop carriers
   there on the left side as you drive   on the right side a few
stands of eucalyptus screening farms from the sea wind   i passed
san clemente   i could tell by the large ridges we passed and a
faint sense of discomfort in breathing   we were beginning the
   smog   but you dont notice it right away   you realize after
a while that youve been sensing a slight increase in temperature
   feeling a slight effort in breathing   and you know youve
been entering the smog   after a while there are more buildings of
   an industrial sort   oil refineries   cracking plants   a gypsum
plant   a holiday inn   youre moving toward long beach
   but you keep going without paying too much attention to the
road   later then youre going through a long stretch of fairly empty
mountains   youre getting closer   you pass a funny shaped
building on your left   a little science fictiony and displaced in
these mountains   then there is another of a different kind

175

also displaced   this time on the right   i think its a bank
and you approach it coming down a hill   its time to make a left
turn onto another road   called the ventura freeway   you
drive on this for a short while   i dont remember how long
     and theres a place to get off   i cant tell you what it looks
like   but when i see it   the angle of light maybe   a cluster
of eucalyptus trees and then nothing   i think   i get off and
find my way left   i go straight ahead until i come to a big avenue
     a kind of more open space   and turn right   i travel along
this street till the businesses get a little flashier and look for the
place   when i am in front of it i recognize it   now i have no
great fund of information about the australian aborigine   but i
have reason to suppose that in some ways he moves around   or
used to move around his own countryside somewhat in the way that
i got to encino   an anthropologist trying to make a map of the
"territory" of certain western desert people   found that "usually
a western desert man will make a small mark representing his birthplace and from it run a line representing his track to farther waters
until he has indicated all his principal camping places"   as you
can see   this is not a map   its a set of "driving instructions"
     and it was only by using a large number of "driving instruc-
tions" that professor tindale was able to construct a "map" of the
desert mans territory   because a map consists of a very large
family of driving instructions   in fact   once a map is put
down from some limited number of sets of driving instructions it
can be used to derive an infinite set of driving instructions
     because once the axis of culture   the left hand right hand
line   the north south line   is oriented to the axis of nature
     the east west line   it is possible by counting some kinds of
units   steps?   degrees?   to get from any place to any
other place within the domain of the map   whether or not they
have ever been of interest to anyone before   hypothetical places
     or conjectural places   can all be arrived at by reference to
known places and the four points of the compass   there are
certainly advantages to this literal career   because thats what it
is   a career   and it was the career of the great astronomical
and agricultural societies in the near east   which became very
involved with regularities   absolute regularities   or as nearly

176

absolute regularities as they could find   one might imagine that
they had a special need for such a career   or rather more precisely
     that such a career was rewarded   under their special circum-
stances of farming on a flood plain   where a great deal of human
     social and economic organization disintegrated when the waters
came   we dont have to hold a functionalist position to suppose
that an ability to reinstitute land divisions on the subsidence of
flood waters   or to predict with some accuracy the approach
of flooding   or to estimate the timing of planting and harvesting
in relation to this water clock   and solar clock   or to dredge
the marshes for cultivation   and allocate regular amounts of
river water to regularly divided land parcels   would pay off
     and maybe even pay off high enough stakes to enough members
of this society   in return for the loss of human freedom that the
regularity would entail   for them to put up with it   and its
not surprising to see trigonometry and geometry and map making
     all together in this growing literalist enterprise   where we
also find   in this hydraulic society   one great center of literacy
     which is again no accident   because if you think of this
literalism as a career   you can also think of it as something like
     the career of a disease   some alien element   perhaps arbitrary
     a foreign body   the first move toward literalism   making
a mark on a wall say   producing a response to that foreign element   recognizing it as equivalent to something or capable of
     being made equivalent to something   always   and extracting
     value from that regularity of equivalence   one mark for the
rising sun to the setting sun   one mark for the number one
     that is for one of anything   two such marks for two of
anything   grasping at the career of regularity in literalism   but
only grasping   because in the beginning making two marks merely
     reenacts the action of counting   "one [makes mark]"   "two
[makes mark]"   it is still a little play   "the sun [he puts his
     stick in the earth making a point and begins to move it] goes from
here to there"   it is still the *act* of drawing   not *a drawing*
     but it is not a long way from drawing   reenacting with the
hand   to *a drawing*   the disease is spreading   once youve
     benefited from any form of literalism it will be easier to try another
and another   and while all these acts of regularization pay off in

some convenience   you will also pay something for them   in
this way most diseases are not so much problems   but solutions
to problems   that youre paying too much for   like athero-
sclerosis   which was solving your diet problem and your lack of
activity problem till it killed you   well now we have a problem
with our overlong career of literalism   overlong and singleminded
      its been so long now that many of us find it hard to understand
the terms of any other possible career   so hard that we must
insist that the western desert man   was not making a map   or
not what we mean by a map   its a pity that tindale doesnt give
a precise account of what the event was like   but that wasnt
his purpose at the time   so let us reconstruct the event as it
probably happened   "the western desert man will make a mark
representing his birthplace"   now how does he do that?   for
a western desert man   "the place where he was born" is not so
much the place where his mother gave birth   that point on a
north-south east-west grid counted off in meters from some objective
physical landmark   it isnt that   his birthplace is the "important place" closest to that physical birth   its the nearest important place   on the famous path   of the "sacred person"
      he will be associated with   a pile of rocks   a small water-
hole   that will be the place of his dreaming   and these camping places   they will lie along the track of his dreaming   more
or less   the desert mans territory is crisscrossed   not by recur-
rent and regularly spaced lines of longitude and latitude   but by
sacred tracks of "first people"   the sacred ones who wandered
through the place   sat down here   went out of sight there
      and left a pile of rocks to mark the place   and placed the
important creatures and plants in the land   now these paths are
not spaced equidistantly   and they do not proceed in right lines
      they wander from waterhole to clump of vegetation across an
arid irregularly watered space covered with spinifex grass and rocks
and scrubby little trees   and because of the way the people live
there   a few hundred people living in an area of a few thousand
square miles   and having to travel in smaller and smaller bands
as the year gets dryer and dryer   most are familiar with some
of each others famous paths   within their familiar terrain
      but less familiar with others paths   though they are from

178

the same group   so what any one desert man has is a knowledge
of roads and driving instructions   some roads he knows better
     than others   now he makes a mark   the first mark he makes
     is for the place he knows best   you ask "how does he know
where to put it   on the paper?"   and thats a good question
     if he happens to make this map on paper   it would be inter-
esting to know does he put it in the middle or near an edge?   is
he an edge person?   because maybe he was born near the beginning of another peoples land or something   but i dont have any
answers for that   professor tindale had something else in mind
and neglected to say whether the western desert man made his map
on paper or on the ground   but i would suppose   that it
would be very unlikely that he the western desert man would line
up the axes of the paper with the sunline and his leftright hand line
before beginning   and it is probable that he would feel more
comfortable laying out his pathways in the ground   with a stick
     and that he would push the stick forward through the ground
as if he was walking in the direction of the stick   unless the habit
of using that stick   his boomerang say   was to pull it toward
him   as when cutting up an animal   but if his working habit
didnt interfere   he would probably push the stick forward and
     reenact his going travelling from his birthplace   to his next
camping ground   try to remember that place and then go on to
his next one   and so on and so on   till he had gone through
all his camping places   or all of them that he remembered
     and while i have no evidence for this   i can point to two
native maps   incised on their spear throwers by pintubi tribesmen
     of the western desert   as these were shown and explained
to donald thomson   who was exploring their country   and
these are certainly not maps in our sense of the word   for one
thing   though both spear throwers   and both maps are from
the same people   the same band even   they are by no means
the same   one spear thrower shows forty-nine water places and
the other shows thirty-six in what seems to be the same territory
     and only eighteen are the same   and while this isnt terribly
surprising   since the drawings   the roadmaps were made by
different people   most likely   what is more surprising is
that these eighteen common places are not in the same place

by which i mean that they are not in the same relation to each other or to the surface on which they are inscribed in the two "maps"   drawings   or more precisely   carvings   but this may take a little explaining   because the carvings themselves exhibit only certain relations found in maps   sequential order and approximate relative proximity and accessibility   how is this the case?   well the carvings consist of more or less circular marks for the camping sites and lines between them for the connecting paths   all of the circles are laid out along one or the other of about three rather wavy lines that parallel the long dimension of the somewhat fishshaped spear throwers   occasionally these circular watersites are connected by crosslines to an adjacent site on an adjoining longitudinal line   so it seems that you can get from campsite 1 to campsite 2 and must then procede directly to campsite 3 and so on   but in other parts of the map it turns out that you can get from campsite 3 to campsite 4 but also to campsite 6 because campsite 3 is connected to campsites 2 and 4 and 6   so what we have is a network of roads   marking accessibility and a sort of serial order   or a choice of serial order and relative proximity   and thats all   now you may suppose that one end of the spear thrower marks north and the other south   but that is not the case   because a place that is at the distal end of one spear thrower may appear either at the proximal end of the other or even at the center   it seems that a sequence of camping sites arranged in the mind perhaps as an ordered list   is laid out in the order in which the sites would be approached ordinarily   first this one   then that one   but that the list is arbitrarily adapted to the shape of the spear thrower   i mean any pintubi would probably know that *wakilbi* would be much further off to the left if he was going there from *kuna*   but if he put it as far off to the left as it ought to be if the law of proportionality was to be obeyed   it wouldnt fit on the spear thrower   so wherever it should really be   it still has to be made to fit on a piece of wood   which was shaped before the map was made   and shaped on the basis of very different considerations   and while this is easy to understand   and a relatively practical solution to a practical problem   making a wide terrain fit on a narrow surface   there is another difference between these road maps

180

and our notion of a map   even when both maps agree on the
watering places they dont always agree on the way to get from one
to another   for example   there are four places   *wirra
wirra   kirindji   kanandibarro*   and *markodarindja*
     and they are laid out on map 1 in just that way   following
sequentially a kind of right angle   of which *kanandibarro* is the
vertex   but on map 2 they are not only laid out in a single line
     but in the order *markodarinjda   kirindji   kanandibarro
wirra wirra*   that is   they are reversed   which is a
trivial difference   because the point of view of the map maker
might have been reversed   but they are also in a different order
     which is to say   if one map has the order 6 7 8 9   map
2 has the order 9 7 8 6   where we would have expected   if
sequence were to be maintained   9 8 7 6   how to explain this
to one who is used to our notion of maps   well   it isnt difficult to explain as long as we remember that this is not really a "map"
     an arrangement that conforms or is congruent or similar in the
disposition of its elements to the elements of the real world   conceived in relation to some fixed axes   if it isnt we can suppose
that the two waterholes   *kirindji* and *kanandibarro*   which
we have called 7 and 8   are neither one of them much further
from or nearer to either campsite 6 or 9   then these two
     kirindji and *kanandibarro*   waterholes 7 and 8   can be
imagined to lie more or less on a straight line   in the real world
     at right angles to a line that might be drawn from campsites 6
to 9   the four campsites would then form a kind of conceptual
diamond shaped parallelogram   and it would be a matter of personal preference whether you went from *wirra wirra*   our number 6   first to *kirindji*   number 7   then *kanandibarro*
     number 8   and then to *markodarindja* number 9   or
whether you went from *wirra wirra* number 6 first to *kanandibarro*
     number 8   then *kirindji* number 7 and then to *markodar-
indja*   number 9   and this transposition of 7 and 8 could be
made either coming from *markodarindja* number 9 or *wirra wirra*
number 6   and the preference that would lead you to make
either choice might have to do with the way in which your particular sacred ancestor happened to go   and he may have gone
one way on one occasion and the other way on another   so that

Map 1

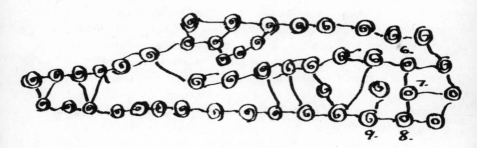

Map 2

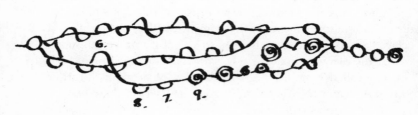

KEY: APPROXIMATE PROBABLE SITUATION

Path of Map 1.
— — —

Path of Map 2.
. . . . . .

6. wirra-wirra
7. kirindji
8. kanandibarro
9. markodarindja

spear thrower "maps" drawn after photographs in d.f. thomson
"the bindibu expedition" *geographical journal* volume 128
1962 pp 262-78   the "maps" are slightly simplified in respect
of possibly significant marks of uncertain meaning on the spear
throwers   the analysis is my own

this is a reason based on history rather than geography   or more
    precisely   on sacred geography rather than geometrical geography
        now this sacred geography   or traditional geography   is
based on these first paths not on literal lines of longitude and latitude which are intended to replicate literally a pathway with respect
to the solar path   what we come back to is a memory of roads
    and places   and it is very much a matter of memory
        because there is no hint on either of these spear thrower road-
maps which waterhole is which   this you have to remember
    and you do it by first remembering the first one   where
you were born?   and then you remember the next one and then
the next one and so on   and if you get confused   there is no
one to correct you except someone elses memory   and as elkin
    the great australian anthropologist says

        sometimes the natives say they know quite well the direc-
        tion and exact location of a certain sacred site [but]
            they seldom approach it by the shortest route   indeed
        they frequently set out as though going somewhere else
        altogether   or they seem unable to find their way to
        the place   the explanation is that the sacred place
        must only be approached by the same path as that taken
        by the hero connected with it   this may lead for
        some time away from it   and some informants may
        have to search round until they find signs of the track
        before they can move with certainty

because in order to come to the right place you have to find the right
    way   which may not mean when you are travelling that you must
    always travel in this order   on these paths   anymore than a
traveller with a modern map must travel along a great circle of the
    globe   clearly you can travel any way you want or have to for
the purposes you have in hand   hunting or whatever   but
you can always locate yourself in relation to these famous lines and
    water places   instead of locating yourself by lines of longitude
    and latitude you locate yourself in relation to famous lines and
famous places   that have one further advantage over arbitrary
    ones   there will ordinarily be water there   you can
probably also regard the celebrated and enormously complex kinship
systems of these societies as also   nothing more than sets of driving

instructions   roadways for distinguishing landmarks in a more or
less indistinguishable terrain of relatively equivalent things
     men and women   and you dont have to suppose any charts
or maps   merely a knowledge of the rules of the road   as
provided by familiar examples   say im supposed to marry my
cross-cousin   some girl   whats a cross-cousin?   in my
case   since im a man   itll be a girl that i should get to by
travelling in the right way   my instructions are "up one generation..."   this roadmap will lead to my patrilateral cross-cousin
     travel up one generation to a man   who will turn out to be
my father   or any man who can be classed as that   which
might be any of his brothers or half brothers   or classificational
brothers   drive left to his sister   or any woman who can be
classed as that   turn back down any number of generations to
whoever is classed as her daughter   and marry her   or any
her you can reach by travelling that road whose father will agree to
     give her to you for whatever wives are going for that year   if
youre supposed to marry your matrilateral cross-cousin   that
merely means you drive up one generation to a female parent
     your mother or whoever you can class as that   turn right to
her male sibling   a brother or whoever can class as that   turn
back down to a woman   his daughter   or whoever you can
class as that   and marry her   for any of these excursions
there are alternate trips   what you might call the scenic route
     you can go up to your mothers mothers mothers mother
     four generations up   as long as you come down four classi-
ficational generations   to her brothers daughters daughters daughters daughter   and at the end of that road there will be a woman
waiting for you   on the other hand   if you happen to begin
with a woman   if you work hard enough   and drive backward far enough   there is an ancestor waiting for you
     which is to say that in kinship also   it is hardly a matter of
who you marry   of finding the right person   it is rather a
matter of finding some person by going the right way   and once
again   so with marriages as with campsites   you may not
choose to travel them   but they mark out the terrain   the
only problem   and it may not be a problem at all   if nobody
makes an issue out of it   is that the memory of relations

landmarks   over any number of generations may become
somewhat vague   in which case you will certainly convert any
   marriage you intend   into a marriage that was arrived at in the
   right way   and you will redesignate all the necessary intermediate
   landmarks   relations   which may not in absolute historical
   fact have been the right relations   to make them the right relations   since there is no such thing as an absolute history   but
   only the memory of history   which you will adapt to the circumstances of your needs and desires   and your sense
         perhaps   of anxiety   which is to some extent the way of
all historians   and possibly   it is an anxiety like this that is
   bound up with   the career   of writing down   some fear
of forgetting   is it an accident that the dakota winter counts
      seem to coincide   that is   their invention and use
      seem to coincide with the sense of the alien presence   of
the white man   some premonition of the loss of their history
      which is really a memory of important things   dimly felt
and worried about   the time they first stole the horses with iron
   shoes   when they first got smallpox   the appearance of the
white trader   the small inroads   spreading an anxiety that
   they might go "out of print"   the recording of history will only
seem necessary   the fixing of the past in some external reservoir
      the message stick the knotted string the cylinder seal the palace
inventory the burial inscription   if there is some danger of forgetting or losing   its an attempt to overcome the deficiencies of
   the human   one deficiency of which is death   by placing
   meaning outside of mind   trying to find some way of bringing
meaning out of a mind and into a place   so it was appropriate
      for that mycenaean society with all its apparatus and gear
      for the minoans   to have a way of keeping inventories and
accounts   but its not all that easy to understand how poetry
came to be written down   or why   i mean if poetry was a
kind of talking   and it had to be if there was no writing   then
   a poet was someone who could talk   when the time came
      could remember other talking   and could tell the important
things   how they had happened and why   and what might
   have happened if these things hadnt happened in the way they
happen to have happened   now i suppose   if the talk seemed

very important   and sometimes it may have been   say that
   the talk was a talking of law   of what was acceptable and right
and what was not acceptable and not right and what then   in
iceland every summer over every three years the law speaker had to
   stand on the law rock and recite the whole law of the land   and
the way that we understand that   is that the law is already
mixed up with writing   because we think of the ten commandments and the code of hammurabi   "thou shalt have no other
   god than me"   or "if you steal from me ill kill you"   but
the law of power is not the only kind of law   that is   statute
law   the law of edicts and statutes and commandments   and
pseudocommandments is not the only kind of law   there is the
   notion of common law   among the germanic peoples anyway
      a law expressing someones views of what is fitting among
equals   if you happen to kill someone   and it sometimes
happens   you have to make restitution of some sort   to his
   people   if you divorce someone   you have to give back her
   dowry   all other things being equal   "have to"?   well
you have to by "law"   it is thought just   and the law will
work   if you   the parties concerned are equal in power
      and can make the "law" work   no   there is an oral law
      sometimes called primitive law   there are courts among
people having no writing   though you may think "if there is no
writing theres no reciting"   and youre wrong   because it is
where there is no writing there is reciting   on the condition that
some particular articulation in talking   was the right articulation
   that one time   "do unto others as you would have others
do unto you"   or "those that have shall receive   and those
that have not   even the little that they have shall be taken
away"   its not hard to remember that at all   give or take a
   little   if its memorable youll remember it   but it will help
if its short and peculiar   jingling and twisted   in some unex-
pected way   its a platitude to say it   that you will remember
   what is distinctive   and that suggests you shouldnt worry about
forgetting   and there never will be writing   because youll
   never need it   but you may think something is important and
it isnt short   it is a long train of events and articulations   and
you are worried that you have to remember it just so   it has the

186

nostalgia of *njal* talking about law   "with law shall our land be
built up but with lawlessness laid waste"   and we must understand that *njal* is probably not just saying that   hes reciting it
hopefully   a kind of proverb   between talking and
writing we probably have reciting   and thats the only way i
could imagine that the talkings of homer got to be written down
otherwise it seems too improbable   that anyone would
want to write them down   not at a time when all of this talking
was going on   as talking   because it would just seem too
freaky an idea   to use a way of mark making that was used for
labels on a can of peaches or a figure in a bill of lading   and hope
it would hold   a way of talking   and i dont doubt that homer
or some other blind man   told those "poems"   because
they just arent put together the way somebody would put them
together if he could lay it out all in front of him and go back
and forth over all that talk   and take out all of his slips and
file away the little side trips that make the talking seem a funny
shape   kind of uncouth as a "form"   but a form only exists
in space   at least it has no objective existence without reference
to some space in which its all together at once   so that you can
inspect all the parts of it   as an overall kind of thing   no serial
art   no art that elapses in time can be looked at all at once
unless it is terribly short   because there is memory again   you
cant flip the pages of memory back and forth to find slips of the
tongue you didnt notice when you made them   or forgot
     and an oral poem is clumsier   if you like literary poems
better   i mean the saga of *burnt njal* is much more elegant than
the iliad   from a formal point of view   and theyre both
terrific   but theyre terrific in different ways   if youre a literary man   homer is something of a slob   the whole opening
of the iliad is something of a mistake   the talker gets caught by a
kind of slip of the tongue and he has no choice but to go right on
     it begins ordinarily enough   as i suppose you all know
     he asks the muse   to give him enough memory to get his
talking straight   you know the way it goes

                                        tell me goddess
          of the destroying rage of achilles   peleus son   that

                          187

loaded all those woes on the achaeans   and sent   too
early   all those brave heros souls down to hell   and
left their bodies for the dogs and all the birds   and yet
it was the will of zeus   and of that first time
          when the son of atreus   king of men and divine
achilles quarreled and drew apart

which is okay as far as it goes   it was the usual thing i suppose
     more or less   but the turning point   the difficult varia-
tion in this opening   something like the dragon variation in the
sicilian defense   is in the next phrase   because up to here
homer could have gotten to the quarrel very easily and worked his
way in from there   but the next phrase goes

          and which of the gods set them on the two of them
          to fight with each other?

which may seem reasonable enough   except none of the gods set
them on to fight with each other   as homer himself will show in
     a very few lines   sure he says it was

          the son of latona and zeus   for he was enraged with
          the king   and he sent a plague among the army
          and the people were dying

which is all very well   but thats hardly what set agamemnon
and achilles quarreling   it merely created an anterior set of circumstances that could have caused any number of things   the
     loss of the war by the greeks   their sailing away from troy in
disgust   their death by the plague   whatever   nothing at
all about achilles and agamemnon   until the plague gets so bad
that hera   zeus wife   takes things into her own hands
          and in a dream she tells achilles to call a council   if there is
no council there will be no quarrel   of divine agents hera is as
good a cause as any   but even thats not enough   its in the
council   when achilles asks for a priest or an interpreter of dreams
          to explain why the disease that calchas stands up and explains
          how agamemnons insult to chryses   the priest of apollo
          caused it all and how to amend it   that the quarrel starts
          now you may say thats all right   the greeks have a funny
view of causality   and i say thats nonsense   homer isnt

188

thinking of causality   as a matter of fact he isnt thinking at all
      hes talking   trying to make his way to the story   which
he intends to tell   this time from the point of view of achilles
      quarrel with agamemnon   who knows why?   and at about
the end of the first request to the muse   hes used to asking
about divine agencies   hes already named the two main human
actors   now its time   or seems to be time to bring in the
gods   hes already talked about the dying and the dead bodies
      and there is the image of them lying on the beach being fed on
by the dogs and the birds   so he may as well   or rather he
may   whether its well or not   talk about the dying   and
just before the quarrel broke out there was a disease that ran
through the army   and it was on homers mind   the dying
men and the carrion birds and the dogs   and there was apollo
      prince of disease   with his arrows   and he was offended
so why not apollo and the story of how he came to be offended
      how agamemnon kidnapped the daughter of apollos priest
chryses   and the old priest came to ransom her   under the
protection of apollo   with the fillet and the ransom in his hands
      and agamemnon drove him away and insulted him as well
      okay   you say why not this way   the answer is that as
soon as homer says "which god set them on each other"   and
names apollo   he has to tell the whole story of the old priest
coming down to the ships with his ransom and politely begging and
bribing the greek kidnappers   and maybe a little threatening
trouble from apollo as well   and homer gives all the speeches
      agamemnons cruel response

            i wont let her go till old age overcomes her   in our
      house   in argos   far from her own country
            working the loom and sharing my bed

and "dont let me find you here again down near our ships"   its
pretty colorful   but the trouble is with the "form"   if you
care about things like that   because in the council that achilles
      calls   calchas will have to tell all over again why apollo caused
all that trouble   and homers just told that story   very well
      and he has to tell it all over again   and its not so good this
time   whereas   if he hadnt slipped into the "which god"

                                    189

gambit   he wouldnt have had to tell the insult to chryses twice
over   in the space of a very few lines   now you may say
theres nothing wrong with repetition   and i would be the last
person to disagree with you   but the notion of "formal" elegance
     is usually related to reduction of redundancy   of pointless
repetition   i mean if calchas told the story the second time in
such a way that it added something   anything   eloquence
     more detail   or more information of any kind   you
could plausibly say it was better written that way   but the passage is nothing of the sort   its a mere statement of the insult to
chryses   and to apollo   and what happened thereafter
     all of which you already know   and know better
     because there isnt much better in the whole poem than the way
apollo comes down from olympos with his shoulders shaking with
rage   rattling the arrows in his quiver   calmly seating himself
on the ground and sending his arrows   rattling   "first into
the mules   and then the swift dogs   and then on the greeks"
     keeping "the funeral fires heaped with the bodies of the dead
constantly burning"   this is all very magnificent   but its the
kind of magnificence that a great chess player improvises right
after a structural blunder   now in a written work   it would
have been very easy to go back   erase the false step   and put
the whole colorful description of the insult to chryses somewhat
     more conveniently in calchas mouth when he explains the plague
in the council of the greeks   but the iliad is not a written work
     and there are some things fundamentally different about an
oral poem   one thing in particular   the technique of erasing
     i mean in a literary poem theres a text and a determined reader
can flip the pages back over and over again   and there is something of an illusion of spatial form   the idea that you can have
it there   all at once   lying under your hands   leading to
the notion of elegant spatial arrangement and its contraries
     clumsy arrangements   all based on fantasies of some spatial
existence that is the result of the minds deceiving itself into forgetting that it has itself constructed this "space" and the "form" that
is an imaginary configuration within it   by mere flipping of
pages and taking this synthetically derived memory   produced by
constant reavailability   and confusing it with real memory

it is this "constructed" literal form which requires the mechanical operations of erasure and excision   the only way you can
get rid of an object is to destroy it   but an oral poem has no
such problem   if you take a wrong turn   make a false start
      you cant "erase" it   but you can recover and you can oblit-
erate it from memory   you can take advantage of the weakness
of human memory   by extending through time some kind of
      diversionary brilliance   if your energy isnt impeded and you
get where you have to go   without looking tired   no one
will remember that it took you a few extra steps to get there   the
principle of economy of form in an oral work is measured out in
energy   not in length   how long is a brilliant passage?
      how short is a boring one?   who remembers?   after
homer told that story twice   remember that story?   the insult
to apollo?   with all those fireworks   who remembers how
      apollo got into it at all?   as a divine agent   what you
remember is the insult to chryses   apollos anger   flying
arrows   the mules and the dogs dying   and the men   and
after the poem was "made"   i mean after a lot of tellings of the
      story   in many different ways   that people "remembered"
      some tellings   and then maybe one telling   or one kind
of telling   seemed very auspicious   and the poet   the
      talker   or some series of talkers   got too fond of their own
bon mots and those of their masters   and there got to be too
much art appreciation and not enough art making   though still
quite a bit   so that the poem was strung out with good phrases
      that by now the overly sensitive younger poets were pretty much
stuck with   because aside from everything else they were easy
to remember and something of a convenience   if you had to do
it while singing   which is a special kind of talking   a little
bit peculiar   like telling a story on a tightrope or while swimming   difficult but not impossible   especially if you had all
those readymade phrases to do it with   so you could save a
      space for the breathing   and also have time to improvise in
another part of the talking   with the arrangement of the story
say   to improvise at all   you need some kind of cliches
      but anyway   with all of this increase in remembering choice
bits   its easy to see   no its not so easy but possible to see how

that making poems   talking poems   could start dying   and
people could start trying to remember somebodys good talking
      and therefore reciting   and from reciting   its not too
far to trying to save it in writing   but we know all about that
      about how writing is about anxiety   trying to hold some-
thing still   and we can sympathize with it   too easily   even
plato   who was afraid of writing   at least socrates was afraid
of it   and says so in the *phaedrus*   how writing will destroy
human memory   that is real memory   because people will
come to rely upon this writing and will not exercise their minds to
come to the truth   and how it   writing   is like the stupid
child of indulgent parents   that will spout words that you will
want to question more closely   and when you ask it more nar-
rowly to tell you its meaning   it will answer nothing at all and
have to run back to its parents to find out the answer   and yet
with all this   platos own theory of forms is the pathetic child of
literacy   the notion of a fixed paradigm   a pattern against
which all exemplars can be checked   or you hope they can
      well maybe it was socrates who saw the trouble coming
      because he committed nothing to writing   and plato com-
mitted everything   but we know this story   how we got here
      its harder to understand what an oral culture is doing when its
making art   say   and easy enough to understand about stories
and talking   but you want to know what about pots?
      because pot making is one of the things they do in oral cultures
      some of them   and some people call those pots art   if
this pot making is art   its the art of making pots   its not the
pots that are the art   pots are the outcome of the art   now
why do i say this   because its sometimes easy to forget this
      and start rushing to the pot to find the art   if pot making is
an art lets think about the way people learn to make pots   in pot
      making cultures can somebody say "here is the ideal pot   in it
is the very idea of a pot   study that pot and copy it"   maybe
they could but they dont   not what im calling oral cultures
anyway   if they say anything at all   which they may not
      they say something like "this is the way to make this kind of
pot   first   you get ready   and you sit down   sit down
      here   no   youre not ready   go away   youre not

ready yet   go think about the clay   heres some clay   take it
   go for a walk   feel the clay go feel the clay"   you know
they may have very elaborate routines   which are from their
   point of view all part of making the pot   and you will find
that in oral societies they frequently have quite elaborate routines
for making all kinds of things   or used to have   in totem pole
making cultures or boatmaking cultures   maybe before you
   make the thing that youre going to make you go out into the forest
and find a branch   and youre not going to "use it"   not in
the sense that it will enter into the boat that youre making or be a
mechanical instrument used in assembling it   its part of the "role"
   of boatmaking   its what "boatmakers do"   you go out and
find this branch and youre getting into the spirit say of boatmaking
       and youre producing auspicious circumstances   the right
mood say   the right set   for doing this thing and then you sit
   down   in an appropriate way and set about working at it   in
an appropriate way   maybe you even talk to appropriate people
       in some appropriate way before you work on it   and then if
it doesnt come out   in some sense we could talk about later
       its symptomatic that something was wrong with the way you
   made it   its not that it was a bad thing   it was that you didnt
   make it right   that is you didnt *do* the right thing   the art
of this particular kind of society is a way   is a way and it leads
   to things   but the things it leads to are only places along the
way   they may be merely stages of the way   so a pot is an
   outcome of a way and its not a prototype   what you do in a
   literal culture is you take a model of a particular pot   and this
pot   this particular pot exemplifies all pots that you want
       as you have someone in a dress factory who works at sewing
the parts of the dresses   of which the factory will make very
   very many   if they are lucky   and she sews much better
       more carefully and accurately to a pattern   that the pat-
ternmaker cuts out of a stiff paper like oaktag   and this seam-
stress who is more skilled than the others   is the samplemaker
       and she makes out of cloth   which is not very much like
oaktag   pieces and sews them into a dress   and if the dress
   fits the dummy   which is the ideal prototypical shape   for
a woman of that size   a twelve say   then they use the

pattern to trace out other ideal sizes   10   14   16   18
by a series of ideal amplifications   bust so much hips so
much waist so much   for the purpose of which ideal amplifications they have an ideal amplifier   a man called a grader who
accomplishes these amplifications and reductions on the same stiff
paper   which he gives to another man called a marker   who
carefully marks these patterns onto a long sheet of paper which
will be laid over the material that they will use in the dresses   by
another man called a cutter   then they will cut up all the cloth
by following the patterns marked on the marker   and the pieces
of cloth cut up in this way will go to the operators   who will
sew them into the dresses that real women will wear   now you
may object that the different sizes of women are not quantized in
such a way that they are proportionally grouped in magnitudes
that are neat multiples of each other   or that an individual
woman may be a perfect 12 at the waist and yet a fourteen at the
breast   which is true   but just too bad   because it is
more convenient to make dresses for ideal women than real women
more convenient for the makers if not for the women   and
all of this is the strategy of a literal culture   tracing off a pattern
and in theory because it is never so in practice   a literal culture will produce things that look more like the pattern than the
pattern after a while   the notion of replication belongs to that
culture   ideally such a society seeks regularity and uniformity
and increases convenience   for the maker   who is fundamentally distinct from the user   because his convenience may
be served otherwise   and this convenience may lead to a total
disjunction between making and using which may reduce to rubble
the whole apparent purposefulness of the initial prototype   now
an oral society does not gravitate to the notion of replication
the ideal example   because as anyone will easily see
there is never a situation without some trivial or not so trivial
accident   in making the pot   the temperature was perhaps
too great   or there was a piece of sand where there shouldnt
have been but occasionally is one   but if you made it the right
way you made it the right way   everybody knows that if you
make something the right way its going to be a little different than
if you make it the right way some other day   in fact you dont

194

even think about it being different from the one you made the right
way the other day   as far as youre concerned theyre quite the
same thing   if you take two pots made by two good potmakers
who are of the same type   belong to the same atelier
perhaps one was the teacher of the other   and theyre both
very good   and if its really an oral culture   more or less
and one pot looks different from the other   to you   you
might have to work fairly hard to get these two potmakers to admit
there was really a difference between the two pots   or finally
to admit that they had noticed it right away but didnt think it
meant a great deal   because they would think that the difference between the two pots was the difference between any two pots
that were made in the right way   now of course you could say
"look the beak is a little longer here   bent a little over here"
and you say "and a little wider over there"   and "yes yes"
they say looking at you like the fool that you are   because it
has always been evident to them that if you can make it the right
way you make it the right way   if this is true   all other
things being equal   we should come to see a fundamental difference between what we are calling oral societies and literal societies
in an oral society they will keep to the right way and in a literal
society they will keep to the right thing   and since the right thing
is itself a literal exemplar of other right things   in such a society
you will have an attempt to adhere rigidly to the right thing if you
are convinced that you already have the right thing   as in
certain hierarchic societies   and if you are convinced that you do
not as yet have the right thing you will try to seek out what that is
by inspecting other things   which are not quite the right
thing   and attempting to finish them to the degree of perfection
that will make them the right thing   but once youre convinced
that you have the right thing youll demand absolute adherence to it
and if theres any difference of opinion about whether it is the
right thing or not   youre likely to have something of a conflict
between the party that believes they have the right thing and the
party that believes they havent   the result of this will be that
any change in any thing will seem much more important
loaded so to speak   when a thing is involved with a notion
of its rightness   so that a literal society will exaggerate any

195

change at all in a thing it takes seriously   and it will seem to this
society   that any changes at all in its things   the things that
it notices   are terrifically radical   and such a society will
imagine itself struggling between order and revolution   however
trivially it may be changing   it is therefore a much more rigid
and inflexible society than an oral society   which we can imagine
as continually accumulating small variations   somewhat randomly
in the sense that the work under hand is continually varying
in the direction of the needs of the moment and habit of the hand
of the human being who is making whatever hes making   and
because there will be no exemplar to hold up the work against
or more accurately   because no one will feel obligated to
hold up the work against any previous work to compare these slight
deviations   there will be a constant fluidity in the working of
this oral society   their workmen artists will always be modifying
things in an easy going way without really thinking about trying
to be different   because whatever difference there may be
this workman will be likely to regard it as the same   which
will lead to the slightly paradoxical conclusion that oral societies
are probably always changing and fluid   and that their changes
may be as great as any changes in any literal society   or much
greater   but they will not flatter themselves   or threaten
themselves   with the notion that these changes are "revolution-
ary" as long as they are made in the right way   because the idea
of a revolution is based on the degree of deviation from a prototype
now all this depends to some extent   the confidence in any
product of the right way   depends on some reservoir of memory
and i think it is more useful to think of this memory as a
group possession   that is   i dont think of this memory as
being an idiosyncratic individual faculty   it involves an individual
faculty that is exercised in a social context   with other similar
faculties   memory of most sorts   of cultural things is
something negotiated by individuals   but negotiated with other
individuals   and "stored" in socially constructed systems like
language   or socially articulated systems like personality   so
that there will not really be such extreme idiosyncrasies in judging
the right way   though there will be considerable biasing in the
direction of single personality or situation if the work at hand is not

196

something that many people must be concerned about in the aspect
   that is undergoing modification   something as socially neutral
as its shape perhaps   now you say that may be true all other
   things being equal   but since they arent always equal what then?
      then there will be change of a slightly different sort   say
among yoruba potters   the nigerian yoruba society was until
fairly recently and still is largely an oral society   but that isnt
   the way change will occur in yoruba pot making   that is
      you can have a family of great potters   the grandmother a
   potter   her daughter a potter and her daughter a potter   and
they may all three have made pots for the same distinctive social
   purpose   a cult purpose say   and all three pots may be quite
   distinctively different   and these pots may seem quite different
to the three potters even though they were all made in the right
way   the granddaughter may say   seeing a pot of her mothers
      which she may not have seen for years   "yes thats a pot of
my mothers they used to make them like that in those days"
      and she will not say "*we* used to make them that way"
      even though she may have been making pots in those days
      why is that?   thats because the yoruba have a "renown"
system   an individual potter can become famous   she may
be publicized by something quite equivalent to an art magazine
      that is   by the religious cult of which she is a member
      she may make pots for the members of this cult   and it will
be through the distribution system of the cult that her pots are seen
      since her pots are commodities   and are commissioned
      it is advantageous to her to have these pots act as her advertise-
ment so to speak   each pot   if it bears the marks of her individual style   is an advertisement of her work   and it turns
out that because being a potter is a profession   and because this
   profession is rewarded by individual commissions obtained from
as far as dahomey   it is practical for a potter to introduce enough
   distinction in her own wares to be identified by   so it will follow
that every professional potter will look characteristically different
   from every other potter   in fact that is probably part of the
   right way   but it ought to be a corollary of this that once she
has achieved a "characteristic style"   she may vary casually
inside of it   but it would be unlikely that she would vary to the

197

point of obscuring the style that is her trademark   so a yoruba
potter will behave something like an american painter of the 1930s
when painters were creating characteristic commodities and
this act was called "finding ones style"   and it is because of this
perfectly honorable but commodity distribution system   and
information distribution system   which has powerful effects
upon the work that is done in its context   that the right way
here intersects with the right thing in a special manner   and why
i am talking about a sociology of art rather than a psychology of art
now it is possible in an oral society to have renown without
commodity   i mean thats what homer was about wasnt it?
praise poets and epic poets and tellers of tales had no commodity   they had a service   you can see that very clearly in
the case of paul radins two winnebago storytellers   the ones
who tell the twin story for him   they both have the right to tell
it   which means they have acquired in a legal way the telling
rights for this story   and the story   in spite of what radin
seems to be saying about it   is not the same   but the blow-
snake brothers appear to be both owners of the same rights
that is to tell a story about a particular pair of important
figures in their own way   and if winnebago society had been in
better shape at that time   they might have been very well known
for their abilities to tell these stories   as it was they had to be
well enough known for their ability to tell these stories for radin to
find this out   but we know that language arts dont have a
commodity in oral societies   what there is is more like a franchise
with rewards for services rendered   you could collect gifts or
whatever   and this would probably promote individual differences among story tellers   which in the nature of things didnt
need very much promotion   but you can also have   in an oral
society   a considerable art that has no reward   no economic
reward for art services   and little renown   take a string-figure
artist like *narau*   the mistress of something over 200 complex and
distinct string figures   made from the manipulation of a 30 inch
loop of kurrajong bark-fiber cord with her two hands   these
figures   made mainly by women themselves or among themselves
with their own two hands   though occasionally they may be
joined by another woman for a four hand figure   now these

198

figures are final configurations that are the outcome of anything
   from 1 to 30 transformations of the original loop   there are
even two known figures with more than 40 transformations   so
     that the string-figure art is a way   an elaborate way   of
   getting to some recognizable place   the figure   which usually
has a name   like emu eggs   two cunts   the morning star
        the menstrual blood of three women   a sea eagle catching
a mullet and so on   which figures are landmarks   of a story
so to speak   the story of the two sisters who came into this part
of arnhem land   *yirrkalla*   invented string figures
        probably string making as well   and named everything
important in sight   that is to say   the story of the two women
is like the string-figure making   a trip through the countryside
   naming important things   but this art   what is it?   a
kind of travelling dance conducted on your hands   maybe
invented sometimes   or at least adapted to your own hands habits
        in the way a dancer will find a way   to adapt a choreography
to her own body or his own   and whether it is a choreography
   with newly invented figures   or improvised figures   *narau*
knew more figures than any other person in *yirrkalla*   and probably 1/5 of all the string figures ever recorded in the world   so
that it is very likely she invented some   and modified others
        and if she modified them   or the way to get to them
        who would know?   at the speed at which she made them
        a transposition of a loop   a mirror image reversal of an
asymmetrical figure   will not be so easy to recognize   and
there will be few to recognize these variations anyway   since
this is not an art played out before a vast admiring audience   or
   even an intent circle of connoisseurs   and if *narau* was a great
artist she was a great artist without a great audience   and like a
lot of artists *narau* practiced an art with no economic and virtually
no social stake   she worked for a biochemist and did her art on
   the side   which from an artists point of view has both advantages and drawbacks   with which we are all familiar   but at
   any rate nobody was in a position to examine the amount of change
she introduced into her art   the main pleasure of which must be
   considered the pure pleasure of transformation   which would
   lead to change   while the secondary pleasure would be the

pleasure of recognition   which would restrain this change
   which we would ordinarily be in no good position to estimate
    except for the accident that an anthopologist observed her
working at a slow motion rate   which he had persuaded her to
undertake so that he could watch her work   and he found that
 when he asked her on one occasion to duplicate an already mounted
 figure she made the "wrong figure twice   by two different tech-
nigues"   on other occasions she proved to be unable to arrive at
  the intended figure at all   but sometimes   while aiming at
 one figure she arrived at another something like it   which is to
  say   that sometimes you get there and sometimes you dont
but sometimes when you dont the place that you get to is right
 enough to call the place   which suggests that a constancy of
naming may disguise considerable change in making   because
    "the menstrual blood of three women" is a good name   and
you may like to find different   very different   figures for
  that naming   so that an art of making or working could give
way   or give ground to   an art of naming   a kind of
  poem   accompanied by a hand dance in a string set

                  two conch shells
                   two cunts
              or one cock and one cunt
                  two bottles
                 two waterholes
                a man lying down
                a leech in a rakia swamp
              three huts
               frog in a pool
             ripples on a pool
             clouds
          menstrual blood of three women
            three freshwater snakes
          three women sitting down
             fishnet
             two catfish
            human shit
             emu tracks
            fire sticks
            yam
           yam

                    womans breasts
                    tree

who knows what possible narratives   can be constructed so?
      while dancing   if you know the story?   in hawaii it was
common to recite a fragmentary journey poem   or topographical
  love poem   that is danced on your hands by your fingers with
  the string

            up rose the sun   in its curved path   the sun
                over the field of ahuena   set in the calm of kailua
                then kona   ·

or to use these figures to "tell stories"   or "to act them out"
      among the eskimos of alaska and indians of canada

            "door boy   door boy   who stands over there
                door boy shut the door   why dont you shut the
            door?"

      "ive got my coat on"   (goes away)

between this string dancing and naming   there is a lot of play
      of room in these hand dramas for variation and change   for
continual   if unemphasized   invention   and change   it
is even possible under some conditions   for making to give place
entirely to naming   as among the duchampian *lega* in their *bwami*
ceremonies   where if there ever was a strong tradition of making
it is now mostly dead   and where a single "sculptured" object
  may be given away casually or broken accidentally   to be
replaced equally casually by some other object that will be equally
  sacred   and not even ordinarily distinguished from the object
it has replaced   though this new object may be an artifact that
looks nothing like the "original"   or it may not even be an artifact at all   but a natural object   a birdsbeak or shell say
      or even a commercially manufactured product   a perfume
bottle maybe   which will be known as the same thing   because
it can be so named   because it is capable of the same semantic
function   so may be named "the same thing"   and no one
displeased or noting the change   but you say "what about

                                                      201

form?" and ordinarily i would be prepared to not understand
you and answer as easily as you ask that question "what about it?"
i mean im willing to assume that any group of people of any
kind whatsoever   in some part of their life   may want to
take advantage   of the literalness that is offered by an object
to turn a meaning   that is only potentially *in* the mind
and actually only in the working of the mind in a situation
or the working of a hand or a whole body   i mean you
may want to get out of that shifty ground that we call the memory
which isnt a reservoir really   but is some action taken in
some place   and you may want to alienate yourself from this
meaning long enough to interrogate it   and convert the act of
meaning into the object of meaning   so you can articulate it
at whatever cost that may require   and so your working
halts   temporarily in an object that you can interrogate   if
only as a station   well then this object will be packed   it
will be something like a condenser   filled with energy
organized energy   that came from some place and can go
some other place   if you understand its organization   if you
know what kinds of leads to take it out on   i mean what is the
"form" of a "sacred bundle"?   here is where the notion of
"form" begins to break down   what about form?   form is
a notion arrived at by subtraction   a residue   in the sense
that the form of the milk is its bottle   which is a notion of
form as a shell or a leaving   fingernails or hair clippings
surely one of the most stupid notions in the history of art is
the notion of "form"   because in the sense in which it is meaningful it is almost totally obvious and trivial   while in the sense
that it is meaningless its so eccentric a theory   so totally freaky
and based on such absurd notions of the human   that it is
hardly worth considering at all   what i mean here is the notion
of some kind of specially "significant form"   the idea that
there is something particularly and universally satisfying about
something like certain simple geometric shapes   and by the way
this is the most modest form of such a claim   because earlier
in the century more grandiose claims were made for the transcendental value of geometricity   but the claim is silly because it is
made in a vacuum   theres just too much evidence that shows

that what is humanly satisfying   or exciting   is too contingent
   to be described this way   i mean you may find plenty of situations where geometrically simple arrangements are significant
      others where it is exciting to find a jumble   and others
where spatial arrangement doesnt seem to matter at all   any
   more than olfactory arrangement might matter in a story   or
a system of tactile values in a play   at the same time   its
totally obvious that the acoustical signs will be important in a radio
piece   because you wont otherwise hear it   and visual signs
   will have to count in a tableau   but who would ever disagree
with that?   and why call the visible signs of a tableau its form?
      as opposed to its content   i mean all content is content
      you say that something has a shape and its shape is "meaning-
ful" and you dont exactly know what that meaning is   okay
      consider the shape of an arrow   the shape of an arrow is
very meaningful   because thats how it enters its object
      when you speak of the form of an arrow what you mean is the
efficiency with which its designed for penetrating what its supposed
   to penetrate   and the difficulty obtaining when you try to
remove it   at least at first thats what you mean   and this
   determines the way its made   with several qualifications   to
obtain an arrow somebody has to make one   right?   you
   dont merely snap your fingers and say "arrow!" and have an arrow
snap into your hand   that way you would wind up with a paradigm of arrow   because whatever design you imagined   your
arrow would entirely manifest your intention   it would be
perfectly designed in terms of your mental definition of "arrow"
      and whatever that might be youll be stuck with it   but
arrows are made out of things   and then there are the ways that
   you make them   ways you like to work   youre a man that
works you may as well enjoy yourself   right?   so you realize
      while working   that if an arrow has a point it will enter
easily   i mean a point is   lets say   a generalization   a
   refinement of a blade   which is merely the principle of the
   wedge or the inclined plane   the australians have a spear that
      terminates in a blade and it kills animals too   but a point is an
   inclined plane considered from at least one or two additional reference planes   at right angles to the planes from which the blade

faces are inclined   and since inclined planes are simple machines
that reduce the amount of force necessary to move a resisting load
      a point should penetrate more easily than a blade   it goes in
easier   and if it widens enough   but not too abruptly to
block the entrance of the arrow   because the steeper the inclined
plane the more force is required to move a load   and if it does
    not widen too slowly to make a large enough wound   when
thrown with the particular amount of force that it is usually thrown
with or shot with   and these are conflicting considerations
      efficiency of entrance   which means maximum penetration
      and maximum wound width   which means a larger surface
tear   and say you add to this a barb   a backwards hook that
makes it difficult to pull out   these are all separate lethal ideas
      all about killing and maiming   penetrating and cutting and
tearing   the point penetrates and the edge that is the intersection
of the inclined planes is a cutting edge   theyre all "functional"
      but not strictly speaking necessary   i mean   the aus-
tralian blade-ended spear also kills   and nobody knows the rele-
vant kill statistics   so while all this is "functional" its not all
      obligatory   and then youve got the stone   if you use stone
      i mean you have to make an arrow out of something   and
if you hit chip or flake the stone the wrong way   it breaks
      so you dont hit the stone the wrong way   that is obligatory
if you want an arrow head   and the arrow head will have the
    marks that are characteristic of the right way or the family of right
ways for hitting that kind of stone   so the marks that you make
will have something to do with the kind of stone you use   but
the stone that you use may have something to do with the stone that
    happens to be around or even more likely with the kind of stone
you happen to like   and you may happen to like it because its
shiny or hard or because it takes well the kind of marks you happen
to like to make   because there may be several available stones
      several adequate ones   adequate for their purpose and for
the tools you have   and for the way you like to work
      because youre a guy who likes to work arrows and you spend
a lot of time working arrows   so youre entitled to your preference   you find "thats a crummy stone   i dont like that stone"
      and there are stones that "look good"   its nice to have slick

snappy arrows   if youre an arrow man you have a thing about
arrows and you like "good arrows"   you have a sense too about
how you might like to make an arrow   like when you flake an
arrow theres a clear mark you can make   a simple intelligible
mark   as opposed to a crummy mark   and after a while you
have an idea of the snappy arrow   the well made arrow and you
have an idea of dapper arrows   sincere arrows (a sincere arrow
goes right to the point)   clumsy arrows   worthy arrows
that are laborious but efficient   maybe the ground point
lacking the boldness of the flaking style   theres no reason
why you wont play   you spend a lot of time making arrows
now somebody looks at that arrow and he says "whats the
meaning of that arrow?"   and somebody says "death"   and
you say "no   its not just 'death'   we also shoot at trees
for fun   we have contests in our village   there are guys
who like to shoot arrows for sheer pleasure   independent of
death   and we have ceremonial arrow shooting   because
killing our food is the way of our life   and we use it in our musi-
cal performances   arrow-target-percussion music   and arrow-
string music   and arrow-wind music   and there is also just
a liking to have arrows   as liking to have a thing that is a pleasure to hold"   and after a while you say "is that the meaning of
the arrow?"   and you say "well there are a few 'meanings' for
the arrow   there are meanings for the arrow maker   its an
arrow he liked   its an appropriate arrow and maybe his distinctive arrow   and belongs to the attitude toward making arrows
of a whole atelier whose character is defined by an arrow of that
sort"   its based on the notion of the snappy arrow or the
stylish arrow   and theres nothing "formal" about chic   this
is not based on a notion of "pure form" or the universal recognition
of some particular family of shapes as better or worse   style is
content   pure content   it is even often   polemical content   and you can hate it or love it   not because of what it
is but because of what it represents   this is all about meaning
perfectly straightforward meaning   it has nothing whatever
to do with pure contemplation or esthetic values whatever they
may be   the notion of pure form and pure esthetic contemplation is a straightforward argument by example for a particular idea

of the good life   which may be manifested in a personal style
   the way people stand say   think of the way people stand
   or walk   as a stylistically meaningful enterprise   in order
to go from one place to another   in a human community
   and for reasons that are not perhaps so functionally clear
   you have to support yourself on your feet   walking   the
way people walk   surely theres more to walking than getting
  from one place to another   because people can get there in a
lot of ways on their hind legs   so you "walk"   if you go out
  into the street youre going to see "english walks"   "dandy
walks"   "struts"   "sexy slinks"   "gunfighter walks"
    "a genteel promenade"   "a cavaliers *paseo*"   "a philoso-
phers *spazier*" (with his hands behind his back peering occasionally
at nearby spectacles   before returning to an absent forward
gaze)   "a tennis slouch"   or a vernacular shambly walk
    just "hulking along"   now all of these walks   are signifi-
cant form to the extent that they represent styles loaded with
  content   these people walking this way are representing themselves to the world and to themselves with these walks   they
  know how it feels and they like it   there are people who like
  to shamble   they sort of "hulk along"   now its not entirely
  a disaster to hulk along   because these people who hulk along
get to places too   often they get there on time too   sometimes more often than other people who dont hulk along   as
they stumble in the door   theres no way of talking about
anything meaningful without talking about it as meaning   there
is no special occasion that can be described as an "esthetic occasion"
  but the act of identifying a totally nondescribable experience
as fundamental and fundamentally nondescribable is a particular
performance   somebody named benedetto croce is performing
some kind of dance   and i dont know whether i like it

    "but what about these forms that are persistent and re-
    main virtually unchanged even in oral societies for gene-
    rations   like benin bronzes say?"

well   im not really convinced that benin bronzes are so unchanged
and there are probably better examples of relatively stable ways of
working with apparently very similar products made by different

artists for long periods of time   and while i can think of examples
they are i believe   the outcome of very special situations   i
can think of this in the situation of a sacred art with a sacred technology and highly valued materials   where the initiates   the
master makers are both makers and users of the art   or where
the audience users are enormously concerned with the precise
outcome of the art making   to such an extent that they take
entire control over the processes of making   controlling the
materials and the workshops   the training of the acolytes
and the quality control over the products of the workshops
like science this is a powerful vested totalitarian art form
what i have in mind is something like the sacred art of radium
poisoning   you have here a combination of the necessary elements
radium is a material of very high value and scarcity   diffi-
cultly obtained   by a severe and refined technology   it must
be handled with care in minute doses requiring elegant measuring
devices   for weighing and testing and preserving   and it is
necessary to use only this means to poison the king   in fact it
is only this sacred material that may be allowed to cause the death
of the priest king   because it is the only material whose value
is on a level with the sacred person of the ruler   the holy king
to be poisoned by the dematerializing force of the holy material
and it is no point to have a ruler who doesnt rule   or whose
life is too short for the society to benefit from the experience he
acquires as a ruler   and moreover there is available a great expertise in measuring out refined doses of radium in millicuries   and
refined magnitudes of damage in becquerels of organic disintegration
and the point of this art form is to sharpen the kings perceptual
field through a domain of gradually concentrating pain   which
will come to isolate him from the distracting pleasures of his own
senses and their easy gratification by a sacred and scientific morti-
fication of his royal flesh   in this system there is for any ruler
a perfect place for his cessation   when this single point of pain
that has been diffused by a kind of leukemia through his body to
his mind renders him incapable of kingship   if the art is to be
successful   that is the point at which he has fulfilled the most
refined and most perfect conditions for this art work   this is
an object for priestly scientific and artistic study   it requires

not only schooling but research   the young prince must be studied
to determine his psychological and physical capacity to handle pain
the psychological and physical durability of the royal person
it will require decisions about dosing and timing of that dosing
and because this is a grand theatrical art   associated with
other arts   of performance   there will be reasons to decide
how the minute quantities of radioactive material should be admin-
istered   to be ingested slowly in his favorite foods and beverages
or to be worked into luminescent jewelry worn close to the
body   so that the young ruler may ride glowing into battle
and one would have to combat the unlikely and unworthy
possibility that he might choose to outlive his term and resist the
wise poisoners   by contriving to avoid the poisons   and
they would be forced to confuse him by poisoning him unawares
in the food he least liked   by working the poison into radioactive jewels or even into perfumes on the person of his favorite
mistress   and then yet   there is one final requirement
that the perfect success of this art form be ensured by penal-
izing all failure severely   by an arrangement whereby if the king
does not die at the appropriate hour   or minute or second
since the technology is so refined   that the chief poison
artist be killed in the interval   and that the assistant poisoners
be killed in succession   as required   during the interval
within which the audience awaits the luminous death of the king
in such a system   if you are not through bad luck forced to
kill off the whole artist population   you could expect a very
stable literal art

208

david ross called up from syracuse and wanted to know if
id do a reading out there at the everson museum   david
was working as their video curator and id met him about
a month earlier when he was here in san diego looking at
some of eleanors tapes for a video show   now he was
back in syracuse and jim harithas for whom david was
working and barbara beckos were putting together a
poetry series and they wanted to know if i was willing
to read   and if i was   who i wanted to read with
*   i had to explain that i wasnt doing any reading any-*
more   or not at that time anyway   that i went to a
place and talked to an occasion and that was the only
kind of poetry i was doing now   but if that was all
right with them id like to read with jackson maclow
*   and it was fine with them   jackson was an old*
friend   a poet whose work has meant a great deal to
me   and i hadnt seen him for a long time   not
since i had left new york for san diego   id run into
him every now and then when i was on the east coast for

readings or some other business but it was always at some
kind of group occasion   a party or a performance
          and we never had a chance to sit down and talk to-
gether in any personal sense or at any length   and his
life was going through some changes   i remember one
time we met at dr generositys   an east side bar in new
york where paul blackburn was arranging readings   at
that time jacksons marriage of years was breaking up
he was very troubled about it and it was all coming up in
this series of poems he was doing that were very simple
and beautiful and humiliating and quite unlike anything
hed ever done before   and we arranged a time to get
together but somehow it just didnt work out   and
now i thought this is the right time   hed be coming
from new york and id be coming from solana beach
california   to syracuse   a town that up to now had
meant nothing to us   and there in that public place
        a museum auditorium   surrounded by total
strangers and new acquaintances and friends   what
could be a better place for our private occasion

a private occasion in a public place

i consider myself a poet but im not reading poetry   as you see
   i bring no books with me   though ive written books   i
have a funny relationship to the idea of reading   if you cant hear
  i would appreciate it if youd come closer   because this is not a
situation where i intend to amplify   thats for the second part
   jackson maclows part   the equipment in back of me on the
stage   its other equipment   im only using this micro bit of
equipment   because its the least equipment i could possibly
manage at this particular time   and the reason is that i was once
  involved with engineering and now im divesting myself of the parts
    there was a time when i would have come with more   a lot
more and not so long ago   but right now i dont want to   its
something like my attitude to the book   from which i dont intend
to be reading   i mean if i were to come and read to you from a
book you would consider it a perfectly reasonable form of behavior
    and its a perfectly respectable form of behavior   generally
thought of as a poetry reading   and it would be a little bit like
   taking out a container of frozen peas   warming them up and
serving them to you from the frozen food container   and that
  doesnt seem interesting to me because then i turn out to be a cook
    and i dont really want to be a cook   i dont want to cook or
  recook anything for anybody   i came here in order to make a
poem   talking   to talk a poem   which it will be   all

other things being equal   because i wanted to talk about something   the situation that comes up when a poet comes to a place
    to do something that is a poem   i mean what am i doing
coming here to talk poetry?   that is if i thought that poetry was
a sort of roman enterprise   if i thought that poetry was a roman
  enterprise i would assume that talking poetry was a reasonable and
clearcut enterprise   i would get to the place and then use all the
wonderful rhetorical charm that i could put behind me and offer
  you poetry   that is i would improve talking   you see
    talking would be just talking   the way people talk   and
poetry would be improved talk   it would be talk that ends kind
  of funny   it rhymes say   or it beats out a tune   or it
does what it does in some unusual and exotic way   theres nothing
wrong with that a lot of people do it   its fun walking tightropes
    its fun talking while drinking water   its fun talking while
standing on your head   i propose not to consider poetry putting
something on top of talk   i consider it   in this case
    coming with a kind of private occasion to a public place   i
mean youre all here   and its a public place   and im addressing
  a public situation   and im doing what poets have done for a
long time   theyve talked out of a private sense   sometimes
from a private need   but theyve talked about it in a rather peculiar
context   for anybody to eavesdrop   which is strange   that
a man would come out here to talk to you   not knowing you
    you not knowing him and you should care about anything he
has to say   and its exotic   theres something strange about it
    except that if we share some aspect of humanness   it may
be perhaps less exotic   that is   people have been known to
walk into a bar   find someone they didnt know   and start a
conversation with this person   tell them their life story
    disappear and never see them again   in fact   i think there
are people who specialize in occasions like this   cabdrivers in
  many cities experience this very often   someone comes in
    tells them a life story which is either true or untrue
    mythical or a poem   they never see them again   and i
imagine that some of the great mythical collections are held by cabdrivers at this moment of time   if they remember the stories
    and in this context i assume we are dealing to some degree in

212

the mythical occasion   because what am i going to tell you?
     something private?   well of course ill tell you something
private   but will you believe it?   now i dont know if i want
 you to believe it   would you believe it if i wanted you to believe
it?   i want to talk about something rather more personal than is
reasonable for a public occasion   just because its unreasonable
     so i want to talk about the way people choose to enter a public
occasion with a large part of their life   now i happen   as
many people happen   to be married   and my wife was travelling in europe having an exhibition or a set of exhibitions in europe
     shes an artist and shes having a video show here   her names
 eleanor   eleanor was in europe and i had the experience of talking
to her on the telephone   at one point   and there was an
operator   with a german accent called on the phone and asked if i
would accept this call from eleanor   and i thought "what would
happen if i said no?"   it would be surprising   i didnt say no i
 said yes   and she called and spoke to me   and she told me
 i said how are things how are things in cologne   now i have
no image of cologne   i havent thought about cologne in years
and years and years   i have no idea of what cologne looks like
now   and a voice was coming to me from cologne telling me
 that she had been in cologne and it was a terrible city   everybody
was awful   they all spoke german   the place must have been
 filled with nazis   i said well thats too bad   i mean why dont
 you leave cologne   she said well i have to see the dealer in
cologne   i said well you have to see the dealer in cologne you
 better make the best of it   she said well   how do you ask for
orange juice   i said well   thats a tough problem   orange
juice   they carbonate all the drinks in germany sorry   i mean
 you may ask for an *orangensaft* all your life but youre not going to
get orange juice youre going to get carbonated orange drink   she
 wept it was very sad   no no she didnt weep but her voice was
trembling   and i was trying to imagine what it was that she was
feeling   she had walked into a signpost outside the kunsthalle
she had become so distracted by the loss of her language in this
 foreign country that she had walked into the sign that was in front
of the kunsthalle opened a cut in her head and fallen down   and
 this is what happened or so she told me   now i have a great

213

faith   in what people tell me   that is   people i know
       because ive learned that people i know have a certain kind of
human reliability   that is   i stand in a human relationship to
  elly and i assume that ellys story is true   and later we were off
    the telephone and i was sitting in   my living room   thinking
about distances   and what it is you believe about people and
what it is you know   that is what there is that you want to know
about people   and what there is in thinking that you know
          that people are what they say they are   now   ive often
said things that i thought were true   many people do that and
they turn out   not to be exactly true   that is   you do the
  best you can   in fact   i was talking to jim   the director
of the museum out here   jim was visiting in san diego and i asked
him how do you like the situation at everson   and that was some
time ago and he said its wonderful   the whole town is up and
   around the museum and we are in the town and there is a relationship   and what we are doing the people respond to   whether
  they agree with it or disagree with it and he painted a picture of
  syracuse   and after it was over i said wow   hes not going to
leave syracuse ever   not for another three or four years hes really
   making syracuse into a scene where all the action in the world will
come   and hell turn it around   and at the moment he said
that he meant it   that is he felt very much that this was the
scene where he was and there was no other where he wanted to be
          because theres one thing about living that one learns   you
learn it kids dont know it   kids dont know it very well because
  kids are always waiting for something   to go somewhere to some
place that will be the scene   but something you learn when you
   grow up   so to speak   to some age   and it may be fourteen for some people or eighty-three for others   and others never
learn it at all   is that wherever you are is the scene   thats
where the action is and it better be there because   at one point
there wont be anything else   and jim was painting a picture
       come in   come in   this is nothing terribly formal and
what poem there is here will be built around whatever happens
          and jim had painted for me a picture of his excitement about
everson   there was the great sioux festival that was to happen and
the video conference that was to happen and all these things

214

were happening and he was filled with excitement about it
because this place is not new york   its not new york city where
you have a scorecard   where people come into an art situation
they look at it and they say   well its not as good as it should
have been   yesterday there was a better one   he did another
one that was just like this one   i mean in a certain sense   this
is a raw community   that is to say this is raw life   raw life
what life is raw life?   no life is raw life   but its not the
new york art scene   which lives an exquisite byzantine existence
which this is not   and he was filled with the excitement of
it in his mouth at that moment   two weeks later i heard he was
going to houston   now jim harithas is not a liar and i didnt mean
to indicate that i suspected that he was lying to me standing there
sitting there   dont hang your head jim   i dont mean to
suggest he was telling me a lie   ive done this myself   ive been
filled with excitement for something and it meant everything   ive
said you cant possibly make a poem that isnt a complete improvisation say   or something like that   and then i figured   as
soon as i said it   a week later i made exactly the opposite kind of
poem   because as soon as you take a position very forcefully
youre immediately at the boundary of that position   which lets
you look directly over the boundary into the other side   and
wonder why you couldnt do exactly the opposite of what you just
had in mind   which has something to do with what it is you
mean when you have an intention   its like an artist says im
going to draw a straight line and he draws something thats   sort
of a straight line   and he organizes all his energy and starts to
make it straighter   and then there is the pencil   and then
there is the canvas or whatever hes drawing on   which is all
focussed and waiting   and theres something else that says "so
what"   and then it moves off the edge and the pencil point breaks
and he likes it   and it smudges on the end   he says i like that
its nice keep it   were not liars when we say something that we
mean   but were not truthers   come on in come on in sit down
make yourself comfortable   you can leave easily   i wont feel
the least bit embarrassed if anybody at some point feels that this
public occasion is not his occasion or her occasion and decides to
leave   and so   i asked myself   what kind of public occasion

215

what kind of occasion did i have for believing ely in cologne?
what kind of occasion did i have for not believing ely in cologne?
i mean why should i not believe her that cologne was filled with
anxiety?   what could cologne have been filled with if it wasnt
filled with anxiety?   glamour?   could i have been jealous of
eleanor?   that is   could i have worried that eleanor would
be unfaithful to me in cologne?   what does it mean for someone
to be unfaithful to somebody?   the idea of marriage is prepos-
terous   and many of us indulge in it anyhow   theres something about the idea of being married thats absurd   its absurd
because its a kind of contractual agreement of an odd sort   well
im forgetting the part of it that doesnt interest me   namely
my marriage was sanctified by mayor wagner of new york
we were married in town hall and i felt it was the first time i
had had any   we were living together and life was very pleasant
and one day we decided to get married   it didnt seem to me
that what was between us our life had any relation to the town or
that the town had any relation to the meaning of anything but we
went to town hall to get married because we thought it would be
the kind of wedding that would be the least sanctified by all the
things we had no relation to   and it turned out to be the most
sanctified by everything we had no relation to   because it was
the state   i mean the least we could have done was pick some
freaky religious operation   because at least it would have had
an idiosyncrasy that we chose   in this case we went in and we
said to ourselves itll be like that   bang bang bang   well walk
in   and we did walk in   with my sister-in-law marcia and her
flamboyantly ratty fur coat   which was an amazing operation
that shed picked up in some high class thrift shop and ely had this
sort of funny looking jacket that she was wearing and i was wearing
a duffle coat with a dopey looking hood over my head and we really
didnt look like we were set for a wedding   we went down there
to be married and we thought thisll be over very quick   we
walked in and the man who was going to marry us looked at us
and intoned in a deep organ vibrato "dooooooo youuuuuuuu
eleanor ..." and we started to laugh   only ely   who started to
laugh out loud   realized that there was something wrong about
laughing at your wedding in this situation   and she was afraid

she said later   she told me   now thats also a matter of
belief   but she told me she was very nervous she was afraid they
would throw her out   say "youre not old enough to be married
youre laughing at your wedding   out!"   she said she had
this irrational fear and so she started to fake crying   this i can
attest to   she was a rather good stanislavsky type actress and
had worked in the theater a while and i saw the way she was working
up the tears   but only because i had seen it before in a professional way   and her sister who was also laughing and infected
by ellys laughing was also working up tears   and she was weeping
and her sister was weeping   and in the meantime jerry and diane
im sure   friends of ours who were also there   couldnt
figure out what was happening except that elly and marcia were
maybe terribly sentimental and breaking up   and all this while
elly and marcia were weeping   tears were rolling down their face
while this man was saying "doooo youuuuuu ..." in his deep organ
pipe voice and i kept squeezing ellys hand saying under my breath
"cut it out youre overdoing it" hoping it would all come to an end
but there we were sanctified by this peculiar legal system and
after it was over we got this piece of paper that said courtesy of
mayor wagner or something of that sort   i dont remember the
words   but i realized i had been sealed by the state you know
        and i thought jesus christ is that what weve been doing?   i
mean we came here in order to have the state make this official and
i guess it is   but people get married   adult people   i mean
many people   with no sense that theyre getting married   lets say
to legalize your childrens status   getting married   people
do get married   and there is a peculiar meaning to getting married
        that is a kind of peace treaty   you might call it that   ˙
        you know somebody signs a treaty and the ambassadors come
and the horses come up on various sides   what is the treaty about?
        i mean in a sense were civilized people   and i say civilized
        civilization is not as it were part of ones body   civilization is
part of ones head   if you like to make distinctions between bodies
and souls or bodies and heads   civilization what kind of civilization does one have?   people who engage in what i would call
        romantic marriages   which are most of the people i know
        mean something different lets say than the marriage of fortunes

217

the alliances of houses and economic arrangements   and mine was
a romantic marriage of the sort   that we were people who
     we were people who liked to sleep with each other and live
with each other and talk with each other   and that is a private
experience and this is as i say a public place   which makes this
a public occasion and youre here at a private experience in a public
place   its what one expects of a poet isnt it?   but what i
     want to say is that there is this image of appetite   that people
have for each other and there are different kinds of appetite
     theres the appetite that one feels for a person   a woman say
     im a man and im heterosexual   that is i like women i dont
like to make love to men   i dont make love to men   so i talk
of appetite and there is this appetite   and appetite is what?
     that its filled with the mind   its filled with the mind and its
filled with the body   but what do you want to do?   sign a
contract that you will only feel desire for the person that you live
with and you will feel desire for nobody else?   i mean everybody
says were civilized   and that makes that contract sound silly
     and on the surface its a terribly silly thing to say and do   but
supposing you dont do that   suppose you sign another agreement
     that is you decide that you have a relationship with each other
which is of such an order that you have   appetite for each other
interest in each other fondness for each other   whatever the
word means you love each other so to speak   but you dont have
any control of each other   that is   as soon as anybody feels
some other impulse he/she goes makes it with whoever he/she wants
     you can try that   its difficult   and i know this kind of
experience   its the kind of experience that takes away   a
kind of evenness   a kind of funny unpressured life   that is
     it puts life at the pressure of a romantic adventure   because
anything can dissociate into its separate parts at any moment   you
can always at the moment of an adventure disappear from somebody
else   its a very distraught and romantic existence and not good
for artists   its not good for artists its good for bourgeois people
     who are they?   theyre the people   the others   its
always the other   you know?   if you want to know who the
     bourgeois are   its always somebody else   nobody here is in
     the bourgeoisie   lets forget that   its the other people theyre

218

not here   this adventurous life its good for the people who dont
have to do anything   they dont have to work for a living in any
serious sense   except to make wages   those people can go in
for instant romance and live a life of total romance   artists are
too busy   so we are practical people   you have to make art
you have to be committed to making art to thinking about art to
thinking about the things that count   "what?   adventure
doesnt count?" you say   sure adventure counts but if it was
always counting you wouldnt have time to count anything else
     because all you would be doing would be counting skirts walking
by   guys walking by   you would have no future that would
be contained in your present because every moment life would move
out   you would have to find a new apartment   let me tell
you you would have to find a new apartment very quickly   why
would you have to find a new apartment very quickly?   i was
     i had a romance with a girl once who lived across the hall from
me and we were going together   we were married in all senses of
the word except mayor wagners sanctification had not been provided
     and we were living together except we were living in separate
and adjoining apartments   which was a very difficult situation
     in fact i met her because we were living in adjoining apartments
     it was a bizarre scene to begin with   i was walking up the
stairs one day and   i lived on the fifth floor of a walkup on jones
street and i was chugging up the last flight with my groceries and
     there was a man kneeling at her door peeping through a small hole
in her door   and i said "what are you doing?" and the guy ran
by me like that as i was coming around the landing past the old
jewelers apartment   and i was coming up and this guy fled and
literally nearly knocked the groceries out of my hands as he ran all
the way down the stairs   and then i was standing there and i
didnt know what was up   for a moment i didnt understand
what had been going on   i didnt know what he was doing and
then i looked and saw there was a minute hole in the door   i
didnt look through the hole   i really didnt look through the hole
     good grief i didnt look through it   as a matter of fact i went
into my apartment and i closed the door and i said to myself
     "should i tell miriam that she has had a voyeur?"   and i
realized that thats loaded with responsibility   that is   i could

ignore the issue and let her find out for herself   i certainly could
wait a decent length of time   provided the voyeur had something
to look at   let us assume that he had good sense and had chosen
what he wanted to look at appropriately   i could wait another
two hours or something   three hours and then call her on the
telephone and at a more auspicious hour tell her that she should
put something over the door or whatever   and worry about it
      but then i was really worried as to whether or not i should even
tell her at all   because i realized once i told her   that there
would be no way for me to extricate myself from a kind of situation
      that would suggest eroticism regardless of what i did   i was sort
of hip   and it wasnt that i was against it   it was just that i
      didnt want   didnt know whether i wanted to as it were get into
a relationship with someone who lived next door to me   under
any circumstances at all   that is   i mean i knew there was no
necessity   by this i dont mean you to assume that i was paranoid enough to suppose that id have to marry her if i told her she
had a voyeur looking in her door   however i was aware that we
had looked at each other with interest   for some time
      casually   if i told her she had a voyeur   into our ambience
of casual concern and interest would have entered a discussion that
      aroused certain knowledge   of what might conceivably be
thought about in the context of voyeurs and i didnt know whether i
wanted to offer anyone an invitation to have a relationship with me
      i didnt know whether i wanted that   some great delicateness
isnt it?   i mean there i sat   so i said "to hell with it ill tell
her   shes going to find it a drag"   maybe thats not why i did
it   i   you know i dont know   now im telling you im an
honest man   what does it mean for a man to tell you hes an
      honest man?   he stands up here and he says to you "im an
honest man" and then you have to judge how honest his honesty
is   well ill tell you something   in this case i dont even know
if i was an honest man   what i did is i waited a decent length of
time   like toward evening i went over knocked on her door and
said "miriam..."   i knew her name wed spoken about something
or other once before   and i said "miriam   you have a voyeur"
      and i knew she didnt believe me   i knew she didnt believe
me at all   she said "what do you mean?"   i said "well theres

220

a hole in your door   over here"   and she looked at it and it
   was a little tiny hole and she said "oh well   ill certainly have to
   do something about that"   she didnt believe it and i   i said
   well dont worry about it   but once that happened it was a
situation from which one couldnt retreat   and the situation
developed that i didnt retreat from and we did get involved   and
were   after some length of time involved in a love affair   i
say love affair because the word affair by itself makes everything
   sound like an affair of state   and we lived together   sort of
      she lived in one apartment and i lived in the other and we
   shared a bathroom   that is we had a bathroom that we had in
   common and it was in the hall   it was a wonderful apartment
that i got for eighteen dollars and seventy-five cents a month   with
   three rooms   and thats why it had the bathroom in the hall
      but it was very nice   it was a nice bathroom   it was a
nice apartment in a nice place   and our relationship was kind of
      stormy   i dont know why it was   somehow there was
something about our belief in each other or lack of belief in each
   other that we had little confidence in each other   and i dont
   know why that is   we liked each other a lot   but maybe we
   were very alien to each other   in some way   and sometimes
   thats good and sometimes thats bad   she was very frightened of
   my background   my background was what?   european intellectual   so to speak   middle europe   and hers was what?
      louisiana mormon   and that was interesting i thought   i
   thought that was kind of interesting and groovy   i mean i liked
   her genteel southern background but she was terrified of mine
      and my friends frightened her for reasons im not at all clear
   about   and she was always in some state of fear that she was
being considered terrible and inadequate or whatever   and so she
   used to produce fits and tantrums   under varying circumstances
      im looking at this to see if im still on the tape because
      though its a private occasion in a public place its eventually
going to have to become something else   because i dont intend
   to let it disappear into this occasion and i want it on tape   somehow this anxiety that she had   converted itself into a series of
   performances that shed put on   performances   that is i
   remember an occasion   a number of my friends came to her house

and we sat there   we had an evening with people over and we
   talked   and i thought that wed all had a very pleasant time
      that is   we had talked about inconsequential things   art
      politics   life   death   inconsequential mainly because
we werent going to change their course at this moment   it was
   chatter   when it was over she got into a kind of hysterical rage
at what she felt were the pretentious concerns of my friends   i
   didnt think there was anything pretentious about it at all   she
   felt they were horrible people   by the end of the argument she
did something that id never seen in my life   she fell down in
   what looked ostensibly like a faint   and i looked at her   at
that faint   and i couldnt quite believe it   that is   in the
   middle of a discussion she sort of keeled over fell down   i
shook her   not with passion but dutifully   because thats
what you do when people fall down you know?   like they fall
   down in faints and you try to revive them   i walked over and
   sort of shook her   i said "get up" you know?   "get up
      miriam"   "get up" and i got some water and i threw it in
   her face and finally she said "well   when are they coming?"
      and i said whos coming?   and she said "when are they
coming?   jack and jerry and barbara and diane"   and i said
what do you mean when are they coming but she said when are they
   going to get here?   you better get the place straightened up
      i said what do you mean straighten the place up? they were here
and left   she was telling me that she had gone through this whole
scene in such a state that she had forgotten the whole existence of
   the event that she had been so terrified by   now either she was
telling me a truth or she was not telling me a truth   i dont mean
   to say that she was putting me on   i mean she could h'ave been
putting me on   but merely my lack of confidence in it doesnt
   make it a lie   and i said come on   i was sitting in the chair
right over there and jack silberg was sitting in that chair over there
      and he asked you that question   you remember that question
about what operas you had in your repertory   she was a singer
   and she had been preparing to be a singer   she had a kind of
coloratura voice   actually she didnt have a coloratura voice
      she had a dark soprano voice and she was trying to get it up to
a coloratura voice   because it was a wiser thing   according to

222

her coach for her to have a coloratura voice   and it was a bad
   scene because she didnt have that kind of light upper range   she
had a very beautiful rich dark middle register and she was trying to
push it up and lose the weight   well shed lost the weight and she
didnt have a very beautiful upper range anyway and it made her
nervous   and jack had been sitting there and hed said to her
   what operas do you have and shed answered him   and i went
through this number reminding her and she didnt remember it and
she sat there flatly asserting that she didnt remember it   what
kind of confidence did i have in this situation   i mean what did i
have?   i had her assertion that she   had not been there
      and i had my experience that she had been there and she didnt
remember it or claimed not to remember it   now i must say this
created a profound doubt in me   about everything about her
      now maybe that was my fault   maybe that was what was
wrong with us all along   that we always doubted each other
      about everything   i mean everything was doubtful   maybe
you know   maybe if it was the right sort of relationship i should
have believed her implicitly i should have absolutely believed it
regardless of whatever bullshit it was intended to seem like   in
fact maybe the whole point of this whole operation was that if i
really cared for her enough i could conceivably have believed this
   incredible piece of romantic amnesiac story and then she would
have felt more comfortable   now i can create a plausible story
for her   but did she do it on purpose?   that is did she come
and tell me this story in order to test me   to see if i would
believe her?   i have no idea   that is i really dont know
      but i didnt believe her and our marriage   our living together
gradually disintegrated along this axis of doubt   there were these
things that we had in common and didnt have in common and we
persisted in living together in our separate apartments which were
right next to each other   which was very difficult to   which
   is really quite difficult to do   because if we were going to get
away from each other in any serious way it would have been useful
   to have a greater amount of distance between us   but we each
   had terrific bargains in our apartments   her apartment was
a three room apartment that cost sixteen dollars and seventy-five
cents a month and mine cost eighteen dollars and seventy-five cents

223

a month   and mine was a three room apartment and hers was a
two and a half room apartment in greenwich village in a very pleasant
neighborhood   on jones street   and you didnt gladly give up
apartments like that because you couldnt find them anywhere
        even then   i guess it was around the 1950s and   at some
point or another i became convinced that she was seeing other people
        now was that bad or good from my point of view?   i dont
know   that is   in a way i hoped that she would go away   i
wouldnt leave my apartment and i hoped that she would go away
        she wouldnt leave her apartment   she hoped that i would
go away and we had a kind of unwritten agreement that we were
        with each other   now "being with each other" in this kind of
contractual agreement   unwritten contractual agreement   is a
kind of compromise   its that you wont do anything to destroy
the other persons image of the future   thats really what its
about   jealousy is a funny image   that is   what is the
difference whether someone that youre not at the moment interested
        in making love to makes love to somebody else?   rationally
        considered   the ideas trivial   i mean it really is it is   at
least as far as i can imagine   and even from this point of view
        consider   you have no appetite to make love that hour
        the woman you live with has appetite to make love that hour
finds someone to make love with and makes love   no one takes
        anything away from you that you   needed   could conceiv-
ably have avoided   you think so?   but nobody thinks so
nobody likes that situation   mainly because what it does is it
        threatens the future   its more than the act of taking a goodie
away   its not like taking a piece of candy away   that is
        what it does   human bodies carry human minds and souls
with them so to speak   we are sort of hostages of our bodies and
        our bodies go walking into places   and they carry you with
        you   and if somebody goes into a romance with somebody else
you say well   thats really what you did yourself isnt it   that
is   you were carried by the same desire the same casual appetite
of the flesh   and something of the mind   and you were carried
        into a relationship that didnt exist before   well   it could
happen again and then you part company   over an hour   you
think about that   and you say well   thats really kind of shaky

and people accommodate themselves to not shaking each others
future   the image of jealousy is like metaphysical doubt   its
like a total notion of not being able to rely on the future   because
after all im in the united states and elly is in cologne   you know
im in the united states and elly is in cologne   let us say elly is
making love to somebody else in cologne   you know   and
im making love to somebody else in the united states   which i
was not   but thats neither here nor there   lets say she was
so what?   i mean im a civilized man   so to speak   so
to speak we are all very civilized   what difference could it make
to me six thousand miles away?   seven thousand miles?   but
the doubt is the issue   that is   no one cares about the sheer
facticity of unfaithfulness or violations of faith   what one
imagines is that a life that one has built that has more moments than
it takes to fuck somebody   can disintegrate into a series of
moments that are equal to about that   and nothing else   now
i dont mean thats wrong   that it should be like that   but
its a scary time   to feel that the world is disrupting from you
just like that   that you could wake up one day decide that youre
no longer going to sleep with that woman or go sleep with someone
else and immediately move in   which is another thing and it
happened   it happened interestingly as a matter of fact   that
this girl that i was living with in the next door apartment finally
got into what i imagine must have been an affair with somebody
else and i remember the feeling of doubt was rather complex   as
to whether we should work out our relationship   that is   she
pretended not to have any other interests than the ones i was aware
of   and i pretended not to have any other interests and we kept
coming back to the same locus of activity   there we were
across the hall from each other   and thats really an awful
scene because youre much better off with one of you in europe and
one of you in the united states at least   at best   you can
manage with twenty-third street and fourteenth street or something
like that   with the bronx and manhattan   i mean you can
manage a scene like that   because its out of sight out of mind
and the bodies are far separated geographically   but we were very
close and we had reason to be suspicious of each other   but we
were having trouble why should we not have wanted to part?

225

why shouldnt i have felt at ease that she was considering going
with someone else into some other romance?   or that i was going
into some other romance and that we would part and life would be
easy again and there would be no more effort   though we were
used to our effort   our effort was like a work that we were
used to doing you know?   it was like having a job   you
know that was like the job we worked at   regularly   and
thats how we knew who we were   we were the people who
worked at that job   you know her name was miriam my name
was david i was the one who had trouble with her she was the one
who had trouble with me   it was well known   it informed my
poetry   it informed her career we knew how our career was
going how it was going to go   for at least a month and a half for
six weeks at least   while she managed to get her upper register
light enough and clean enough to run scales while i was doing something else   i was working in those days i was writing stories
    and i was writing stories and i was working my story paragraph
by paragraph and i knew what kind of story i was writing and i knew
that i had to get to the end of it   i was in the middle and there
we were   i was doing it about a paragraph a day   in those days
i worked very slow and it was hard going and   i said well   i
know who i am   but there was this feeling of suspicion   she
was suspicious of me and i was suspicious of her and one day i
went over to borrow a cake of soap and she was in bed with somebody else and there was an enormous feeling of relief   you know
there was this funny feeling of shock and relief   because it
wasnt suspicion   that is   like i said excuse me and it was over
    and i said gee weve split   thats wonderful   didnt feel
wonderful but i knew it was wonderful   you see now im trying
to remember what it was really like   it wasnt bad it was much
better than being in doubt   and it was bad for her too   why
was it bad for her?   that is it was bad for her in being in doubt
    it wasnt bad for her being in bed and certain that she was being
in bed   and it wasnt bad that i appeared at the scene of her being
in bed so that finally she was committed to getting out of the life
    you see   because it was important that she get out of it
    and she couldnt get out she didnt have the nerve to get out of it
    just as i didnt have the nerve to get out of it   we had just

226

about enough nerve to suffer together   you know?   which
   was really a drag   because we had a sense of responsibility and
we were responsible people   and there we were   out of it by
   definition   out of it is a whole other thing   now there i was
as i said sitting in new york   now in that case i was in new york
          in that other one i was in new york   and now here i was in
california and i was in california saying to myself   what do we do
to believe in ourselves this way?   believe in contracts that we
   dont go off to make love to other people because well shatter our
      faith unless we do it flatly out in the open you know like by decla-
ration and fiat   you live your life and people send you a formal
   notice   at six oclock in the morning tomorrow im going off
with somebody else   or im going to enter into an engagement to
   become interested in somebody else next week   you need preparation   is that better or worse?   now this is the counter
side of the romantic position   that is   you have the problem
          your life is defined by history and history is the outcome of
having a future   that is you project a future which gives you a
   present   and you have a trajectory in which you make it your
   life   and there we are in a marriage   and our marriage is
going to be imperiled   finally we say   or maybe we dont
      maybe we say how will it not be imperiled?   supposing elly
and i live our careers where were flipping around the country sepa-
rately for long periods of time   i mean were human   complicated   physical   you go to another place what do you do?
          you play out this old game of marriage and fidelity in the old
way?   you play it out in a new way?   it seems to me that
what you face here is another image of what life is about and you
say to yourself "are we going to split finally   when your career`
takes you to a european circuit for three weeks once again were
   over?"   do i say that do i say i dont go and travel the circuit
myself   what kind of agreement do people make to live a human
   comfortable life   do we travel around with each other all the
time?   i always grab my wife and travel with her she grabs me
and takes me with her as we attend each other like children on a
leash   its a very strange situation for people who are both human
   and not siamese twins   siamese twins have it easy siamese twins
dont have any problem they have a physical relation thats continuous

227

and permanent   short of a disastrous operation they dont become
two people and they cant afford to act as two people even together
      and it is in this sense moving around the idea of marriage that
you say why do people enter into it at all?   and you enter into it
      marriage   at least i had i see it now as one enters into it in
relation to a kind of self definition in a public place   because
marriage is a public place   marriage is a public place in the sense
that   your self   your self is a private self you see it as a private
self   because you always see it inside your own head   which
is a private place so that your self as it is   when you see yourself
      is a private occasion in a private place   and you emerge   you
see yourself emerge   for a moment   before you lose sight of
yourself into a public context by being with another   any other
      i mean you see yourself emerge for a moment before you lose
sight of yourself in being in that   place   which is a public
place   anyway for a while   and the reason people like me get
married and now i dont mean the others   the bourgeois people
      we dont worry about having children and legalizing things
      its mainly because it produces   an externalization of ones
life and intentions   one plays it out in a public place   that is
one puts it in public   like in a government place so to speak
      one arranges a government by treaty with somebody else
      and its a dangerous treaty that covers a territory for coming
together with another   but imagine the opposite   imagine
never putting anything into a public place   imagine only talking
to yourself   imagine only living inside yourself   and youre
your own actor and audience   youre the audience of your own
intentions   in fact the only thing you can do is listen to your
own intentions with total doubt or total faith   the total
      either total   doubt or acceptance   are indifferent
      because really what happens is that in order to perceive your
intentions   you have to stand so far in back of them   step so
far back that you perceive them before they emerge   and they
depart from you as soon as you come up with an idea of   seeing
them   its impossible to speak a language alone   that is the
idea of a private language is silly   because there would be no
memory system on which you could rely for that language to be
encoded stably   there would be no set of rules and regularities

228

the meanings of the words could shift   youd come up against that
kind of wittgensteinan situation in which when you say "i"   by
the time you heard the word "i" you might intend something else
someone else   who do you mean by "i"   "i" is who?
   it happened at the turn of the century that there were a lot of
people who were concerned with where that "i" comes from when it
speaks and there was the famous case of a woman   a woman in
new england   a young girl actually   who spoke with this "i"
   only the "i" was different each time she spoke   or rather
she had four different "i's"   for whom she spoke to this psychiatrist   or neurologist   they didnt have psychiatrists then   a
man named prince   morton prince   and she spoke to him a
different person each time   and each of these different persons
   each of these different people were defined in relation to other
parts of her   character   and each one recognized its self
alone   so she was sort of "sleeping margaret"   or "dangerous
sally"   or whoever she was   i dont remember their names
   but each time she was another person and that other person was
always pretty consistent   there was a reckless one who caused
trouble for all the other ones and went out and provoked sexual
encounters   and there was a very good girl who always did the
right thing and there was another depressive one   nearly catatonic
one   who did very little except be depressed   and all these
different people spoke to the psychiatrist in different voices   they
addressed him with a different sense of style this person who was
willing to let these "i's" play themselves out   or else help them
invent themselves   because these "i's" didnt exist before that
   one girl in that one body found her neurologist   there was only
one person there whose name i think was   sally beauchamp
   pronounced "beecham"   or that was the pseudonym she
was given in the book by the neurologist   who spelled her name
"beauchamp" and said it was pronounced "beecham"   which i
remember struck me as odd   but anyway she was only one
person sally beauchamp and she was having difficulties and she went
to visit this neurologist on the advice of her family   i think
   and the neurologist spoke to her long enough for her to stop
being one person and become four   and each one of these people
had different desires and intentions   but one of the things that

interests me in this is not so much that she became four separate
  "i's" as that each one formed its coherency in relation to the
  memory of the psychiatrist   that is   it was the neurologists
  mind that held them together   it was like a ball game   a kind
of handball court against which "i" banged itself off and got a return
  from the psychiatrist and saw where the ball bounced when it
came off a particular spot on the wall when it was struck in a particular kind of way   now i dont know how many "i's" might have
come out of it but the "i" that went to the doctor was the "i" that
  her family had created so to speak and the social environment
  created as a handball court   that is there had been these
  intentions toward a self   in self realization and self determination and she had said "i   sally" and they had said "you
  sally"   and they knew that sally would do the right thing
and sally would go to school and sally would do her homework
and sally would be modest and sally would wear dresses and she
  wouldnt run after boys   this would be "sally" and everyone
knew what "sally" did she was a good girl   and then sally went
  to the neurologist and he didnt have any such expectations or not
all of them and soon you had a whole set of other girls along with
sally   a depressed girl and a sexy girl and a violent one   who
tore up the other ones notes   they used to write notes to each
  other   several of the "i's"   and one of them used to tear
up the other ones notes and throw them away and write nasty
  things   and the other one wrote very politely   and one of
them spoke french and the other didnt   which was sort of
interesting that one of them was capable   the one who was
educated by the family in boston spoke french   the other one
  didnt speak french   resolutely couldnt understand a word of
  french and that was the way that the one of them could write
  messages to the neurologist that the other one   the nasty one
  couldnt understand   by writing them in french   and she
  would slip messages in french to the neurologist   who understood   which created a kind of illicit alliance between one self
and one neurologist   now i think in some sense people get married
  in order to define a self   a kind of yet private self that is still a
public self   that is   my kind of people do that   but defining
  a self is   a matter of hope and expectation   that is   i hope

to be somebody   that is   i am somebody i am somebody i am
somebody jim harithas is somebody jim harithas adored syracuse
     he hoped to love syracuse and he has loved syracuse and hes
done great things in syracuse   dont be embarrassed jim you did
     what youve done in syracuse is really a rather considerable
achievement   you wanted to love syracuse   i wanted to love
miriam   and i loved miriam   which is about the same thing
     and then one day miriam and i stopped loving each other
     and i dont know exactly how you handle that kind of situation
     that is   who speaks for me when i speak?   do i have a
quorum?   im here in this public place talking in the context of
some old friends some new ones and people who have come here
with expectations maybe of what a poet is   you know?
     what a poet will do   what hell talk about   and i come
here with my private thing so to speak   and i tell you im here to
define myself and im telling you who i am and what im doing it
for   and you can believe it as much as you can believe me or
any poet   or as much as you can believe your wife   or your
child   or yourself

we were going to perform jacksons pieces right after a
short intermission but there was some trouble with the
electronic equipment that was needed to get the degree
of amplification that jackson had wanted   we would
be doing his word event performance pieces   some
of the gathas and the pieces on peoples names that jackson
composes something like the game of "constantinople"
by taking a friends name and using it as a source of
letters for all the words he can or wants to draw from it
which he then sets down all around a page that he
then uses as a score for performers to read or intone or
sing   as usual everything finally worked out and we
performed together   jackson and sharon mattlin and
his two kids mordecai mark and clarinda   listening to
each others voices and sending out whatever messages we
felt like finding or hearing or sounding from the score
of MICHAEL WIATERs name   like WATER and AIR
or WATCH MALICE WITHAL or CHARM ALICE or
RAMA CLIT HEAT LETCH or merely the sounds of the
letters as phones or as tones of a scale for singing   and
it got so late that we all had to rush down to the airport
packed into david rosses small car in such a hurry that
jackson lost his favorite winter gloves and was disturbed
about it all the way back to new york   on the plane
ride back clarinda and i had a long conversation about
what communists were

jackson and i finally did get together because i had to hang
around new york for a few days in order to do another
talking piece at bernadette mayers workshop at st marks
in the bouwerie   so a few days later i took the subway
up to the west bronx where jackson was still living even
though hed been planning to move back downtown for
a long time   jacksons one of those people who finds
it hard to change anything once he starts doing it   or
stops   hed had another apartment over on hoe avenue
in the east bronx for over ten years   a huge walk-
through that id helped him move some furniture into and
i know it was at least that long ago because castro was in
new york for a un meeting and had just gotten kicked
out of a park avenue hotel for holding cockfights in the
living room and slaughtering chickens in the kitchen and
hed moved over to the hotel teresa in harlem so that
when we passed through east harlem in my old sunbeam
talbot with the convertible top down to get the table
into it a little black kid spotted us   me with my bald

head and jackson with his black assyrian beard   and a
look of astonishment went over his face and he yelled out
"HEY! KRUSHCHEV CASTRO!"   jackson was the
same way with jobs as with apartments   he was an
amazingly hard worker and a very good one   and
when he had a job he would just wear it out   hold it
until the company went out of business or relocated or
something   hed had an editing job over at funk and
wagnalls with paul blackburn till they finished the ency-
clopedia and all got laid off   and then hed had a job
teaching english to foreigners for years until nyu got hit
with a budget cut   but he was the same way about
not having a job as having one   he would just stick
with it till it went away and sometimes his jobless periods
would last for years   jackson used to think of this
pattern as a problem he was stuck with through bad luck
       he once explained to me how all his other problems
had gotten cleared up back in the fifties as a result of
studying zen with suzuki and going for psychotherapy to
kurt goldstein   which i remember thinking kind of
surprising because i remembered goldstein as a great physiological psychologist whose course i had sat in on in
college and what i remembered most about him was his
       admirable distrust for the theory of the neuron   that
he persisted in referring to as the "so-called neuron"
       but apparently goldstein had a keen if critical interest
in psychotherapy which he practiced as an experiment
       though i believe jackson was his only patient   but
for jackson the experiment was a nearly total success
because   between them   suzuki and goldstein
       all of jacksons problems seem to have cleared up

except that suzuki went back to japan and goldstein
suddenly retired just as they were getting around to
jacksons job problem   right now he was in one of the
jobless periods   spending all of his time working on
his poetry and taking care of the kids   so we were
able to spend a whole day together   trying to readjust
those ideas of each other that tend to drift away from
their objects during long absences   david ross had
found the gloves and mailed them back   they were
the kind of brown cotton gloves that workmen often use
in lumberyards

i had dinner with vito acconci and nancy kichel   rob
stefanotty was opening a new conceptual gallery and he
had been spending a lot of time talking to vito who he
was interested in attracting into the gallery and nancy
was working on a series of anxiety fantasy pieces   the
kind of things that go through your mind if your boy
friend shows up a couple of hours late and you imagine
him run down by a cab or fallen down a manhole or run
off with the girl cab driver or the lady construction
worker who came out of the manhole   vito had come
home late the night before and she worked out this terrif-
ically detailed set of logical and absurd incidents that
came to a kind of conceptual crescendo in the piece
*   just to explain vitos delay in coming home   which*
turned out to have resulted from nothing more than a
long business conversation with rob   i asked her
*   since the fantasies were all absurd anyway   why*
she didnt imagine an affair between vito and rob   but
i guess she thought that was too absurd even for art

vito told me that the performances started around nine but
he didnt sound too sure about it and when i called bernadette she was pretty sure it was 8   but i called her
around 11 oclock in the morning and she sounded as if
she was still asleep   it turned out i was way over on the
west side the evening of the reading and i had to catch a
cab to get over to st marks by 8:15 but there was nobody
there and the church was all locked up   it felt like old
times   in the beginning when the poets had left the
metro and paul blackburn and carol berge arranged with
the church to hold readings in the basement   and nobody could get it quite all together   not even how to
arrange the seating   the main difference here was that
bernadettes workshop met in the vestibule on the first
floor between the main entrance and the body of the church
      pretty soon bernadette came by and managed to get
the doors open and then people started drifting in in twos
and threes   mostly old friends like george economou
and rochelle owens and hannah weiner   or st marks
regulars that i didnt know because this was about the
fourth or fifth generation downtown   ed friedman
came by   he was running the monday night readings
now   and cathy acker   the black tarantula
      had just come in from the west coast with her hair
chopped off looking like elton john   she was in to do
some kind of art piece with alan sondheim who was also
there   alan and i had had a brief correspondence about
the possibility of a basis in the structure of the brain for
the idea of number   a notion i dont think of as very
promising   i suppose because i prefer to look at it in
terms of human experience   like that of our two

*handedness and two leggedness and the mode of our loco-
motion   which would seem to have more to do with
our notion of number through counting by stepping off
and matching   as the notion of even and odd could
easily derive from our manner of walking and standing
          one leg advanced in walking is odd bringing up the
other and standing is even   and i tend to doubt that
otherwise human beings who happened to be armless and
mounted on wheels would arrive at our notion of number
          as they might not arrive at our notion of geometry if
instead of standing vertically upright by an act of will from
a horizontal ground they floated leaning every which way
effortlessly above it   hannah was also deep in numbers
and id heard that she was having numerological insights
into people and occasions   sometimes reading a number right out of the air over somebodys head   carrying
some significant message and this seemed like a bit of a
coincidence because on the subway that day id been reading george kublers* the shape of time *and he was doing a
number trip too   proposing to group the art works of
an age into a silent series of self-sufficient self-propagating
primes restoring art history to a sequence of numbers
          by about 9 the place was getting filled up   george
quasha came in with his tape recorder and it seemed time
to start*

a more private place

you were right vito   it begins at 9 oclock   its ok   i used to
think of new york as always beginning on jewish time   we used
to arrange to meet people at 9 oclock and show up at 10   and
        nobody minded   at least not in those days   times may have
changed   but i still dont think anybody minds terribly   not
in my world at least   i had asked for this kind of situation where
there wouldnt be very many people   mainly because im a little
tired of talking under the circumstances of a rather large auditorium
        which is a little more theatrical and a little more public   and
at the moment im not especially anxious to talk in public terms
        ive just come back from talking at everson   the everson
museum in syracuse   and it was in a funny auditorium   i was
up there with jackson maclow and we had to decide whether or not
to take advantage of i. m. pei's medieval futurist court that looked
like it was set up for a fascist oration or an indian rope trick
        il duce could have come out to speak from the little balcony or
judy garland   wearing long gloves could have come down the
winding staircase   but for my talk it was impossible   so they
moved us into an auditorium and the auditorium had a no-stage
stage but youre on it   and then there are two hundred and fifty
        people   sort of   or two hundred and fifty seats and some
number of people that approximate it but theyre outnumbered by
the chairs   and even if only twenty people come to an auditorium

239

like that its still a theatrical situation regardless   a public situation
      and so i had to deal with the problem of coming with a private
occasion to a public place   come on in   come on in   were
among friends   theres room   i knew this would happen
      thats why i have a tendency to begin slow   i think there are
more chairs somewhere   yes i feel like im back in a jewish center
again   yeah maybe it would be a good idea   as rochelle
suggests   not to smoke   rochelle has asthma you know   i
mean if we smoke too much we   will all become extinct
      probably tonight   because were all so close   now at
everson what i was trying to do was test out the situation   of
coming with a private occasion to a public place   and the hope
that i had   in coming here   was in speaking in a smaller place
      that the place was not so public   as the occasion was not so
public   but the idea of the not so public   occasion   is a
rather elusive one   i mean i know many of the people here and
and many are friends and acquaintances   and on the other hand
no occasion in which you speak in any sense at all turns out to be a
private occasion   in fact the idea of a private occasion in the
act of talking is somehow   almost a contradiction in terms
      you come into a situation   prepared to externalize   or
prepared   i try not to be too prepared   i mean im aiming not
to be prepared   so that i can do what i dont expect to do   in
terms of something i want to say   and which is what one means
by improvisation   to do something you want to do in a way you
didnt know you were going to do it   which is to do something
new   and what you mean by improvisation is coming and saying
something you dont know   perhaps discovering something you
dont know   and in doing that you circle around the things you
do know looking for an opening between what you know and what
you dont know   and before you take your move into what you
dont know you go over   in a sort of family way and pat the
things you know on the head nicely   things i know about improvisation   namely that improvisation needs a sort of warmup
      you kind of warm yourself up to the situation and pretend youre
talking to yourself   but im not really talking to myself   and
i wanted to talk not to myself and thats why i came out   out?
      what was i in that i came out of?   i suppose theres a comedy

240

involved in this idea of an inside and an outside   you know
        the hand inside the glove the glove outside the hand   intimacy
            you take your hand out of the glove   its a funny idea   i
mean the idea that the self is inside   is itself a funny notion
        whats inside? and inside of what?   i mean im not even inside
of myself if i come here and talk to myself   or if i sit in my own
room and talk to myself   what do i see as my self?   the part
    that comes out?   see   i cant get out of saying out   it
keeps coming "out"   as i say it it comes out and i suddenly see ıt
    out there   and seeing it out there i hear what i say and then i
    know what i mean   now its probably no different for anybody
else   im really convinced   i mean im as convinced as im convinced of anything that im an honest man   so i say im convinced
        you should believe im convinced   that talking is thinking
        my kind of talking is thinking anyway   i used to   for
years i used to say people couldnt talk   i mean it bugged me
terribly   i used to go around complaining nobody could talk
any more   i moved to san diego and i said gee   nobody talks
        and finally i found out that nobody meant what i meant by
talking   i kept saying they dont talk any more nobody wants to
sit down and talk   and they sat down and they talked   so to
speak   i mean they spoke   and they listened when i spoke and
    they spoke again and they would mutter or shout   but nothing
would happen   i mean we had a different vocabulary   i mean
nothing would happen and i assume talking is making something
happen   and it didnt happen too often   but in any case if im
    going to make something happen and not talk to myself   in a
way i have to come here with my intentions to talk to people   as
i said   that i partly know partly dont know   which is a con-
    dition not very like living with people that you think you do know
        or living with yourself   because if im standing here resisting
as it were entering into the water of a discourse   to take a bath
in public so to speak in my own intention   its not because im shy
    of all the people here   i mean i could probably be as autobio-
graphically revealing   send out   say   the same banalities
    that you could reveal to me at any moment   and i would be
    hopelessly trapped if you revealed yours to me as i might hope-
lessly trap you later on by telling you mine   im circling

because in a way im dealing with the ritual of my own image of
honesty   an absurd image   but honesty is a funny thing for
people who talk   i mean honesty is about truth   or adequacy
     you say somebody says something and hes honest   which
is to suppose that at the time he says it hes saying what he intends
to say   and that it corresponds to something he knows
     whether hes right or wrong   i mean imagine somebody says
something and he says it in public and he believes it and its not true
hes an honest man so to speak   well hes honest in a manner
of speaking   but very often you say something in public when
youre improvising   when youre talking and moving and youre
saying something that you dont entirely mean   and while youre
saying it you know that you dont really mean just that   the way
it comes out   i was talking to a friend the other day and he was
very disturbed about something that appeared in a magazine and he
had been improvising   that is he had been talking in a staged situation and he had been talking about a number of things and started
talking about several people he knew   very rapidly and   i
think in a context not unlike this one   though maybe really
different   and not expecting to be held to the letter of the word
     or to see the letter of the word   he said of two people he
knew who were his friends   something about "those second
raters"   talking of   dan graham   who is a friend of both
of us   and john perreault who is also   and i didnt do all this
to entangle you vito   i really didnt mean to entangle you in
this thing merely for the sake of entanglement but because im prepared to defend   in a way i love dan graham and in some way
maybe you do too   im prepared to say that while you didnt really
not mean it you didnt really mean it either   that is   in what
way is dan graham?   and i dont know how many of you know
dan graham   dan graham is not a second rater   dan graham is
someone who has a very mad sense of america   a very strange
sense of american mania   staten island italian houses   the
internal decor of staten island houses that were sold by developers
     and he noticed this a long time ago   the "musical" way they
were sold   you added one room to a normal ensemble of utilities
and it was a "sonata"   you expanded it a bit by the number of
bedrooms and it was a "trio"   if you made it a bigger house

242

with maybe a patio and a roof over the garage it was then a "concerto"
    he fastened on these houses and the art manias of america but
he didnt fasten on them all the time in a way to advance himself in
    an appropriate way   because in some manner dan graham was
very confused   hes a very beautifully confused discomforted
man   wandering around somehow in europe as an artist doing
things that maybe he could do better   and for reasons i dont
    understand he admires sol lewitt   now sol lewitt has done some
very nice things   and sol lewitt is nice enough to be anybodys
    uncle   but i dont see any reason why anybody should   admire
sol lewitt   or more precisely i dont see why dan graham should
    admire sol lewitt   sol lewitt who is a man who has done very
nice things is now resolutely putting lines on a wall   has resolutely
    put things in a serial   systemic form   and when i say "reso-
lutely" i am talking of something that may be admirable   but
when i say "serial and systemic form"   in the art world i mean
something that is at best dopey and at worst trivial   like mel
bochner   because what you mean in the art world by "serial and
systemic" is something you could count on your fingers and all of
us can count and i dont think thats very surprising   but sol
    counted resolutely   he gave people instructions to make things
        make lines and do things you could count and then he stood by
and looked as contented as an uncle   and there was something
about that avuncular style   its persistence that poor dan admired
        here was dan graham who is probably the worlds greatest
authority on hawaiian guitar music   on ukeleles on arthur godfrey
on why dean martin and america are one   and on eisenhowers
paintings   dan graham knew more about the important things of
america than sol lewitt will ever know whatever his virtues   but
dan graham admires sol lewitt and sol lewitt probably doesnt admire
dan graham   and in some sense the verdict of the art world has
    not been to admire dan graham   who i admire   i admire dan
graham but i wouldnt envy dan graham   and i think i understand
    what vito meant   vito did not mean that dan graham was a
second rater but he meant something else   he meant that other
people   who vito takes seriously will not admire dan graham and
they wont take him seriously enough   because he wont let himself
    be taken seriously enough   theres something not resolute

enough   not remorseless enough about dan graham   and theres
something not resolute enough or remorseless enough about john
perreault   who is also my friend   who is also our friend
        john perreault is one of the few people in the world when he
writes about something that happened in the art world   if you
havent been there you still know what its like   hes one of the few
people in the art world who when he describes an event you know
        whats happened   thats not a trivial thing   to be able to
know something on the basis of a report   but yet it is not in the
art world important   and many people hold that it is not important there   where there are other kinds of importance   as for
example to construct an allegory out of this event   or at least
invent some reason for supposing it to be important   provided
that you do this only for such events as some of our friends
        vitos friends   already suppose are important   but yet
again   i dont want to make an issue of this   its about improvisation the sense of talking out of   being on your feet and
when you say something fast and its in accordance with where youre
going you have a feeling that youre speaking appropriately   and
you go and you say it and you dont expect to have it come back at
you   you dont expect a deposition in court   "did you really
mean that?"   "i dont know what i meant   i said it"   i mean
you mean what you say   or i suppose it depends on how you say
it and how you mean it   at everson i was telling a story about
myself   it was not entirely about myself because as i said
        when i speak   if i speak about people who are real and are
here   under any circumstances   and i can only speak about
        people who are here if i know them   but im here and im speak-
ing about myself now   you hold hostages in your mouth   in
        the sense that youre going to talk terrible lies about them   and
you think of what i could say   terrible things   that i could
say about myself or anybody else   i mean thats not really the part
of it that makes any difference   the problem of honesty and
improvisation or   honestys not enough   i mean you can be
        honest and its not adequate   but as you can make a representa-
tion of the real that is fundamentally inadequate isnt that the same
as being false?   because being false is only possible   youre
only capable of being false if you have a notion of truth and falsity

244

that is sufficiently binary for you to bring things up to that binary
test   normally anything that counts requires a more complicated
model   something like a map   and you make a map of what
happened   an event say   and the map has a lot of parts
      supposing you get a map from someone and it has a river on it
and it has a town by it and a hill just outside the town and it has
  some indication of mileage and it tells you where the gas station is
      and youre driving along using that map and you find a gas
station and you stop at the gas station and get gas   if theyve got
gas   and you drive further   and you stop the car   youre
tired you get out and you say "well   im going to go look at the
  river"   you go look at the river and the rivers not there   so
the rivers not there what do you mean the rivers not there? its on
the map   its a false map   but the gas station was there
      the road was there   the town was there   but the river
wasnt there   now you can say its a false map and go home say
"its a false map the river wasnt there"   or you can park the car
and go look for the river   now there are several possibilities
      lets say you get out and go looking for the river and you find
the river after a long time   you know   youve been walking
      and walking and youre tired and you go on and you find the
river   its not really much of a river   its sort of a slim river
and you say "its a river and he didnt know where he was putting the
  river"   and you go back and you say hes not a good river marker
      but the map is not exactly false   you know there could have
been a better marking for the river   or supposing you dont do
that   supposing you go out you go looking for the river and you
  go looking for the river and there just is no river   theres a dried
up river bed   now it happens that there are some territories
      like say mexico northern mexico   that have a lot of places
where there are rivers some times of the year and there are not rivers
other times of the year   and you know you go back to the gas
station and you say "hey i have this funny map says theres a river
here" and they say at the gas station "oh theres a river here but the
rivers only there in april"   it didnt say that on the map but its
an april river   you say "oh   april river"   there are alternatives to truth and falsity when youre dealing with something in the
world   even when youre dealing with something other than a

245

map   and you have a whole set of structural assumptions that
have to be taken as an ensemble   you take them as a package
  and then either the package is good enough for the purposes or its
  not   but that depends on what the purposes are   and sometimes on whether theyre good enough for the package   if you
see me looking at this thing its because its only a funky little tape
recorder and i dont always know how much time is left on it   but
  i wanted to talk about the self and my own peculiar sense of the
self   that came up recently   it came up in a rather odd way
      a kind of trivial way but an odd way   i was in california and
elly   who is my wife was having a series of exhibitions in europe
      she was travelling in europe   she was away for a couple of
weeks   and i was home doing a number of things   i was busy
teaching and doing other things and she was traveling and we were
separated for some time   as i said a period of about three weeks
      and letters dont travel fast between here and there as you may
know from italy   letters between italy and the united states are
not exactly prompt   in fact some of the letters   shed been
back a week and a half and some of the letters were still getting here
      which is interesting   you can write yourself all sorts of
documents and then answer yourself   its a kind of amazing situation in the postal service   but at some point i figured id hear
from her and i did   she eventually called she called after   at
  a disastrous place   when she was in cologne   and she hated
cologne and cologne depressed her terribly   and i heard this sort
of frantic voice and i said "well how are things?"   and she said
oh the show is fine the show is fine   the shows were fine but
  cologne is terrible   in the meantime i had not known she was
  going to be in cologne   in fact i thought she was still going to
be in italy   so i   i was not quite clear and i was trying to get
information from her about how things had gone in italy   because
thats where the shows were and she couldnt talk about anything
except cologne because cologne is where she couldnt get orange juice
      because in cologne they carbonate these drinks and you could
keep asking for orange juice forever but whatever you ask for you
wind up with a carbonated fruit drink in germany and if you dont
like carbonated fruit drinks   tough!   dont drink   go to a
  private home and squeeze their oranges   but she was far from

DATE 4/13/90

NAME

ADDRESS

SOLD BY	CASH	C.O.D.	CHARGE	ON ACCT.	MDSE. RETD.	PAID OUT

QUAN.		DESCRIPTION		PRICE	AMOUNT
	1	Autm			3 95
	2	Tallerny at the			27
	3	Boundaries			
	4				4 22
	5				
	6				
	7				
	8				
	9				
	10				
	11				
	12				

CUSTOMER'S ORDER NO.   REC'D BY

me and   i remember sitting down after the phone call and wed
   talked   and i had this funny image   this funny interesting
alienated image   that is i said to myself you know ive been
married for   oh i think we got married in 1960 so i guess weve
   been married fourteen years   we were married fourteen years
        which is a very monogamous arrangement and   i said to
myself its strange   i mean weve never been   so far away from
each other for such a length of time   and thats both a reasonable
   and dangerous speculation   theres something about human
relations of pairing   that is   couple formation   marriage
being lets say only a formalization of that   that is very fragile
        that is you dont know whats going to happen as soon as you
   move out of the room   in a sense   if you let it   if you and
someone with whom youve been living a kind of marriage life   i
say a marriage life because that means something in which you play
   a role   a role   that is you engage in an adventure of self
   determination   of self definition in relation to someone else and
you do it as a pair   you do it as a pair   you invent as it were a
structure of the real thats filled with assumptions about people
        its filled with past and its filled with future and its filled with
expectations   but introduce for a moment the terrifically com-
monplace doubt you know?   about someone whom youve been
   living with   "i dont know what shes doing over there in europe"
        you know?   is she making out with somebody else in europe?
        now you say thats trivial   of course its trivial   i mean as
i was talking to a friend of mine i said "you know   what difference does it make if shes fucking somebody else in europe?"   i
mean in a really serious sense what difference could it possibly
make?   i mean were all civilized people   arent we?   i mean
i dont believe in the instantaneous passage of bodies across time and
space   and im sitting in california   specifically sitting in solana
beach on a cliff over the sea in a living room   and whats more
   im tired   i cant send myself across there and i couldnt make
love to her at that moment and if she had to make love to somebody
   and shes in cologne   in a serious sense what could that possibly
matter to me   right? i mean were all civilized arent we?   but
are we   now?   i dont know how seriously i now remember
whether or not i felt alienated on grounds like that at all   but if

247

you introduce a moment of doubt into a relationship like   what
if we decide to split?   you know   what if we suddenly decide
to split   she comes back i go away you know   what if we do?
    well what happens is that what you imagine is that the shape of
your life has suddenly changed   and you resist it   the terrific
anxiety lets say that comes up   and it comes up for anyone
because it structural   it comes up because when two people in a
    kind of romantically existential situation play out a coupling   i
mean i can imagine people playing out tripling   though usually
    thats only another complicated way of coupling   with at most
three couples in it   but dont suppose im now discussing monogamy as if monogamy   monogamous heterosexual marriages
    as if they were the only possible kind of grouping   i mean
its really that im relatively pedestrian in my sexual choices   i can
    imagine   i have friends who do it otherwise   i confess   i
personally confess that i find it hard its hard for me to imagine homosexual pairing in quite the same way   its an inability on my part
    mainly because it seems somewhat preposterous to me and thats
so and it may be purely an inadequacy on my part   but it
always seems to me that homosexuality is a comical thing   and
    most homosexuals have a loveable sense of the preposterous   its
like turtles and peacocks you know?   theres a story   konrad
lorenz tells a story about a peacock falling in love with a turtle
    theres something of that in homosexuality that i kind of admire
    but remotely   and only remotely and the idea of making
love to a man strikes me as one of the funniest things in the world
    and i understand from some of my friends that its the only
thing that turns them on   and theres no telling what turns people
on and i   its just that evolution has its pedestrian manner of
operating and i have a rather dull heterosexual sense of whats interesting   now thats only a mild issue   i mean that i dont even
mean that to enter in to define the thing   this coupling   because
    that might be the way you might choose to do couple pairing
and one could choose triple pairing   or tripling or quadrupling
    we all know of *menages a trois* of some sort or another no
matter how temporary or unstable they might be   but theres no
reason one couldnt imagine them working out   maybe quadrupling more easily than tripling   again im not theorizing on this

with a view to how people should live   i dont really care how
people live but i am interested in what view of the self they set up
in the way they live   for example imagine someone who sets up
and will not be as it were   shaken by jealousy and doubt   in
order not to be shaken by jealousy or doubt   which has nothing
to do with the probability of the event   of betrayal let us say
     you need a situation in which youre not really seriously defining
yourself against the behavior of another   and thats really what
makes a very big difference   for example   imagine you lived
the life of adventure   that is "im an adventurer"   romance is
as it were multiple and profoundly rapid   there is a turnover in
pairings   one two three four every time i see a skirt pass in the
street im attracted   wonderful possibilities   my life will
change i move from forty-second street to central park south
     from central park south down to the village   up again next
time then im in iowa finding myself in bed with a coed   leaving
you know   its terrific   what a scene   and it goes by
like that   you dont have to define yourself because youre
travelling too fast   that is you travel so fast   see theres one
thing about lovers   that theyre more like each other than theyre
not   you know?   and so if you go through a multiplicity of
couplings the one thing it has is an equivalence   after a while
     and the advantage of that is that you dont produce self defini-
tion in the same way that people who do the coupling number   i
mean its a terrific number   this also   its the hall of mirrors
     what you do is you produce a dazzling blur of adventures and
its kind of terrific and you travel at great speed and you get flickering
images of yourself across all of them   generally you see yourself
the same way in all of them because you dont have time enough to
meet resistance   you see its sort of nice   what happens is each
one treats you with enough   they dont have enough time to treat
you to all their own particular characteristic quirks of humanity because the only quirks they can really treat you to are the ones that
you meet with over coffee in the morning or in bed   and those are
relatively restricted   there are more characterological quirks
that develop over a longer period of time when you live with
people in a kind of social circumstance   so you reduce the possibility of receiving any information about yourself thats more

complex and threatening and puzzling   in fact what you do is you
receive a kind of confirmation of all your initial assumptions and
thats in a sense what i suppose is terrific about the don juan role
but it takes a lot of time and its filled with energy and its a
drag for artists   because they have too much to do and   you
know   its a nuisance   right?   you dont want to do it its
hard to do it you have to keep up and you have to have second wind
and it isnt easy   it involves traveling fast too and you drink so
much bad coffee in the morning its terrible   because you cant
tell anybody how you like your coffee   and besides which
its not a role that seems to me to be committed to this kind of
existential self definition   but the self definition role   i mean
the monogamous dull one you know   the romantic monogamous
role   and i say romantic meaning its not a marriage of convenience
very many people have marriages of convenience but not too
many that i know   i say this out of statistical faith   i mean i
assure you i havent made a count   but this image of self definition and monogamy is a funny thing   you have somebody whos
another insider   thats how i got into this thing   we were
talking about the relation of public to nonpublic   what i really
wanted to get at was this being an insider and an outsider   the
thing of living with somebody is that theyre sort of insiders
theyre probably as much insiders as you are   inside in your
own sense of inside   they know you very well   sometimes as
well as you know yourself   which may not be terrifically well
except in terms of the things you say or characteristically say or
think you want to say and they know they see it coming   i
mean they say "oh hes going to say that again" you know?   like
"i heard that line before   thats a nice one   i like that one say
it again its terrific   i remember when you said it last week" you
know?   and you have this sort of insider you live with who
youre an insider with also   in a sense youre both insiders
whos inside everything its possible for another insider to be
inside of   and everything is perfectly understandable   to the
extent that its understandable at all   and youve been living the
coherent life   and youve been doing regular things   what
have you been doing? youve been working at some job youve been
making your art youve been living in the same house for six years

and everybody knows that people suddenly embark and leave it
      you know   not everybody but theres always a case some
case where someone whose always been right   you know i have
a lot of friends who whatever they do theyre doing it right   i
mean that whatever they do however mad or freaky or accidental
and arbitrary what theyre doing happens to be it has always been
perfectly planned   from the day they were born   and then
something new and freaky happens and they do something else
      separately   and theyre in another life   and you say
"well   but what happened?"   and then they explain how it
was the only thing that they could do   and how what they do is
just right and though its another life its now this life in which they
were always right and not the last life   and they suddenly are
divorced they have a new pair of children they live an entirely different way and yet they were again living the right life the only life
they could possibly have ever lived   and you know when you
see this happen it could happen to you   because its happened
before   i mean it happened to me   i mean i was living the
only life i could live and then i stopped living it and started living
another   and you know i recognize theres an ambiguity in the
sense of confidence with which i say "i"   normally we ride in
with terrific confidence in saying "i"   i mean "i"   who do i
speak for?   im here i say this and i   when i say "i" im talking
about my life   what do you mean "i"?   who do i answer to?
      the people who call me "david"?   from the beginning of my
life people have been calling me david   long before i was consistently "i"   that is long before i was consistently going to answer to
that name in quite the same way   they had very consistent expectations   the people who called you "david" or "baby"   they look
at the child thats there and they say "hey   baby" you know and
baby says something back or doesnt say something back and gradually
baby reaches the assumption that its probably convenient to respond
regularly to that name as if it were a consistent entity   baby keeps
finding it convenient to be "baby"   that is   "baby giuseppe"
turns out to be consistently "baby giuseppe"   now "baby giuseppe"
may at some point sense that probably he could desert   you know
      abandon ship they would call "baby giuseppe" and he walks
out the door   you know   but he doesnt do it because there

are advantages   you get fed you get taken care of they clean you
up you get nice clothes to wear   besides they amuse you   and
everything around you combines to help you stay stable   when
they talk to your "i"   you find it interesting you tend to respond
and when they give you your name you answer to it because you
can get things from it   that is   if you turned out be different every time they called you you would disappoint them but
they would disappoint you even more   and its a bad scene
      how much they would disappoint you   and what you do is
you react to your life in a funny way   you imagine that the
reason you have such terrific confidence in the coherency of your
life is because you see it as shaped by your past   at least i do
anyway   i think most of us have a way of seeing our lives as
connecting with a past   you think of your life it unfolds in time
      you know you have an image of it as being temporally consistent
      i do anyway   but i can imagine different kinds of temporal
consistency i mean it doesnt have to be like an unrolling rug
      imagine a life   you know   a self thats like a sequence of
numbers   you can imagine all kinds of number sequences and
they can be pretty freaky   i mean they dont have to be the
simplest kinds of number sequences   imagine that each number
corresponds to an event   you know?   and if you live a freaky
life you still can have an image of a freaky sequence this way
      imagine that its a random number series   the events them-
selves are drawn randomly but theyre drawn this way   theyre
drawn from a box of numbers   the box contains only the
natural numbers   integers   whole numbers   its still a
random series   there are an infinite number of whole numbers
and you dont know which ones will get picked or in what order
      but maybe that isnt freaky enough for you   for your image
of your life   well you can imagine several boxes   youve got a
box of all the rational numbers   youve got a box of irrational
numbers   youve got a box of transcendental numbers and youve
got a box of imaginary numbers   and each one is a different
kind of event right?   i mean imaginary numbers are drawn out
by an entirely different process than rational numbers   imaginary numbers are what you might call freaky irrationals   because
you have to create them by a process that is unlike the four

252

fundamental operations of arithmetic   you have to extract them
   as roots of negative squares   which is totally impossible   and
   you cant extract them   you cant get down to their root because
   nobody knows what that means   to be a negative square
      because if you square any number at all the result will not be
   negative   so these numbers you cant get down to the root of
   these imaginary numbers are what you would call profoundly irrational numbers   theyre the freakiest ones   but otherwise there
   are very clear relations between rational numbers and irrational
   numbers   whats a rational number?   a rational number is any
      number you can describe as the quotient of two integers   you
   can never not find one right?   theyre all and only the numbers
   you can construct by dividing one whole number into another
      and thats sort of simple   everybody knows what a whole
   number is and how to divide   so its no problem   you divide
   one integer into another and you can make the whole field of
   rational numbers   you can always find a way to do it   but
   they can be pretty freaky those rational numbers   i mean you
   may not think much of rational numbers because theyre so low and
   cartesian like   but they can really be kind of odd   if you
   start doing them the right way   i mean you can start by dividing
   a hundred and sixty seven into a hundred and thirty eight   you
   can produce some very funny numbers   now if you think of this
      number sequence   lets think of this number sequence as a
   sequence of events   real events in life   now im just using
      numbers as a convenient way of describing events   because
   numbers can be produced infinitely   and obviously if you look
   at your life you can find   depending on how close you look
      an infinite number of events in your life   if youre really
   concentrating   depending on how much you concentrate and the
   angle at which you look and how close you come   your life
   doesnt have a finite number of events   because the number of
   events it has is directly related to the ways you look at it   now
   let me suppose something   let me suppose just for the sake of it
   that the way you define yourself is really in terms of prime numbers
      lets call them each one a prime event   in the beginning all
   events are prime events so in the beginning of your life no event is
   not prime   because a prime event is an irreducible event   its

253

irreducible   a prime number is a number that is divisible only by
itself and one   thats an irreducible whole   and you can
imagine that beginning a life all events are prime   because you
have no past into which to reconstitute it   that is it wouldnt be
divisible into other recognizable integral factors   so you begin
one   the first event   you recognize as an event its a prime
number   for our purpose   one is an irreducible prime
two?   its an irreducible prime because two and one are its
only factors and you cant make anything else out of it   three?
prime number   you get to four you remember   you have
memories of two   four   not a prime number we came upon
our first unprime   after a while the prime numbers are going to
stop coming up so regularly   that is to say four is not a prime
but five is prime again   six? not prime   you can remember
three you have nostalgic memories of three and two   youre
flirting out there with your memories of other times and other
events   seven? prime number   eight you got too many memories   two and four   and four reminds you of two again
twice and you remember it   as you remember nine because of
all those threes in it   not prime   and you say "well ten?" not
prime   you have to wait for eleven to come to another prime
now think about that for a minute   if you go on   think
about the whole field   you know its not a field   im sorry it
isnt a field   i dont want to describe prime numbers as if they
were a field   if there are any mathematicians here its not a number field the way the rational numbers are a field   lets call it the
run of prime numbers   the whole run   nobody knows how to
generate the whole run of prime numbers   i mean its totally
impossible to do that   but we know a lot about prime numbers
i mean i can tell you something about prime numbers very
quickly   by just inspecting them   supposing you considered
that your life oscillated   i mean you can think of oscillating lives
you can imagine a self that isnt consistent in a simple way but
that oscillates   jumps back and forth in some way   thats
what we started out to imagine before   that the events of our life
might have oscillated in some way between rational numbers and
irrational ones rational events and irrational ones   so lets assume
your life jumps in certain ways   lets assume your life is something

254

like a sequence but not a random sequence   you didnt randomly
pick from here and there   because events your events turn out
to be characteristic of you in some way   i mean you recognize
yourself in your events   but lets not be so simple about how you
recognize yourself in events   suppose you come off a rebound
lets think about rebounds   you say one is a prime number
for us   its your first event and its irreducible   and you
think of your life as somehow a sequence of events that are related
even if in a simple way   so you suppose you have this event
your first prime number and thats one because you remember it and
its important for you and what happens is you come to your second
prime number and thats two   and because you remember the
first one and youre aware of the second you compare the two
because thats the way you develop your self   in comparing
your primes your prime experiences   you express this comparison
as a ratio   you divide one into the other   so what happens
you divide one into the other   what happens when you
divide one into two?   you have two   right?   and this is
quite obvious   i mean i dont want you to suppose im doing
something very profound   and you say ok   now the next
prime is going to be three   and you divide three by two because
it was the last prime experience you had   this ratio is in a simple
way an approximation of your consciousness   i say simple
because lets say you dont have a terrific memory but at least you
have a kind of simple persistence   that lets you hold your
memory of your last prime experience when you come up to your
next one to compare it   so in a simple way you can think of
your self   of your life   as the sequence of the ratios of successive primes   and you can consider it   so you divide three
by two and you get one and a half   very soon you recognize
something in this sequence   even if the numbers are bouncing
around   it turns out that the first number   ratio   two
divided by one is two and you divide three by two and get one and
a half   you jump to the next and divide five by three and get one
point six something or other   and you look way ahead   to say
nineteen divided by seventeen   and you realize that ratio is
going to be considerably smaller than one and a half and even if
youre very dumb and have to go on to thirty-seven say or much

further you very soon realize something about the way these ratios keep bouncing   you know after the first two primes   one and two   youll never have a ratio as big as two again because it couldnt be prime   and youll never have a ratio as small as one   because the only number that will divide into another number and give you the ratio one has to be the same number   which is also obvious and not very important   but you know that whatever kind of oscillation theres going to be in this life of successive primes is going to bounce between two and one and never reach either again   you also realize that there is a way these ratios of any succeeding prime to any preceding prime will tend to move between a higher and lower figure   and that this lower figure which you may approach somewhat irregularly   will over time get smaller and smaller   as if the sequence of these ratios was like some strange pendulum   receiving an occasional push but   over the long run   constantly declining   now i cant prove that   because i cant generate all the primes or a method for generating them   though it seems intuitively likely   that for the whole run of the primes   there will occur at various times successive primes that are twin   that are separated by only one number like 11 and 13   and if this is true as the prime numbers get higher and higher the ratio of these twin primes will become smaller and smaller and come infinitely closer to one which no ratio of successive primes could reach   so it is like a kind of strange damping   this sequence of the ratios of successive primes   now if all this sounds somewhat remote from a life consider   im living my life   i was jumping from my "one" state say   my orderly monogamous life   to my "two" state   my wild adventurous life   say   and i can hold the two in my mind all together   now i remember moving from an opportunist advantageous life   where i proceded in a rigorous way to advance myself   lets say an academic or business career i was once in a business   i once ran a scientific publishing company   it may not look like it   it doesnt look like me but i was the scientific director for an american division of sarpedon press   its embarrassing to think about it and i can hardly recognize that life   and i jumped out of that life a long time ago   and it wasnt much of a jump it just seemed to go

256

away   i mean somehow or other it really went away very easily
one day i went into the office of the rumanian vice president
after i had finished discussing it with the swiss controller and i told
the rumanian vice president that i really wanted to be fired   and
he said "why do you want to be fired?   wouldnt you like to go
to another office   maybe you could take over in paris"   i
said i dont want to take over in paris i want to collect unemployment
insurance   he said no no no he said youre doing very well
you know even if you did make a mistake and make a lot of
money for us and we had to pay higher income taxes that was all
right   dont worry   it was a minor blunder   we could give
you another job that would be more interesting   where would
you like to go?   we have a printing plant in czechoslovakia
it was terrific england had resources that were coming from
czechoslovakia in return for assets that had been seized during the
second world war and by some enormously complicated and sophis-
ticated scheme this publishing company had managed to get printing
done in czechoslovakia for the money owed to other perhaps now
nonexistent english businesses   and it was very cheap printing
it was terrible printing   which shouldnt astonish anybody
but it was very cheap it was almost for nothing   and you
know maybe i could have gone to czechoslovakia   and think of
all the wonderful things i could have done in czechoslovakia   i
could drink slivovits and go to avant garde theater and live in prague
but i wanted unemployment insurance   and he didnt understand me   because he was from my other life   the other part
of my cycle   that is he was at one of my maxima or maybe
minima   and i said let me out of here and he said "now look
thats not a reasonable way to talk" because there i was wearing
a suit   it was my one suit   it was my business suit my looking
for a job suit   my soft english tweed suit with the expensive
english cut that i never wore except to special conferences when i
needed something and there i was wearing this suit and he was
wearing a suit too   and we sat upstairs in a brownstone building
in an office over the buckingham book shop and we looked at each
other seriously and he couldnt believe it   that a man sitting
across the desk from him wearing a business suit wanted unemployment insurance   i said look   i have an apartment that costs

257

$18.75 a month and its got three rooms and its in a very nice part of town and i can live very well on unemployment insurance   and he said but do you realize what that means   you could be making a lot of money   and i said i know and he said dont you want to do that   make a lot of money?   and i said im tired of making a lot of money thats why i want unemployment insurance   well i got unemployment insurance and i was in another life   but the point is   that at one moment i was in that life and it was my life   and then i was in another   now i can predict certain possibilities in my own life   if i act as a historian   i could act as a kind of bold historian of my life   survey it from wherever i happen to be   look back at what i can see and make some kind of formal prediction of my future   theres nobody in this world   i dont care what kind of wonderfully gifted pyrotechnical psychopath you are   you can always make some kind of prediction of your moves   within limits   i mean if you have trans- cendental numbers in your sequence system you know perfectly well that theyre going to come up in some relation to the non- transcendental numbers of your system   a transcendental number is a number that cant be derived from some finite number of equations with rational coefficients   okay?   i mean a number like "e" the base of the natural log or *pi*   is a transcendental number and *pi* can be expressed as a simple geometric ratio   of the circumference of a circle to its diameter   but anyway say you have this reservoir of transcendentals and you pick from it   occasionally   and you cant exactly say when   so you cant predict everything   but you can predict a lot   sometimes even too much   when youre more or less likely to choose a rational   an irrational   a transcendental number or even an imaginary number   because there is this self that you feel that youre wearing   you know you go along and feel that youre wear- ing it   this self   maybe the way i was wearing that suit and still you say "im an honest man"   what does it mean to be an honest man?   its a man with a very reliable sense of the tracks on which hes running or on which you feel that youre running   if you happen to feel like a train   i mean youve been going along and you feel that youre coming along this way   and you look back and it looks like theres this track   in back of you

now you knew the last station   and you predicted the next
station and   thats why you feel very nervous   at junctions
      the idea of running off the tracks is not a good one   i mean
people usually feel bad at running off the track   at least its supposed to feel bad   and i know that its not entirely true   there
are times when people love the idea of going berserk   thats what
it means to jump the tracks   and try for another life   though
the other life may be merely an inversion of the one youve been living   its a negative number   for example youve been wearing
your suit and   come on in jackson youre not interrupting   and
vasile who is my boss my vice president   he looks at me and he
doesnt believe what i say   he doesnt believe i want unemployment insurance   he thinks i mean something more devious   like
some other business   i will go to work for his competitor with what
i learned here   he has no idea of what i mean   so what could i
do i could become the first buckingham bookshop streaker   i was
sitting there across from him in this wainscotted office i could divest
myself of my clothes and run madly across the room and   he
would let me go   he would let me go if i did that   going berserk
is to violate the track right?   you jump the track and pull it up
with you   thats what everybody does when he does that   and
you could get very good at doing it   people who go berserk are
usually well appointed for that trip   and what they do is well
pointed in relation to what they neglected to do before   theyre
terrific at finding the place at which the track is going to be difficult
to stay on and they know just how to edge right off   first one
wheel tilted slightly then the next and   jump theyre off   going
berserk you kill your relatives   or people you think should be
your relatives   its wonderful how when people go berserk they kill
the people they should be killing or the kind of people   and they
usually are very good at it   they sweep out the field in relation to
their track   theres a wonder of logic in this   ill tell you a story
about this   i mean its not like i needed this story   because i
could have gone on in the other direction but i wanted to come
around the edge and i remember this story   it was told me by
someone and i dont know if its true   though it may well have been
true   and it was told to me as a true story by somebody who didnt
usually tell lies   i think it was told me to show how terrible women

259

are   and that may color the story   which i think is probably
true in spite of that   this guy was a songwriter and chess player
       he was a mediocre songwriter and mediocre chess player   but
he made money writing songs and doing arranging and he didnt make
money playing chess   and   he had a talent for acquiring depen-
dent women   he was very good at it and they were drawn to him
like a magnet   a magnet is maybe the wrong word   you know
       he was pointed in their direction   pointed at their weakness
       and they sensed the intensity and decisiveness of this pointing in
their direction   its violence and interest   and they came toward
him to be impaled   it was reliable he was beautiful at it and the
experience was intense   he performed a major service for a large
part of the female population that was seeking an intense experience
       they moved in swiftly   were impaled and fell down   then
they would sort of be carted away   or they would walk away and
enter another life   in this sense he was a life changer   he
diverted people from one life into another   well one girl had been
going with him   a woman   had been going with him for some
long time and had been suffering in this painful and intense relation
       and finally she gave him up   yes   and she was about to get
married to some other man   and she was on the way to her wedding   shes driving with her groom and some of their friends and
she says youve got to stop the car over here   ive got to get out and
see somebody for just a moment   the car stops   and they wait
with an idling motor   she runs upstairs into the apartment where
the songwriter lives   and she comes in   theres a whole crowd
of people sitting around in the apartment talking   and she starts
this mad romantic scene with this songwriter   the guy she just
gave up   now there must have been fifteen people in the room
drinking beer and listening to music and maybe just talking   and
       this is the way the storys told and it may not be true   and i
dont have to believe it and you dont have to believe it   but
surrounded by all these people who know her   while her groom
is waiting outside   shes crying and sobbing and grabbing at this
guy and she forces him into his room throws him down on his bed
and sucks him off   now you say to yourself what is it that shes
really doing?   forget whether its true or not   you can imagine
it   and i can imagine it too   not because women are like this

260

or people are like this   i can imagine that in a funny way
this is a metaphysical crisis   that is to say   which life is she in?
shes at the point of a life jump and shes trying to bring the two
parts of her life together closing a circuit   she wants to test
where she is   its a philosophical act   and people who live
philosophical lives are always absurd   and shes living the philosophical life   shes at the point of going from one life to another
and wants to hold both in her mind at once to compare them   its
like in a poker game youve gotten this hand and youve taken it
this far and its a hand you can play and youve played it   youve
been playing and raising and other players have raised you back but
youve got to see the hand out and call it   because youve got too
much invested in it not to see the hand out   to see what it is that
you really have   because you dont know whether youve won or
youve lost   because the question is what your hand really is
not what its supposed to be   the question is whos speaking
you dont know who you are   the reason you dont know
who you are is because you dont have a track in back of you any
more   the sense that theres a track in back of you is what makes
your self   if youre contemplating going from one track to another you dont have anything to rely on any more   all youve got
to do is go fast   what you need is energy   its a jump   you
know   bang   from here to there   if you stop   start to
worry with one wheel still on a track youre not going to go anywhere except into a wreck   and there is something about this in
the whole business of my saying   here i am sitting there   in
a calm quiet place   sitting carefully in my living room listening to
telemann   i mean theres nothing can disturb my life except   i
dont know whether im in one place or another   and i say to
myself what a funny sense of where i am   what a strange sensi-
bility im in   i mean what do i have to doubt about anything
about my self   that i want to change my life?   i dont
even have a rumanian vice-president i could go in and talk to   i
mean i cant go over to someone and say   i want to live the artists
life   im already living the artists life   so to speak   im
living the artists life   im teaching   you know   since for
most people thats what happens to most artists is they teach   i
mean the role of the artist in this society is largely being subsidized

by educational institutions   because from a practical point of
view their art doesnt get them anything else except credentials
     most artists i know get subsidized in some manner for another
kind of irrelevant work   its not the kind of work that goes
directly into their art   i think if you took a statistical survey youd
find that educational institutes subsidize artists   poorly   and
the majority of them are subsidized in such a way as to give the
illusion that theyre teaching art   and they do the best they can
     normally they do the best they can in that educational institu-
tion   which often does the best it can   bad as that may be
for reasons beyond anybodys direct control   so you say im living
the artists life   i do what i want as an artist   i dont work
that hard   i have enough money to survive   but im not mobile
     because the college says to me you have to be there a certain
number of days of the week   more or less   because i can
always manage something   i mean as long as the students get
taught   i can get somebody to take a class for me   i can
rearrange things   i can call the twenty-two students   or my
seven   or the ones who are there and i can say to them lets meet
at some other time when we can all make it   and we do   the
term is now over and im going to meet my class im going back
there tomorrow and im going to meet with them once more
     even though the term is technically over my class is going to
meet next week   were going to meet twice more   because
though they might have gladly stayed away i suppose i had a sense
that what i had to say to them was probably more meaningful than
most of the things that get said to them most of their life and they
might as well come twice after the term is over and hear what i have
to say   its a sort of confidence i have in myself and ill find out
whether theyre there or not whether they have equal confidence in
me   under the circumstances its a test of sorts   but what sort
of sense do i have that im going to change my life   i dont know
     but it provokes me   to the edge   any shift in your life
can provoke it   this sense   and you start playing with it
     do i want to change my life   what do i want to be?   who
do i want to be?   do i want to change into being somebody else?
     i think of a man who made a break   and you sometimes
think that you want to make a break   you want to pull from

262

another box   the imaginary numbers   ive never pulled from
the imaginary numbers ive pulled from the rational numbers the
irrational numbers   the transcendentals   but ive never done
an imaginary number   think of what that could be id love to do
that and i think   of ansel bourne   ansel bourne was a carpenter
seventy-five years ago or so in new england somewhere in new england   i dont remember exactly where   and he was a man who
was filled with a religious experience and he became a preacher for
some peculiar denomination a minister   and he delivered inspiring
sermons and he gave up carpentry   which he was apparently all
right at but he gave it up for his calling   and he was living the
ordinary artists life of a minister in his home in new england and
made bank deposits and had a house   and one day he took the
horsecar to providence withdrew some money from the bank and
disappeared   he was gone   several years later a man showed
up in a town outside of philadelphia with a little shop   that sold
bits and pieces of things and stationery   a notions store   and
he sells things and lives quietly in the back of his shop and hes a
member of some kind of odd denomination religious organization
     and he makes a few trips into philadelphia to replenish his stock
     and otherwise he goes nowhere except to his church   where
on one sunday he was said to have given a rousing sermon   now
that doesnt seem like too much of a break   this imaginary number seems like a very ordinary form of a very ordinary number
     maybe even a deprived form of ordinary number   and if
somehow under some circumstances something happens to him and
he goes to see someone about this   this deprived number
     maybe he sees a neurologist   who knows all about diseases
of the nerves   the way psychiatrists know all about diseases of
the mind   and they talk to each other say and it turns out that
they agree hes really ansel bourne   everybody agrees say   in
the ansel bourne life   which the people outside of philadelphia
cant know but accept say   but what does he do   he cant put
the pieces together   he could believe it   both numbers
     by checking it out with his bank and his wife if he had a wife
and his customers and his congregations   but he couldnt put it
together the two trivially similar different lives   in which there
was something wrong   i mean what did he do   change houses?

263

sleeping partners?   the girl at your side has brown hair she
used to have blond hair   and this has stylistic significance   i
   wouldnt deny it   and you could go even further on stylistic
   grounds   and ive known people to do it   theyve been living
a kind of normal domestic sexy life   and they decide   on
stylistic grounds   because thats what they usually are   to go
   do the homosexual life   and it happened to numerous people
that maybe we all know   and there are as they see it powerful
stylistic meaningful reasons for doing this   theyre making a
break   and then they live a normal domestic homosexual life of
   the same sort that they lived when they were not living a homosexual life   which is not exactly what you meant by making a break
   its not always possible to do that for seemingly trivial reasons
   comical debts to the residue of your own life that make it impossible or at least very difficult for you to do some things   you
cant even unlearn speaking the way you do   i mean you can learn
another language its easier to learn another language and come on
differently in another language than it is to relearn you own language
   im sure it would be easier   i mean if i want to change my
life i dont think i could unlearn the way i speak english   it would
be a disaster   theres no way i could learn to speak english say
like an academic poet   i mean colleges are filled with poets of
that sort and if i go to an academic meeting and i have nothing to do
      and i hate committee meetings   i go there and i try to estab-
lish their phonemes   its really terrific i go there and try to figure
out what country they come from and it turns out they dont come
from any country but they once studied somewhere in england
   you know they were born somewhere in iowa but they have this
scholar abroad accent   and i could try to develop a sound like
   that   you know i could develop a broad ahhh and lose my new
york sound   it would be funny to hear me talking like a poet
   with an english accent   now that i say it it sounds kind of nice
      i could get myself a little tattersall vest   i dont know if they
wear tattersall vests any more   id get a little tattersall vest and
   sort of stand a little taller   and write rhyming poems   and
develop an appropriately clipped sound   that was maybe inap-
   propriate for an englishman but very appropriate for a man from
iowa   but it doesnt work   it would be easier to go and learn

french   much easier   i mean theres a great alternative   and
i couldnt bear to learn parisian french in a really serious way
because i learned it to begin with   the important thing to do
is go to marseilles and develop a fierce street dialect   and then go
to paris and talk to intellectuals in street marseilles   for years ive
wanted to bug parisian intellectuals   i hate parisian intellectuals
it would be wonderful to go to paris and insist on having intellectual conversations with jean luc godard   i mean i met godard
so i ought to be able to go talk to godard with my marseilles street
accent   it would be terrific   you know?   but what a job
could i do it?   could i develop a low southern accent like a
sailor and seriously put down marxist avant garde esthetics?
what a terrific scene   you could yell at him you could yell
at him in southern french style   tell jean luc hes full of shit   i
mean it would be great   you know   a cigarette hanging out
of the corner of your mouth   suddenly i see my future its alive
its great   you get a job somehow you convince them to give you
a working card you become a longshoreman   you become a
longshoreman   you know? youre living your new life   and
you get a sort of chunky wife a sort of terrific sort of chunky wife
with funny shoes and at night you go down to the cafe and you talk
to your friends you do a max jacob kind of routine   i guess i
guess i dont have the energy for it   it takes too much energy
but you get a feeling youd like to do that and if youre going to
do it you might as well really do it   if you can   and then you
find out you have weaknesses that develop character weaknesses
characteristic weaknesses   which is the problem   i have
character weaknesses in my style   they keep creeping back
its those damned tracks   the tracks follow you   you know
like you jump the tracks and suddenly you find yourself on another
track that feels kind of familiar   you begin feeling that youre
leaning at the same angle and you can feel that sort of rocking sensation under you   its this urge to divest   which comes up and
which in all honesty weve been discussing   i mean i have to say
it with as much honesty as we deserve   as i deserve anyway   i
dont know how much honesty you deserve   i mean what
honesty do we owe each other   as long as i know you dont feel
terrible about it   yet i dont know if theres anything that i could

divest myself of so easily in order to become something else that
would be of any consequence   so easily   it would require an
   investment of an enormous amount of energy and i dont know if i
   have that kind of energy   children always have lots of energy
      theyre always becoming this and that or the other but forty
years of experience   forty years of events   if your life is a
   series of prime numbers and the ratios of successive prime numbers
      one of the things when you get further out in the numbers is
      not only is it a matter of where they come up and how often
      but if you get far enough out you cant even tell whether its a
prime number any more   i mean who can tell me whether thirty-
seven-thousand-four hundred-and-fifty-three is a prime number   i
mean it takes a lot of effort to figure out whether youve even got a
   prime number when the numbers get very high   and thats a very
   bad thing   i mean if youre going to do major transformations
      because if you dont know whether its a prime number you
   dont know whether its a prime experience   its very dubious
      you dont know when youve had a prime experience at all was
that a prime experience?   was that an integral ensemble unlike
anything i ever experienced before?   somehow it seems vaguely
   like a lot of others and i might be wrong   what if it was a prime
   experience and you didnt know it was a prime experience?
      which seems to be more like what life is like now than it used
   to be   you dont know whether you had a prime experience
      were you at the right place for a life transformation?   was
it the next prime number?   one two three five seven eleven
theyre very easy to recognize   thats the point but one thousand
two hundred and fifty seven who knows? until you start working
   on it   and when you get over ten thousand it gets very hard
      and thats not a very big number   and when you get to the
real big numbers the factors can be very large   and its too time
consuming to exhaust all the possible factors that might be in it
      even though you can discount many numbers   like the even
numbers because theyre certainly not prime   and though that
   cuts the problem in half it doesnt really make it easier   and
      mathematicians feel very embarrassed at being unable to develop a
   system for generating the primes or a method that will instantly
tell you whether theyve got a prime number or not   but there is

this inherent difficultness of inspectability   that may be built
   into the system of defining a prime   which is only prime if
youve discarded all possible factors smaller than itself and larger
   than one   so that the larger the number becomes the more possible factors it may contain and the harder they are to discard   so
   as you go on youre worse off than with the problem of having a
   prime experience or not   you can have a prime experience and
not know it   and the system of increasing doubt becomes more
   threatening because you dont even look for a change   because
   at this point i dont expect to change   i dont expect to see
myself change really   though i may change by anybody elses
   standards   i mean maybe i will go to paris after i study up in
marseilles   maybe ill do that you know?   and if i do that i
   dont know if thats such a big change   for me   i go around
bugging people all the time   why cant i find the factor of marseilles   in what im doing now   i mean can i find a way to be
somebody other than i am now?   in principle   yeah   but
   in practice who else would that be?

afterwards we got to talking about numbers and hannah
asked me what i thought about numerology   and i
dont know much about numerology but what i do know
is that it depends on reducing the great domain of number to one of the nine digits which with zero form the
basic morphemes out of which the great family gets all of
its names   and i guess i just dont see human experience
as being any more reducible than the great family itself
        so i tend to like more generous and less elegant and
minimal formulations   and george quasha wanted to
know what i thought would be the human equivalent of
an imaginary number   which he pointed out was a
name that most mathematicians except maybe spencer
brown tend to regret   and i suppose they regret it for
the fairly good reason that the usual sense of the word
"imagination"   is a faculty for conceiving of the fantastic and false   the nonexistent   so that "imaginary
numbers" become "nonexistent numbers"   thereby
depriving many mathematicians of a large part of their
world   but i dont think its so terrible to call these
 numbers "imaginary"   because there is something
freaky and fantastic about them   like the way you
arrive at them   by talking   the way you arrive at
everything else in mathematics   by talking in what
seems like a perfectly reasonable way   and then it turns
out that what you find yourself saying   in a perfectly
 reasonable way is quite fantastic and freaky   because
what youve always assumed when you talked arithmetic
is that when you multiply one number by itself
        you arrive at a number from which you ought to be
able to get back to the original number   which is the

root of that number   that square   and thats what
you mean by its square root   and at the same time you
also have a perfectly reasonable way of dealing with the
direction or sense of a number   its sign   by which
you suppose that when you have a number with a negative sense a minus sign   and you multiply it by itself
      by the same number with a minus sign   minus 1
times minus 1 say   the two negative signs reverse each
other and your result comes out with a positive sign and is
called +1   while you assume that if you multiply the
signed magnitude +1 by itself the two plus signs will confirm each other and the product of this multiplication
will also be the signed magnitude +1   and this way of
proceeding which has seemed reasonable to generations of
arithmeticians leads to an ambiguity when you want to
find out what the root was   of what you were assured
was the result of a squaring operation that led to this
signed magnitude +1   because   you see   it turns
out you cant be sure of that   you can only be sure
that it was either plus 1 or minus 1 and thats all you can
say   now it turns out that there are many more things
that are sayable than thinkable   or maybe thats not
quite true   but there are certainly many things that
are perfectly sayable and equally unthinkable   for
example a square that is a negative number   because
as soon as youve conceived of the procedure of squaring
      multiplying a number by itself   and you have
conceived that the outcome of this process is a number
      you can conceive of it as a number with a sign   +4
      +16   +37   and after youve said these things a
few times   it comes fairly easily to your mouth

just as easily in fact   to say -1   -4   -16
so there you are   youve said it   and youve
said that these signed numbers are squares   and so they
may be but can you conceive any way of reversing this
squaring process and finding the root of these squares
if you insist on remembering the rules that youve
accepted for multiplying signed magnitudes?   according to which the product of two negative numbers must
have a positive sign   so you have a choice   you
may say dont say these things   forbid yourself and
anybody else to mention these things   or you could
say dont worry about it how we got to these freaky
squares   somehow we got here thats whats imaginary
and unthinkable how we got here   but now that were
here lets deal with whats here because we can conceive of
a way of dealing with these freaky squares   more or
less   its easy to see that the square root of -4   whatever it is   is twice the square root of whatever -1 may
be and the square root of -9 is three times the square root
of whatever -1 may be and the square root of -16 is four
times the square root of whatever the square root of -1 may
be and so on   and this proves to be a very promising
reasonable way of proceeding   now that were
here and have to go on and thats why i suppose i can think
of a perfectly satisfactory way of conceiving what the
equivalent of an imaginary number in human experience
would be   i mean think of an experience that somehow
you cant possibly imagine getting to   and then somehow youre there   now i can imagine a whole family
of them   these impossible to generate experiences
that somehow i couldnt imagine arriving at   and then

somehow i was there ordering them   as a family
        i remember once   and for me this is an imaginary
number because it was a situation which occurred and i
cant imagine ever getting into it   or getting into it in
        the way i did   and yet i did   i was living in a place
        on jones street in the village   and i was coming home
on the train late at night   and normally when you
        come home on a train in new york late at night   this
was in the early 60's   or maybe at the end of the 50's
        you dont pay attention to other people on the train
        not too much attention anyway   and im not too
paranoid about new york and riding on subways in the city
        and the subways were not so entirely crazy then
        but you just dont get involved with other passengers
on the train like that   yet somehow i did   there
was this very unattractive kid   tall and pimply and
gangly   a red haired awkward ugly kid with reddish
        hair who i got into a conversation with and it turned out
he had no place to go   really no place to go   and
        im a native new yorker   as all new yorkers know you
dont worry about things like that   which is one of
the reasons you dont talk to people on subways   but
it was a cold winter night and he had no place to go and
no money to go there with and he looked kind of miserable
        so i said he could stay at my place and then go on his
way in the morning   and he was on his way to somewhere in new england   and in the back of my mind i
        thought maybe this is not really a good idea   and
        though i wasnt worried about it   i mean it wasnt a
sense of physical danger or anything   i felt quite confident i could hold my own if i had to against this frail

awkward kid   but the point is i kept thinking "you
dont really want to do this do you?   i mean i dont
really want to do this number"   he came out with me
and i gave him some cocoa i think and he poured a ton
of sugar into it as i remember   and we talked for a
while and then i sent him off to bed in my extra room
          and something about the tone of that experience
gave me the sense that this was not a right move   not
my kind of move   but i did it   i did it with these
mixed feelings of whether i should do it or not   but i
did it   and in the morning we talked some more
          and he told me he was in the marines   on leave
          and hed lost all his money i forget how   and he
was on his way home to new england and i didnt believe
he was on leave   if he was in the marines   he was
probably awol and probably not in the marines anyway
          but he didnt have any money and he had all this bar-
racks room wisdom   hed gotten drunk his first night
on leave and picked up this street walker   a young
spanish girl   who took him back to her place but
wouldnt let him fuck her and kept showing him her breasts
and asking him if she was heautiful   which made him
very angry and he snarled at her "yeah like hedy lamarr"
          so she told him she couldnt fuck because she was
sick and he was so drunk he gave her his last twenty bucks
for a blowjob and she gave him a handjob instead   and
here he was camping on my doorstep without any money
waiting to get some money to go on to boston   so you
see he wasnt even a very attractive kid and i didnt really
like him even though i felt sort of sorry for him   though
even that didnt matter very much because we already had

*this kind of   relationship   that i was letting him
stay there till he could go to the bloodbank and sell some
      of his blood to get his fare to boston   and somehow
      he hung around for a couple of days without going off
      to boston   maybe the blood bank was closed or he got
there too late or he got lost just walking around new york
            which was a city he was unfamiliar with   and it
was getting hard to get rid of him   because we had this
      relationship   i had been friendly to him   invited
      him in   listened to his ridiculous stories   about the
      marines   about women   and hed keep coming
      back and id feed him   it had become a paradigm
            and now i was the sort of person who invited people
into his house and i had this lost waif and he was there
      one day   and he was there two days   three days
            and all the time he kept saying how it was getting
      time for him to go on to boston or wherever the hell he
was supposed to be going   and id encourage him id say
yeah   thats right   id direct him to the greyhound
      terminal or id tell him how he could manage to hitch out
      of town   and you know i realized all the time that this
was an absurd role for me   and i continued to play it
            and in the meantime im trying to steer his life around
            i see that hes starting to get kind of jumpy and some-
thing feels odd about it   and he keeps telling me his
problems and i figure hes kind of hung-up   so i say
      well why dont you go pick yourself up a girl or some-
      thing   go to the museum of modern art   you can
      always pick up girls in the museum of modern art
            the museum of modern art is where everybody picks
everybody up   go stand in front of the guernica*

have a cup of coffee in the cafeteria   walk through
the sculpture garden   there are always girls there
and i remember him looking at me like i was nuts
and i begin to realize that theres something about this
whole number thats wrong   somehow hes been reading
something   some of the signals the information ive
been giving him   and i realize hes been reading this
information thats been coming his way to mean something
else   somehow something i said initially started him
reading things this way   that id picked him up because i
was queer and id intended some kind of romance   and
now that the signals that keep coming wont confirm this
its a way of reading hes stuck with and he keeps read-
ing it   because there are enough signals left   maybe
to suggest this   to him   the art   the con-
versations about sex   an excessive kindness   so he
probably decides that im shy and hes waiting it out
now i didnt realize this very clearly at the time   i
didnt even clearly suspect it   or i could have told him
forget it   and as i gradually began to suspect it
somewhat more precisely   i had the problem of
telling him   like how do i disabuse him of this illusion
that he hasnt put directly forward either   do i tell him
youre out of your mind kid   i mean i didnt want to
hurt his feelings either   in this strange gentle state of
mine   youre out of your mind kid   the last thing i
want to do is make love to a man but if i wanted to
youd be the last man in the whole fucking world i
could have thought of making love to   so there i was
in this dumb thing and i wasnt getting rid of him
finally he says that hes going   and he takes off in

the morning for the blood bank and i figure im rid of him
and late that night   about 3 oclock in the morning
i hear somebody knocking at the door and im sort of tired
and dazed   and i open the door   and there he is
come back   i said how come youre back   and
something happened to the money and he didnt have his
fare anymore   and this time i figure thats it   in the
morning i call up the bus terminal and find out how much
he needs for bus fare and i give it to him and tell him to go
and i go out myself to spend my time out in the street
away from this ridiculous scene thats been going on for
days now   though i dont want you to think that was
the only thing going on with me at that time   that is
my whole life wasnt as wrapped up with this set of
circumstances as the way ive been telling you this story
might suggest   you see   just at this time i was be-
ginning to enter into an affair with a girl who lived next
to me   you see   she lived in the apartment across
from me   and we were seeing each other every time
my kid marine would go away   see   hed go away
and id go visit my friend in the next apartment   and
we had not made love or anything   wed been sitting on
her couch and talking and drinking coffee together
and listening to music together   im describing the
tempo because its part of the situation   in which the
tempo was very important   that we had not gone to
bed with each other but that we were contemplating
going to bed with each other   you know   in a rea-
sonable and slow and casual manner   mainly because
we were cautious   and circling each other like cats
and then we decided   well you dont really decide

you go to bed   and we were in bed with each
other   were in bed and i hear this knocking on the door
of the next apartment   and its my door   and i hear
this sound that i at first dont quite make out   and its
      knock   knock   knock   getting progressively
louder and clearer with each successive knock   and its
finally pounding on the door of my apartment and i say
      miriam whats that?   and she says a sound at the
door   i think its him   youd better go answer it   i
said im not going to answer i said you answer it   hell
ask if you saw me   you never saw me im not there
      finally i figured out the way to get rid of him
      miriam put on her robe went to the door and in her
very sweet ladylike voice lied me out of the situation
      denied any knowledge of me and my whereabouts
      and he went away   and i stayed in her apartment
for five days and he came back dutifully two or three
times   and then disappeared   thats my imaginary
      number

we talked a while longer about changing lives and imaginary numbers and a few people remembered their own
      imaginary number stories and after it was all over berna-
dette came up to me and told me i was wrong

New Directions Paperbooks

Walter Abish, *Alphabetical Africa.* NDP375.
  Minds Meet. NDP387.
Ilangô Adigal, *Shilappadikaram.* NDP162.
Alain, *The Gods.* NDP382.
David Antin. *Talking at the Boundaries.* NDP388.
G. Apollinaire, *Selected Writings.*† NDP310.
Djuna Barnes, *Nightwood.* NDP98.
Charles Baudelaire, *Flowers of Evil.*† NDP71.
  Paris Spleen. NDP294.
Martin Bax. *The Hospital Ship.* NDP402.
Gottfried Benn, *Primal Vision.*† NDP322.
Wolfgang Borchert, *The Man Outside.* NDP319.
Jorge Luis Borges, *Labyrinths.* NDP186.
Jean-François Bory, *Once Again.* NDP256.
Kay Boyle, *Thirty Stories.* NDP62.
E. Brock, *The Blocked Heart.* NDP399.
  Invisibility Is The Art of Survival. NDP342.
  Paroxisms. NDP385.
  The Portraits & The Poses. NDP360.
Buddha, *The Dhammapada.* NDP188.
Frederick Busch, *Domestic Particulars.* NDP413.
  Manual Labor. NDP376.
Ernesto Cardenal, *In Cuba.* NDP377.
Hayden Carruth, *For You.* NDP298.
  From Snow and Rock, from Chaos. NDP349.
Louis-Ferdinand Céline,
  Death on the Installment Plan. NDP330.
  Guignol's Band. NDP278.
  Journey to the End of the Night. NDP84.
Blaise Cendrars, *Selected Writings.*† NDP203.
Jean Cocteau, *The Holy Terrors.* NDP212.
  The Infernal Machine. NDP235.
M. Cohen, *Monday Rhetoric.* NDP352.
Cid Corman, *Livingdying.* NDP289.
  Sun Rock Man. NDP318.
Gregory Corso, *Elegiac Feelings American.*
  NDP299.
  Happy Birthday of Death. NDP86.
  Long Live Man. NDP127.
Kenneth Cragg. *The Wisdom of the Sufis.*
  NDP424.
Edward Dahlberg, *Reader.* NDP246.
  Because I Was Flesh. NDP227.
David Daiches, *Virginia Woolf.* NDP96.
Osamu Dazai, *The Setting Sun.* NDP258.
  No Longer Human. NDP357.
Coleman Dowell, *Mrs. October Was Here.*
  NDP368.
Robert Duncan, *Bending the Bow.* NDP255.
  The Opening of the Field. NDP356.
  Roots and Branches. NDP275.
Richard Eberhart, *Selected Poems.* NDP198.
Russell Edson. *The Falling Sickness.* NDP 389.
  The Very Thing That Happens. NDP137.
Paul Eluard, *Uninterrupted Poetry.* NDP392.
Wm. Empson, *7 Types of Ambiguity.* NDP204.
  Some Versions of Pastoral. NDP92.
Wm. Everson, *Man-Fate.* NDP369.
  The Residual Years. NDP263.
Lawrence Ferlinghetti, *Her.* NDP88.
  Back Roads to Far Places. NDP312.
  A Coney Island of the Mind. NDP74.
  The Mexican Night. NDP300.
  Open Eye, Open Heart. NDP361.
  Routines. NDP187.
  The Secret Meaning of Things. NDP268.
  Starting from San Francisco. NDP 220.
  Tyrannus Nix?. NDP288.
  Who Are We Now? NDP425.
Ronald Firbank, *Two Novels.* NDP128.
Dudley Fitts,
  Poems from the Greek Anthology. NDP60.
F. Scott Fitzgerald, *The Crack-up.* NDP54.
Robert Fitzgerald, *Spring Shade: Poems
  1931-1970.* NDP311.
Gustave Flaubert,
  Bouvard and Pécuchet. NDP328.
  The Dictionary of Accepted Ideas. NDP230.
M. K. Gandhi, *Gandhi on Non-Violence.*
  (ed. Thomas Merton) NDP197.
André Gide, *Dostoevsky.* NDP100.
Goethe, *Faust,* Part I.
  (MacIntyre translation) NDP70.
Albert J. Guerard, *Thomas Hardy.* NDP185.
Guillevic, *Selected Poems.*† NDP279.

Henry Hatfield, *Goethe.* NDP136.
John Hawkes, *The Beetle Leg.* NDP239.
  The Blood Oranges. NDP338.
  The Cannibal. NDP123.
  Death, Sleep & The Traveler. NDP393.
  The Innocent Party. NDP238.
  The Lime Twig. NDP95.
  Lunar Landscapes. NDP274.
  Second Skin. NDP146.
A. Hayes, *A Wreath of Christmas Poems.*
  NDP347.
H.D., *Helen in Egypt.* NDP380
  Hermetic Definition NDP343.
  Trilogy. NDP362.
Robert E. Helbling, *Heinrich von Kleist,* NDP390.
Hermann Hesse, *Siddhartha.* NDP65.
C. Isherwood, *The Berlin Stories.* NDP134.
Gustav Janouch,
  Conversations With Kafka. NDP313.
Alfred Jarry, *Ubu Roi,* NDP105.
Robinson Jeffers, *Cawdor and Medea.* NDP293.
James Joyce, *Stephen Hero.* NDP133.
  James Joyce/Finnegans Wake. NDP331.
Franz Kafka, *Amerika.* NDP117.
Bob Kaufman,
  Solitudes Crowded with Loneliness. NDP199.
Hugh Kenner, *Wyndham Lewis.* NDP167.
Kenyon Critics, *Gerard Manley Hopkins.*
  NDP355.
P. Lal, *Great Sanskrit Plays.* NDP142.
Tommaso Landolfi.
  Gogol's Wife and Other Stories. NDP155.
Lautréamont, *Maldoror.* NDP207.
Denise Levertov, *Footprints.* NDP344.
  The Freeing of the Dust. NDP401.
  The Jacob's Ladder. NDP112.
  O Taste and See. NDP149.
  The Poet in the World. NDP363.
  Relearning the Alphabet. NDP290.
  The Sorrow Dance. NDP222.
  To Stay Alive. NDP325.
  With Eyes at the Back of Our Heads.
  NDP229.
Harry Levin, *James Joyce.* NDP87.
García Lorca, *Five Plays.* NDP232.
  Selected Poems.† NDP114.
  Three Tragedies. NDP52.
Michael McClure, *Gorf.* NDP416.
  Jaguar Skies. NDP400.
  September Blackberries. NDP370.
Carson McCullers, *The Member of the
  Wedding.* (Playscript) NDP153.
Thomas Merton, *Asian Journal.* NDP394.
  Gandhi on Non-Violence. NDP197.
  The Geography of Lograire. NDP283.
  My Argument with the Gestapo. NDP403.
  New Seeds of Contemplation. NDP337.
  Raids on the Unspeakable. NDP213.
  Selected Poems. NDP85.
  The Way of Chuang Tzu. NDP276.
  The Wisdom of the Desert. NDP295.
  Zen and the Birds of Appetite. NDP261.
Henri Michaux, *Selected Writings.*† NDP264.
Henry Miller, *The Air-Conditioned Nightmare.*
  NDP302.
  *Big Sur & The Oranges of Hieronymus
  Bosch.* NDP161.
  The Books in My Life. NDP280.
  The Colossus of Maroussi. NDP75.
  The Cosmological Eye. NDP109.
  Henry Miller on Writing. NDP151.
  The Henry Miller Reader. NDP269.
  Remember to Remember. NDP111.
  The Smile at the Foot of the Ladder. NDP386.
  Stand Still Like the Hummingbird. NDP236.
  The Time of the Assassins. NDP115.
  The Wisdom of the Heart. NDP94.
Y. Mishima, *Confessions of a Mask.* NDP253.
  Death in Midsummer. NDP215.
Eugenio Montale, *New Poems.* NDP410.
  Selected Poems.† NDP193.
Vladimir Nabokov, *Nikolai Gogol.* NDP78.
P. Neruda, *The Captain's Verses.*† NDP345.
  Residence on Earth.† NDP340.
New Directions 17. (Anthology) NDP103.
New Directions 18. (Anthology) NDP163.
New Directions 19. (Anthology) NDP214.
New Directions 20. (Anthology) NDP248.

New Directions 21. (Anthology) NDP277.
New Directions 22. (Anthology) NDP291.
New Directions 23. (Anthology) NDP315.
New Directions 24. (Anthology) NDP332.
New Directions 25. (Anthology) NDP339.
New Directions 26. (Anthology) NDP353.
New Directions 27. (Anthology) NDP359.
New Directions 28. (Anthology) NDP371.
New Directions 29. (Anthology) NDP378.
New Directions 30. (Anthology) NDP395.
New Directions 31. (Anthology) NDP404.
New Directions 32. (Anthology) NDP412.
New Directions 33. (Anthology) NDP419.
Charles Olson, Selected Writings. NDP231.
Toby Olson. The Life of Jesus. NDP417.
George Oppen, Collected Poems. NDP418.
 This In Which. NDP201.
Wilfred Owen, Collected Poems. NDP210.
Nicanor Parra, Emergency Poems.† NDP333.
 Poems and Antipoems.† NDP242.
G. Parrinder, The Wisdom of the Forest.
 NDP414.
Boris Pasternak, Safe Conduct. NDP77.
Kenneth Patchen, Aflame and Afun of
 Walking Faces. NDP292.
 Because It Is. NDP83.
 But Even So. NDP265.
 Collected Poems. NDP284.
 Doubleheader. NDP211.
 Hallelujah Anyway. NDP219.
 In Quest of Candlelighters. NDP334.
 The Journal of Albion Moonlight. NDP99.
 Memoirs of a Shy Pornographer. NDP205.
 Selected Poems. NDP160.
 Sleepers Awake. NDP286.
 Wonderings. NDP320.
Octavio Paz, Configurations.† NDP303.
 Eagle or Sun? NDP422.
 Early Poems.† NDP354.
Plays for a New Theater. (Anth.) NDP216.
Ezra Pound, ABC of Reading. NDP89.
 Classic Noh Theatre of Japan. NDP79.
 Confucius. NDP285.
 Confucius to Cummings. (Anth.) NDP126.
 Gaudier-Brzeska. NDP372.
 Guide to Kulchur. NDP257.
 Literary Essays. NDP250.
 Love Poems of Ancient Egypt. NDP178.
 Pavannes and Divagations. NDP397.
 Pound/Joyce. NDP296.
 Selected Cantos. NDP304.
 Selected Letters 1907-1941. NDP317.
 Selected Poems. NDP66.
 Selected Prose 1909-1965. NDP396.
 The Spirit of Romance. NDP266.
 Translations.† (Enlarged Edition) NDP145.
Omar Pound, Arabic and Persian Poems.
 NDP305.
James Purdy, Children Is All. NDP327.
Raymond Queneau, The Bark Tree. NDP314.
 The Flight of Icarus. NDP358.
Mary de Rachewiltz, Ezra Pound:
 Father and Teacher. NDP405.
M. Randall, Part of the Solution. NDP350.
John Crowe Ransom, Beating the Bushes.
 NDP324.
Raja Rao, Kanthapura. NDP224.
Herbert Read, The Green Child. NDP208.
P. Reverdy, Selected Poems.† NDP346.
Kenneth Rexroth, Assays. NDP113.
 Beyond the Mountains. NDP384.
 Bird in the Bush. NDP80.
 Collected Longer Poems. NDP309.
 Collected Shorter Poems. NDP243.
 Love and the Turning Year. NDP308.
 New Poems. NDP383.
 One Hundred More Poems from the Japanese.
 NDP420.
 100 Poems from the Chinese. NDP192.
 100 Poems from the Japanese.† NDP147.
Rainer Maria Rilke, Poems from
 The Book of Hours. NDP408.
Arthur Rimbaud, Illuminations.† NDP56.
 Season in Hell & Drunken Boat.† NDP97.

Selden Rodman, Tongues of Fallen Angels.
 NDP373.
Jerome Rothenberg, Poems for the Game
 of Silence. NDP406.
 Poland/1931. NDP379.
Saikaku Ihara, The Life of an Amorous
 Woman. NDP270.
St. John of the Cross, Poems.† NDP341.
Jean-Paul Sartre, Baudelaire. NDP233.
 Nausea. NDP82.
 The Wall (Intimacy). NDP272.
I. Schloegl, The Wisdom of the Zen Masters.
 NDP415.
Delmore Schwartz, Selected Poems. NDP241.
Stevie Smith, Selected Poems. NDP159.
Gary Snyder, The Back Country. NDP249.
 Earth House Hold. NDP267.
 Regarding Wave. NDP306.
 Turtle Island. NDP381.
Gilbert Sorrentino, Splendide-Hôtel. NDP364.
Enid Starkie, Arthur Rimbaud. NDP254.
Stendhal, Lucien Leuwen.
 Book II: The Telegraph. NDP108.
Jules Supervielle, Selected Writings.† NDP209.
W. Sutton, American Free Verse. NDP351.
Nathaniel Tarn, Lyrics for the Bride of God.
 NDP391.
Dylan Thomas, Adventures in the Skin Trade.
 NDP183.
 A Child's Christmas in Wales. NDP181.
 Collected Poems 1934-1952. NDP316.
 The Doctor and the Devils. NDP297.
 Portrait of the Artist as a Young Dog.
 NDP51.
 Quite Early One Morning. NDP90.
 Under Milk Wood. NDP73.
Lionel Trilling, E. M. Forster. NDP189.
Martin Turnell, Art of French Fiction. NDP251.
 Baudelaire. NDP336.
Alan Unterman, The Wisdom of the Jewish
 Mystics. NDP423.
Paul Valéry, Selected Writings.† NDP184.
Paul Van Ostaijen, Feasts of Fear and Agony.
 NDP411.
Elio Vittorini, A Vittorini Omnibus. NDP366.
 Women of Messina. NDP365.
Linda W. Wagner. "Speaking Straight Ahead":
 Interviews with William Carlos Williams.
 NDP421.
Vernon Watkins, Selected Poems. NDP221.
Nathanael West, Miss Lonelyhearts &
 Day of the Locust. NDP125.
George F. Whicher, tr.,
 The Goliard Poets.† NDP206.
J. Williams, An Ear in Bartram's Tree. NDP335.
Tennessee Williams, Camino Real. NDP301.
 Cat on a Hot Tin Roof. NDP398.
 Dragon Country. NDP287.
 Eight Mortal Ladies Possessed. NDP374.
 The Glass Menagerie. NDP218.
 Hard Candy. NDP225.
 In the Winter of Cities. NDP154.
 One Arm & Other Stories. NDP237.
 Out Cry. NDP367.
 The Roman Spring of Mrs. Stone. NDP271.
 Small Craft Warnings. NDP348.
 Sweet Bird of Youth. NDP409.
 27 Wagons Full of Cotton. NDP217.
William Carlos Williams,
 The Autobiography. NDP223.
 The Build-up. NDP259.
 The Farmers' Daughters. NDP106.
 Imaginations. NDP329.
 In the American Grain. NDP53.
 In the Money. NDP240.
 Many Loves. NDP191.
 Paterson. Complete. NDP152.
 Pictures from Brueghel. NDP118.
 The Selected Essays. NDP273.
 Selected Poems. NDP131.
 A Voyage to Pagany. NDP307.
 White Mule. NDP226.
 W. C. Williams Reader. NDP282.
Yvor Winters,
 Edwin Arlington Robinson. NDP326.